EDINBURGH
EDUCATION AND SOCIETY
SERIES

POVERTY AND WELFARE
IN SCOTLAND
1890–1948

IAN LEVITT

EDINBURGH UNIVERSITY PRESS

© Ian Levitt 1988
Edinburgh University Press
22 George Square, Edinburgh

Set in Linotron Palatino by
Koinonia, Manchester and
printed in Great Britain by
Oxford University Press

British Library Cataloguing
in Publication Data
Levitt, Ian
Poverty and welfare in Scotland 1890-1948.
1. Scotland. Welfare services, 1890-1948
I. Title
361'.9411

ISBN 0 85224 558 0

CONTENTS

ACKNOWLEDGEMENTS

I am greatly indebted to the following for their kind permission to consult and quote from manuscript sources; Ayrshire District Archives, Edinburgh District Archives, Edinburgh Public Library, Central Regional Archives, Fife Regional Council, Glasgow Mitchell Library, Midlothian District Council, the Public Record Office, Renfrew District Library, Strathclyde Regional Archives, the Scottish Record Office, Tayside Regional Archives, and West Lothian District Library. Their staff – archivists, librarians and clerks – laboured hard to satisfy my thirst for new sources.

I am also indebted to a large number of colleagues who assisted (often unwittingly) in developing my thoughts. In particular I would like to thank Frank Bechhofer, Roger Davidson, Bob Morris, Christopher Smout, Alan Deacon and Gordon Brown. I hope what I have written does not do too much violence to their own views.

I must also thank Susan Tolan whose assistance with an earlier draft of this volume laid the foundation for its publication.

This volume is dedicated to the memory of Tommy and Mary Steel.

1
INTRODUCTION

At the end of the Second World War there occurred a dramatic shift in British political opinion. With Labour sweeping the country to claim a victory as large as the Liberal landslide of 1906, a new era in political administration was quickly established. By 1947 the shape of welfare in that administration had become clear. There was to be a free and national health service, overcoming both the old division between voluntary and local hospital control and the haphazard nature of general practitioner care. An integrated and compulsory national insurance scheme covering the unemployed, the sick and the retired was to be introduced. Local authority services were to be completely revamped, with particular emphasis on the provision of domicilary support for those elderly, children and disabled not requiring medical or monetary assistance. A new national assistance scheme for those disqualified from insurance benefit, sweeping away the last vestiges of a locally based Poor Law, was to be introduced. In its provisions, not only was the Government going to assume a responsibility for monetary benefits, but the whole ethos of meeting need was to alter. Out went a legal-bureaucratic system of welfare, in which claimants had clearly defined rights, and in came an administrative form of welfare, based on regulation, where a claimant's needs were to be periodically reviewed and assessed.

Past experiences and much debate had led to a decisively new format for the provision of assistance to those in need. Thus when Government Ministers rose to introduce the National Assistance Bill in late 1947, they scarcely disguised their enthusiasm for its contents or their optimism about the future. Arthur Woodburn, the Scottish Secretary of State, in a highly charged speech, summed up their views by stating:

> We establish in this Bill one of the greatest ambitions of our movement – the establishment of work or maintenance as the moral principle governing the treatment of people who are in need. Under this measure those who get assistance get it without humiliation or abuse. Perhaps the greatest thing about this Bill is that it removes from the treatment of people who are hard hit in life the humiliation which accompanied a great deal of charity in the past. I think that the greatest injury done to the poor in the past was not the fact that they were deprived of food or nourish-

ment, but that they were deprived of their self respect. The destruction of the dignity of man was the great issue amongst the poor in days gone by.[1]

And as an afterthought, he declared: 'This Bill wipes out poverty as we know it, and any shame attached to need.' With unusual ferocity he and other Labour M Ps demolished all Conservative attempts to suggest that the position of the poor might not be radically improved.

In retrospect, although Labour's plans for a Welfare State did enjoy considerable electoral support, poverty – as the Conservatives sensed – was far from being 'wiped out'. Indeed as the 'rediscovery of poverty' in the 1960s and subsequent studies have all indicated, the post war scheme fell far short of Woodburn's assertion. But the abolition of poverty through a massive redistribution of income was not necessarily the issue regarded by Labour and the working-class electorate as the most vital. Equally important to them was the creation of a system that would overcome the personal shame and public humiliation of a structure still rooted in 19th-century philosophy. The final abolition of the Poor Law, with its pecuniary practices, its local authority staff trained in the traditions of the past, and its failure to meet need, was the immediate priority. Labour's post-war welfare plans were therefore as much an attack on the continuance of a particular method of relieving poverty as an attempt to provide the poor with extra monetary resources. Indeed, when the family means' test and other pre-war benefit regulations are discounted, there is comparatively little difference between the scales of benefit before and after the war. The increases that were provided can be almost wholly attributed to Labour's pegging benefits to rises in real wages.

This book then sets out to explain certain adminstrative aspects of the Welfare State's derivation, the reasons why Labour Ministers were so ferocious in their attack on the existing system, and why working-class opinion had been so decisively acknowledged as important in any restructuring of provision. Such an understanding is important for two reasons. Firstly it helps explain why the Welfare State has lasted so long and secondly, why, as the coalition of ideas and interests that brought in the reform have all but disappeared, Britain enters a post-Welfare State. Nevertheless one important element needs to be stressed, the evolution of welfare policy was not something that occurred in isolation from other social and political developments. As one writer has suggested:

> The growth of state involvement with the social welfare of its citizens can be related to the development of an industrial society and its subsequent maturation, or perhaps decline, into what some writers have described as 'post industrialism'. Alongside this industrial development are political developments associated with the extension of the suffrage, involving citizens more

thoroughly with the activities of the state. The result is a package of developments – of the state's role, the character of the economy, and the nature of the political process.[2]

Thus in providing a detailed analysis of events and policy, six factors in particular require consideration. These will be outlined in turn.

The first relates to the nature of class in industrial society. In the 19th century wealth was created on a scale previously unknown or thought possible. But because that in turn created inequality and social dissatisfaction, the working classes constantly struggled with employers over the distribution of rewards for their labour. The former had a basic material interest in increasing their share of the social product, whilst the latter an interest in preserving private property and maintaining profits.

Second, it is important is to look at the way in which ideology and institutional framework were combined during the early years of the 19th century to create a particular welfare hegemony. The middle classes believed that if the workforce was adequately motivated then the problem of maintaining public order would be secured. In an attempt therefore to ensure a sense of participation and benefit from capitalism, they sought to instil the values of hard work, thrift, and the notion that economic rewards would accrue to the virtuous. They needed to create welfare institutions which, while offering assistance, did so in a way that bound the less fortunate to capitalism's predominant ethos. Thus the starting point for an analysis of late 19th century policy change must be to regard the existing system of welfare as a 'moral' order in which virtually everyone, from pauper to property owner had come to view the New Poor Law, temperance reform, voluntary hospitals and the zeal of the Charity Organisation Society as 'right and proper'.

The third factor relates to the way in which property-owners perceived political enfranchisement as necessary to maintain the legitimacy of the existing mode of production. The relative decline of the British economy in the late 19th century shattered working class expectations about the ability of the existing system to sustain living standards. Thus by conceding the vote and incorporating working class views more formally into Government, property-owners could offer them the prospect of achieving their material interests through 'negotiation' rather than violence. But the consequence of enfranchisement had to be met with new strategies. If the working classes found they could adjust the tools of Government to their own satisfaction, then those who owned property had to become far more subtle about protecting their interests.

This leads to a fourth factor, the way in which those operating welfare institutions can display their power and effect changes in policy. An enfranchised society creates a wider diversity of means towards achieving particular welfare goals. Thus although class divisions provide the perimeter for a discussion of social policy, it becomes important to emphasise micro-political processes as the basis for understanding how forms of welfare came to be accepted as legitimate. Moreover, it is the shifting balance of power within these processes, and the ability of various social factions to manipulate their institutional environment, that ultimately determines the general order and pace of welfare development. Under certain circumstances individuals can react to events not simply according to their objective class positions but because of other factors such as their religious beliefs, or in the case of welfare administrators, their statutory goals. Thus during the period before 1945, property-owners rather than simply exercising crude class power, could 'play politics', make 'concessions' and develop new forms of welfare.

In consequence a fifth factor needs to be taken into account: the way in which the different classes began to perceive the State's administrative powers as a method to obtain material well-being. Thus it has been argued that the more open, 'contestable' nature of 20th century society saw the development of social policy being guided by the search for the maintenance of popular support. On the one hand the Conservatives with the promise of efficient and mildly redistributive policies, sought the votes of skilled workers, and on the other Labour, by backing away from implementing revolutionary slogans, the votes of the property-conscious middle class. Both Parties realised that moderating class based ideologies was essential if the middle ground of politics was to be secured. As a result, in any analysis of policy development it is important to understand the way in which both political and professional administrators begin to present themselves, not as the 'instrument of a single ruling class' but as the 'moral arbiter' between conflicting claims of industry and worker.[3]

Armed with these factors a much broader interpretation of philosophies and aspirations can take place. But there remains one final factor that needs to be stressed: an analysis of the kinds of conditions that led to State involvement becoming 'regarded as imperative'. In consequence a more distinctive methodology is necessary, one that looks at the 'purposive actions' of individuals and groups in pursuit of their own ends.[4] It is vital to take into account how individuals defined poverty, pauperism, their statutory duties (if they were administrators), the power of other groups to influence the enfranchised workers and the ways in which they sought to articulate their interests. So it has been suggested that:

> no explanation of policy development in terms simply of the requirements of capital accumulation, the selfishness of sectional interests or the dictates of societal devlopment can be adequate in as much as any of these would presume an essentially reactive role for the mass of citizens.[5]

Thus within a more subjectivist approach it is necessary to recognise the process of 'collective learning' through which electors, administrators and social groups come to some form of consensus on what constitutes an ethos and practice of welfare. Understanding the nature of electoral experience and its critical appreciation of prevailing welfare forms is therefore an essential element in any analysis of policy development.

In summary, then, although 19th-century industrial development offers some models, the battle for 20th-century welfare may be seen as a unique process, involving many different groups pursuing their own aims and interests. Moreover the perspectives on welfare and the evaluation of alternative strategies need not be class based. The underlying concern is the way in which policy came to be structured around enfranchised and politically equal citizens. As a result, the core of any critical analysis must be an examination of the changing role of the State, the process of decision-making as it actually occurred, the values attached to welfare and the evolution of a distinct code of welfare conduct. In an attempt to explain the origins of Labour's plans, this book will discuss the events surrounding the downfall of one institution, the Scottish Poor Law, from about 1890 to 1948. It has been chosen for a number of reasons.

First, throughout the period the Poor Law was the last bastion of public support for those both 'destitute and disabled'. New institutions may have been established and developed, but in real terms more was being spent on Poor Law provision in 1938 than in 1890. Indeed not only did it continue to meet a wide variety of needs, but it also acquired a number of new statutory duties – ones that greatly broadened its criteria for assistance.[6] Second, the 1890s was a time when the deteriorating nature of urban-industrial living began to destroy the existing pattern of working-class material well-being – and nowhere was this more obvious than in central Scotland. As a result poverty became 'a settled condition' from which a growing number of Scots 'could not escape.[7] Third, it was a period when the working class acquired the vote in both national and local elections. There was therefore a whole range of new public institutions through which their interests could be directly articulated. Fourth, because of its existing philosophy and practice, it was this particular institution that engendered so much of the early Labour Party zeal for reform. This must be appreciated if Woodburn's assertions in his parliamentary speech are to be understood. Fifth, the sheer complexity of administrative tasks and the number of political units within the comparable English institution has prevented a full appreciation of the National Assistance Bill. Recent accounts of the English Poor Law have largely focused on particular aspects, like income maintenance policy or the workhouse, rather than presented a broad sweep of its administrative practices, changing perceptions of need and the role of the State. Neither legal developments nor events in the 1930s have been adequately covered. Next, events in Scotland had a special impact on Labour's plans. Not only did its 19th-century welfare have a distinctly harder element – many of those assisted in England could not be in Scotland – but the inter-war depression caused a much sharper edge to deprivation. In consequence not only was working-class reaction far more bitter, but others in Government felt Scotland required a different response than the British State seemed willing to provide. Finally, it is an area of Scottish history that has remained sadly under-researched. Although a considerable amount is now known about this period's political and industrial development, little is known of social policy, the extent of Scottish poverty or their relationship to the developing class structure. Until more detail is provided, no definitive statement of the way Scottish society changed be formulated.

Thus this is an attempt not only to indicate the evolution of Scottish Poor Law policy, but also to aid an understanding of the origins of the British Welfare State – and the difficulties it faces today. Careful attention will be paid to local events, policies and conflicts, in the belief that this kind of analysis best illustrates the difficulties of early 20th-century welfare: how capitalism maintained its legitimacy in a period of increasing urban malaise and an assertive working-class electorate. A detailed account of the debates surrounding the emerging ethic and conduct of welfare will also be provided. Of course such an account of British social policy can only be partial; Scotland had only one eighth of the UK's population and a separate welfare administration. But the issues across the border, as indeed in other western industrial countries, shared a common theme, 'the civic reintegration of the labour force' during a more advanced phase of industrial capitalism.[8] The first step in that analysis must be to consider the nature and form of welfare as it emerged in the mid-19th century.

NOTES
1. Second Reading (24.11.47), in *Hansard 444 (Fifth Series)*, p.1653.
2. Hill, M., *Understanding Social Policy* (London, 1980) p.14.
3. Pinker, R., *The Idea of Welfare* (London, 1979) p.235.
4. Goldthorpe, J. H. (1962), The Development of Social Policy in England, 1800-1914, in *Transactions of the 5th World Congress of Sociology* (London, 1964) pp.41-56.
5. Room, G., *The Sociology of Welfare* (Oxford, 1979) p.80.
6. In 1934 at the height of the Depression, 426 000 Scots were on Poor Relief, some 9 per cent of the population. In 1890, it had been 82 000, or 2 per cent of the population. See Appendix 1.
7. Comment by Scrymgeour, E. (Dundee) during Committee Stage of the Poor Law (Emergency Provision) (Scotland) Bill (24.2.27), *Hansard 202 (Fifth Series)*, p.1983.
8. Kerr, C. (*et al*), *Industrialism and Industrial Man* (London 1964) p.187.

2
VICTORIAN SOCIAL POLICY:
CREATING PAUPERISM

The veteran Labour politician Tom Johnston once remarked that, after the 1845 Poor Law Act, the Scottish working class achieved their legal right to State welfare.[1] The Old Poor Law, he said, had failed to provide a decent standard of living. Johnston knew he was giving an over-generous view of the New Poor Law, but the system based on a local inspectorate, a central Board of Supervision and easier access by claimants to the Courts, indeed made a significant change.

Yet the history of the New Poor Law was dominated by one fact: that by 1890 it was assisting fewer than at any time since the 1830s.[2] This chapter will explore how this came about; how, as Scottish society settled down to a period of unrestrained economic development, the philosophy and practice of welfare changed; how in fact a distinctive ideology of pauperism – adequate but discriminatory relief – was created. To do so, it is essential to look at four aspects of 19th-century policy. First, the nature and form of Government control; second, the restriction of relief to the unemployed; third, the growing demarcation between the statutory sectors of welfare; and finally, the growth of middle-class charitable action.

Although the Board of Supervision had been established as the central authority, it had not been given the same powers as the English Poor Law Board. What powers it had and how it influenced parish action were explained by a later Chairman:

> The Board, while they have no power to issue Orders similar to that which I understand is exercised by the English and Irish Local Government Boards, are in the habit of issuing general regulations, rules and minutes for the guidance of Parish Councils. These are, for the most part, in the nature of recommendations, expressions of opinion and records of decisions given by the Board. They may inquire into the management of the poor in every parish, hold inquiries, examine witnesses on oath, and appoint commissioners. The Board... exercise certain controlling powers in regard to the erection of poorhouses, their maintenance, management and discipline. They consider complaints of inadequate relief (made by an individual pauper)... The Board to a large extent control inspectors of poor and regulate the administration of their duties. These officials can only be dismis-

sed with the sanction of the Board.[3]

This lack of overt control in fact reflected Scotland's political status. Although the Lord Advocate was nominally responsible for Scottish affairs, his Office – a legal department – could not be expected to implement the Act. The Board's parliamentary head was therefore the Home Secretary. This meant that the parishes authorities, composed almost entirely of owners of large property, would have to accept direction from what was a sub-department of the English Home Office, something – another Board Chairman said – they would not readily do.[4]

The Government in 1845 had recognised the issue and in an attempt to overcome it constituted the Board on a 'representative' basis. Apart from a Chairman and Secretary, the Board included the Lords Provost of Edinburgh and Glasgow (the two principal cities), the Sheriffs of Perth, Renfrew and Ross-and-Cromarty (agricultural, mining and highland counties), the Solicitor-General and two Crown nominees. Nevertheless the first Chairman, Sir John McNeill, a distinguished diplomat and brother of the Lord Advocate, felt the representation was not enough. As he later explained to one Poor Law Inquiry:

> I have always thought it very important to the Board, and to the smooth working of the Board, that there should be a representation of the landed interest of the country in the Board. I do not believe that the proprietors in Scotland would have worked as smoothly with the Board if we had not had amongst our members two recognised representatives of that class; they felt that what these men concurred in was not hostile to their interests, and we have all along had. . . landed proprietors of considerable weight on opposite sides of politics; for from the commencement I was exceedingly desirous that the Board should not only be free from any party bias, but that it should be free from any suspicion of party bias.[5]

This 'representative' and non-political status was further enhanced by the fact that the first two Secretaries were advocates. Until the early 1870s (when the volume of Board work increased with the Public Health Act) they provided parishes with free arbitration on settlement and other issues.[6]

Throughout the 19th century, then, the Board retained considerable independence and in practice parishes were only too willing to accept what advice was given. For instance the Board understood it could not compel parochial authorities to board out (foster) children. But through the exhortations of its Minutes and Annual Reports which all stressed the importance of family life (and its cost effectiveness) hardly any were kept in poorhouses.[7]

Another example was the use of poorhouse accommodation. The 1845 Poor Law Act had specifically said:

> . . . for more effectually administering to the wants of the aged

and other friendless impotent poor, and also for providing for those poor persons who from weakness or facility of mind, or by reason of dissipation and improvident habits, are unable or unfit to take charge of their own affairs, it is expedient that poorhouses be erected in popular parishes.[8]

Within a few months of the Act's implementation, a number of Highland parishes sought the Board's advice on offering only poorhouse relief.[9] The numbers on relief had substantially increased. The Board declined to give an authoritative judgment – that, it said, was a matter for the Courts – but it indicated that offering only indoor relief would involve 'considerable hardship' and in many cases would be an 'act of great cruelty'. A few years later, after further parish inquiries, the Board issued a more formal circular:

> The altered feelings of the poor in regard to parochial relief, their more perfect knowledge of their rights, and the facilities which the law now affords for enforcing these rights, have caused a strong pressure on parochial boards from a class, whose claims it would be unsafe to admit without testing the truth of the allegation on which these claims are founded. For this purpose a well regulated poorhouse is the best of all tests.[10]

But at the same time the circular went on to re-iterate what the Board had already stated:

> Any systematic attempt to refuse all relief, except such as may be received within the walls of a poorhouse, would excite a baneful spirit of discontent amongst the poor, and that part of the population with which they are most closely connected, without effecting any saving to the funds of the parish; and, far from being countenanced, would scarcely be tolerated by public opinion in this country[11]

As McNeill was later to say, although parishes were urged to provide poorhouses, the Board was against the 'test' being used 'oppressively'. To back this up parishes were told that where they had been too 'harsh' and the pauper subsequently appealed to the Board, the Board would support a further appeal to the Court of Session.[12]

What then of the second issue, unemployment relief? From the evidence presented to the 1844 Poor Law Commission and from earlier parliamentary accounts, it is clear that some parishes before 1845 were in the habit of giving 'temporary' or 'occasional' relief to the unemployed.[13] Usually this occurred when the harvest was poor and landowners felt it necessary to provide some assistance. It is also evident from these accounts that after 1800 many in the more industrial parishes began to object; such relief undermined a free market economy. But when a severe trade depression occurred in the late 1830s an anti-*laissez-faire* campaign emerged. A leading proponent of this campaign was Archibald Alison, the Tory Sheriff of Lanark (and brother of Dr W. P.

Alison). Alison based his critique on a radical view of how industrial society created apathy and estrangement:

> When wealth increases, manufactures spread, and society assumes a complicated form, the opulence and greatness of the higher classes, and the grandeur of the whole fabric of society throws into the shade the humble individuals by whose labour it is maintained, and renders the success of their exertions the means by which the distance is increased between the higher and lower orders of the state.[14]

For him the only redress was to ensure that the poor did have a right to relief:

> . . . the claims of the poor for relief are not of the nature of a petition, to be admitted to the benefits of a voluntary donation, but a legal right, founded upon the claim which the destitute and impotent poor in a complicated state of civilised society everywhere have to reasonable support from the more opulent and fortunate classes of society, who have been maintained by their labour. . . The wisest and most benevolent system of legal relief that human wit could have devised, would in practice, be soon rendered almost nugatory, if the power of judging in the applications for a share of its benefits were wholly vested in the ratepayers, or any persons under their control.[15]

Thus the Commission, set up to review existing practices and recommend a new policy had a difficult task in reconciling two equally 'established' but totally opposing perspectives. The Commission noted the Alison view that there ought to be a statutory right to receive relief.[16] But it also noted the view expressed by the opposition and epitomised in the evidence by the work of Thomas Chalmers, that local administration should be based on voluntary giving and be more discriminatory.[17] The consequent Act tried to balance these perspectives and stated that '. . . all assessments imposed and levied for the relief of the poor shall be extended and be applicable to the relief of the occasional as well as the permanent poor: Provided always, that nothing herein contained shall be held to confer a right to demand relief on able-bodied persons out of employment.'[18]

The Lord Advocate, Duncan McNeill, also a Tory, told the Commons that the Act was to preserve 'use and wont'. If other mechanisms of relief, such as appeals for charitable funds, failed or were found to be inadequate, then the new parochial boards could assist those out of work. Others did not share this view. To them the new Act tipped the balance towards indiscriminate relief.[19] By allowing easier access through the appeals system, by employing local inspectors of poor (who, once appointed by the parish, could not be dismissed without the sanction of the Board) and by having the widespread use of legal assessments, the unemployed would have a right to demand relief.

In the early years of the Act, after some clarification from the Board, many parishes did provide the unemployed with assistance.[20] The Board even circulated parishes on the relative merits of offering indoor relief and a labour test.[21] Nevertheless some of the larger urban parishes appeared not to have been happy at the Board's circular and, in agreement amongst themselves, initiated 'test' cases through the Courts. These soon cut away at the grounds of discretion. In one, in 1852, the House of Lords declared first that, 'an able-bodied man has no right to parochial relief for himself though unable to find employment and destitute of the means of subsistence' and second, that he could not claim relief for his dependents because, 'the Poor Law does not recognise children as distinct from their parents when they are living in family together, and that the children can only claim through their parent, who represents them and to whose control they are subject'.[22] Another a few years later, made the position still clearer: 'an able-bodied man has under no circumstances whatever a legal right to parochial relief either for himself or his family, and that by an able-bodied man is meant one who suffers under no personal inability, bodily or mental, to work'.[23]

Not all parishes agreed with this line of reasoning and backed by the Board continued to provide 'occasional' relief when they felt unemployment was severe.[24] A final ruling was given in 1866. The House of Lords, overturning a Court of Session judgment, stated categorically that 'the right to give and receive relief was correlative and if there was no right to demand relief there was none to give relief'.[25] That opinion had altered was seen when Sir John and Duncan McNeill drafted a Bill to restore what they thought the Act had intended. Urban parishes combined with the large landowner, and the Bill never left the Lord Advocate's office.[26]

It was not until 1878 that the Board made any attempt to review the position. After some exceptional winter weather caused a sudden upsurge in unemployment, a number of parishes asked the Board what they should do. The Board were emphatic that the judgment was firm, but said:

> It must be kept in view that Parochial Boards have no power to expend any of their funds in the relief of persons who are not both destitute and (wholly or partially) disabled. In considering the question of disability, however, in case of a person really destitute, the Inspector should not carry the letter of the law to an extreme, and cause delay in a doubtful case by the necessity of an appeal to the Sheriff. Moreover, it is obvious that if a person is really destitute, no long period would elapse before he also became disabled from the want of food.[27]

It then continued:

> Besides the class of persons. . . who are legally entitled to relief. . . there falls to be considered the best mode of dealing with able-

bodied persons rendered destitute by being out of employment. The legislature had entrusted the safety of these persons to the voluntary benevolence of the public, and that trust has never yet been found to have been misplaced.

Although the Board would allow parishes some discretion to prevent outright starvation, unemployment remained a matter for private bevevolence.

What of the other two issues, the demarcation of statutory assistance and the growth of middle class charity? The older Poor Law statutes, by the generic phrase, 'crukit folk, blind folk, impotent folk, and waik folk', implied that the sick should receive care. But before 1845 medical assistance had hardly existed, and outside the large towns poorhouses was almost unknown. The same lack of development also affected voluntary hospitals and, by the time of the 1844 Commission, Scotland had only twelve, with less than two thousand beds in all.[28] These hospitals would have been difficult to define as medical institutions. Since there were few poorhouses, infirmaries had been established by the wealthy for those the Poor Law had neglected, the sick poor requiring institutional care. Many provided treatment free of charge. Some, like Edinburgh Royal Infirmary, had a charter specifically prohibiting paying patients. Others, like Inverness, Dundee and Glasgow, were still free to the patient, but admission was based on a 'subscriber's' line – the amount of donation a local landowner, burgh dignitary or parish had given. In many cases nominations and admissions continued to be made, even if the donation had lapsed. Before 1845, the casual nature of this system, admitting not just the sick but the mentally insane, the aged and even tramps, prevented the development of all but the university teaching hospitals into purely medical institutions.

In their evidence to the Poor Law Commission the Alisons had argued for an improvement in medical care. They had suggested not only more poorhouses for the aged and chronically sick but also an outdoor service based on local general practitioners. The existing service was even worse than the indoor one, with many parishes having no doctor at all.

The 1845 Act allowed parishes to continue their contribution to the voluntary infirmary and encouraged an outdoor service by specifically stating, 'it shall and may be lawful to provide for medicines, medical attendance, nutritious diets, cordials, clothing for such poor'.[29] With a Government grant available from 1848 virtually all parishes established an outdoor service, though the lack of doctors and the inclination of some parishes to insist that medicines should be paid for by the doctor meant wide variations in practice.[30]

The Act also allowed groups of parishes to combine more easily for building poorhouses. But as they could still contribute to voluntary hospitals, no English-style workhouse infirmaries were established. Instead the new poorhouses developed as mixed institutions; the sick (those the infirmaries rejected), the chronically ill, the aged, the unwanted child and, until 1866, the unemployed, all had to be housed under one roof.[31]

Similar problems also affected the early development of the care of the mentally ill. If poorhouses accepted the insane then they had the problem of segregating them from other inmates. If the voluntary hospitals accepted them, other more curable patients would be excluded. Thus in many of the towns that had infirmaries, separate mental asylums were established.[32] But it was not long before these too became overcrowded; families saw the advantages of depositing their relations in safe and secure institutions. The same was true of parishes.

The solutions – rate-aided asylums – posed many problems. Parishes were too small to raise large capital sums; linking care with the Board of Supervision would mean many respectable workers would have to mix with paupers; and the legal restraint necessary for a national policy to work was against the prevailing notions of 'liberty of the individual'.[33] It was not until 1857, after an American lady, Dorothy Dix, exposed the chronic lack of asylum provision, that a Royal Commission was established and an Act eventually passed.[34]

The new Act created district boards (combinations of parishes) to ensure the development of asylums. Those whose families could not pay the necessary fees were to have their costs met by the parish, without themselves becoming paupers.[35] To underline the separation of care from the Poor Law, a new central authority, the Board of Lunacy, was established. It was to be staffed by part-time, unpaid 'men of affairs and independent means'.

When fever crises occurred in the early part of the century, infirmaries unfailingly opened their doors to the infectious sick. During the 1830 cholera epidemics, the larger local authorities pressed for and received some legislative control over 'public nuisances'. By the time of the 1845 Act a rather haphazard system of controlling infectious diseases had emerged. Infirmaries, poorhouses and local authorities all provided crisis accomodation. At the beginning of 1848 when another cholera epidemic broke out, the Board hastily became involved in the various control measures. But due to medical and burgh opposition, the Board was granted no lasting powers to become involved.[36] Infirmaries, poorhouses and specially constructed local authority fever hospitals continued to function whenever need arose.

It was not until both Edinburgh and Glasgow found many of its slum houses falling down and endangering passers-by that greater legislative powers to control defective housing and epidemics was granted. The permissive Burgh Police and Improvement Act of 1862 allowed the appointment of local medical officers of health and the creation of permanent fever hospitals. After a further wave of epidemia, the Board finally decided to press the Lord Advocate for more power and in 1867 a new Public Health Act was passed.[37] All local authorities (the parochial boards in rural areas) could engage a medical officer of health and a sanitary inspector. The Board was created the central authority, but, to allay burgh concern, no powers of compulsion were given. If the Board felt that local needs were not being met, it could apply to the Courts for an appropriate order.[38] The Act also stated that 'The local authority may provide within their District Hospitals or temporary Places for the Reception of the Sick, for the Use of the Inhabitants. Such Authority may build such Hospitals or Places of Reception, provided the Board approve of the Situation and Construction'.[39] This section was intended to allow local authorities (burghs and parishes) to build general hospitals, not just fever ones, in areas insufficiently provided for by the voluntary movement. None were built. The complicated nature of the Act's rateable provisions together with parish lethargy led to the creation of less than 1 500 hospital beds by 1890 – all for the infectious sick.

During the 1870s, a clear demarcation in the structure of medical welfare had evolved. Voluntary hospitals were freed from the necessity of dealing with the infirm, the chronically ill, the insane and those affected with infectious diseases and so could turn their attention to acute illnesses and the newer horizons of surgical medicine. The rapid increase of beds, the extension of hospitals throughout Scotland and the upward trend of admissions all testify that this was what they did. Voluntary contributions did not seem a problem.[40]

Other non medical charities also flourished. Throughout Scotland, the number of parish and burgh trusts doubled and even trebled.[41] In Edinburgh the number of new charities grew from twenty-seven between 1800 and 1850 to thirty-six between 1850 and 1875, and eighty-four between 1875 and 1900. The pattern was the same in Glasgow. The orphan homes run by William Quarrier found little difficulty in attracting donations: between 1880 and 1900 annual income more than doubled to well over £20 000.[42]

The majority of these charities, like Quarrier's, had been established for a specific purpose. This was often visible in their names; the Flora C. Stevenson Committee for the Feeding and Clothing of Destitute Children; the Home for Crippled Children; the Falconer Rescue Home. But many of them were in open competition for funds. Those who were fully endowed jealously guarded their autonomy and often refused to co-operate over individuals in need or in local strategy.[43] Some philanthopists began to see this independent action as likely to cause more harm than good and in the late 1860s new supra-charitable organisations emerged. The Association for Improving the Condition of the Poor in Edinburgh (1868) was followed by a similar society in Aberdeen (1870) and a Charity Organisation Society in Glasgow (1875). They sought to co-ordinate all charitable activities in their area.

Although the new charities were not as successful as perhaps they had hoped, their philosophy had very real consequences for the poor and for statutory assistance. What they wanted was a system of welfare that enhanced family life and moral respectablity; although they accepted that some causes of poverty, like orphanhood, were not the fault of the individual, others – like family desertion, illegitimacy, crime and drink – were. They epitomised individual selfishness and the capacity of society to decay. Borrowing the language of Thomas Chalmers, the new charities suggested that the only way to save the poor from further 'degradation' was to carefully investigate any application for assistance, assess a person's character and then offer, through one agency, appropriate individual support. Monetary benefit was a secondary consideration. They also felt the Poor Law was, at best, a necessary evil: it encouraged the belief that the State would ultimately provide. If the Poor Law was to survive – in areas where charity had not been sufficiently organised – it too should become more discriminatory, more reformatory and more rational.

The late 1860s was therefore a watershed in the development of voluntary welfare. Yet what the new philanthropy was suggesting was somewhat at variance with the the intentions of 1845. The Act had been born out of a Tory concern for the poor and this was reflected not just in McNeill's appointment as the Board's first Chairman, but also in the choice of his Secretary. John Smythe, another Highland (and Tory) landlord, had been responsible for drafting the Commission's Report. Although not as 'advanced' in their views as the Alison brothers, both McNeill and Smythe fully accepted the criticism of the old system. Indeed McNeill's philosophy mirrored Archibald Alison's. Explaining to one Poor Law inquiry why he thought the poor no longer had any 'pride' in keeping themselves off the Poor Law, he said:

> I see every day instances of a most creditable struggle to keep off the roll, a creditable struggle not to sink into pauperism. [But] in a country where the occupations between man and man is a matter of bargain and contract, you cannot keep up that feeling. As to the feeling of independence, I do not know that a man who went about from door to door begging for his food, was a more independent man than a man who comes to a parish and demands the relief he is legally entitled to.[44]

He told another inquiry that although it was important the Poor Law was managed by those who provided the 'funds', public opinion remained firm on the need for adequate relief. Such relief could only come through a statutory system, and although that involved extra expense, a balance had to be maintained:

> You can never by any arrangement make a public management precisely as economical as a private management may be; you are to balance between the inconveniences and dangers of the two modes of proceeding. In the one case, if you narrow your circle

too much, you may fail to provide the necessary funds; in the other case, if you extend it too much, you may destroy husbandry and economy.[45] Smythe held similar opinions. Ultimately, he told one inquiry, the Poor Law had to accept paupers as they were and offer adequate relief – 'even in cases of improvidence you could never allow a man to starve'.[46]

Board policy until McNeill's retirement in 1868 was dominated by these considerations – a fatalism about human nature and a belief that industrial society created the conditions that made State welfare necessary. In practice this meant both a steady increase in the numbers on relief and in the amounts they were offered. By the 1860s Scotland had a similar proportion on the Poor Law as England.

It was not until 1865 with the appointment of Alex Campbell as the Visiting Officer for Lowland Scotland, that any real hint of change occurred. During his poorhouse inspections he urged the introduction of 'task' work – 'universal idleness', he claimed, was 'evil' – and for the closer segregation of 'immoral' inmates from the more respectable.[47] But in 1867, when he met his replacement, a fellow-Conservative called Malcolm M'Neill, a different policy was formulated. M'Neill, though Sir John's nephew, was clearly shocked by the Board's policy and as he later explained to a friend, he quickly 'conferred' with Campbell (who had moved to be the general superintendent for the the the South Highlands) 'on the expediency of a united effort to check outdoor pauperism'.[48] A year later with Sir John gone, William Walker (the new Chairman) insisted that the outdoor inspectors spend time with the Board on developing a common policy (previously they had been left very much to themselves).[49] As a result, M'Neill was sent to review English workhouse practice and on his return he made it clear that poorhouse management had to change – some Scottish paupers were being overfed.[50] The Board agreed and at the end of 1869 altered the diet for those of 'doubtful' character.[51] The meat was to be left out of their soup. Since poorhouses could discriminate more precisely between paupers, both M'Neill and Campbell urged parishes to offer the 'test' to a wider range of claimants. It was, said Campbell, impossible 'to work a Poor Law without one'.[52]

Outside the Board others also felt the Poor Law had been lax. In 1866 Edinburgh City Parish urged that some review was necessary, costs had risen too sharply.[53] The cry was taken up by other city parishes and by one of the new charities, the aptly named 'Chalmers Association for Improving the Condition of the Poor'. It wanted the Poor Law's complete abolition and a return to the old principles of voluntary care.[54] A number of MPs supported the Association and in early 1869 the Lord Advocate agreed to a Parliamentary Select Committee on the Poor Laws under Edward Craufurd, the Liberal MP for Ayr.

Craufurd's Committee, although it retreated from suggesting the Poor

Law should be abolished, made it clear that a new guiding principle
was essential. Poor Relief might well have been a legal right, but the
Committee was in no doubt that far too many had been assisted. It
concluded:

> The mere fact of legislating in favour of the poor tends to create
> a conviction that the law will do everything for them and to destroy
> industry and self-help in themselves, while drying up the natural
> flow of charity and assistance form others. The only means of
> diminishing these evils is by insisting on the application of the
> most stringent checks in the administration of the law. The provi-
> sions of the law should be such as sternly to reject all considera-
> tions but those of strict justice; to relieve none but those whom
> their relatives are unable to support; to admit no arguments of
> mere sympathy, and to leave all questions of benevolence to be
> dealt with by private charity.[55]

Bolstered by the Craufurd recommendations, M'Neill continued to
press parishes to reassess what was meant by adequate relief. One group
singled out for special attention were mothers with illegitimate children,
as in his 1872 Report to the Board.

> The system of granting outdoor relief to women who claim on
> behalf of their bastard families is now, practically, without defen-
> ders among persons professing acquaintance with the subject.
> Parochial Boards should ask themselves whether, if the poorhouse
> had been offered, and outdoor relief denied, it is not reasonably
> probable that the production of additional burdens to the parish
> might have been discouraged; but, assuming that the family is
> already large, it is not, I think, over-sanguine to believe that an
> adherence to indoor relief in such a case might produce in the
> minds of observers an indisposition to incur the same treatment,
> and might thus conduce to the dimunition of illegitimacy.[56]

M'Neill had strong views over what kind of institutional care such
women should receive. Comparing their treatment with that of a widow
whose children required medical assistance, he said:

> The nominally respectable woman should occupy another dormit-
> ory, should have more frequent and easy access to her children,
> and should receive such extra diet and liberty in consideration of
> her labour as the rules of the house may permit; while on the
> other hand, the dissolute woman should not be permitted to
> exceed the prescribed working diet and should be deprived of all
> indulgences.[57]

Both Campbell and M'Neill felt the 'test' should be more broadly
applied. As M'Neill reported:

> Without the protection of a poorhouse, Parochial Boards are
> powerless to resist the claims of persons well known to be fully
> supported by their relatives; still more so to ascertain the true

condition of others in whose cases the assistance of relatives is said to be withheld, or has not been earnestly sought. . . It has occasionally been urged in particular instances, that the pauper is a person of good character, or old or infirm; but I have uniformly declined to accept these as valid arguments for relieving the relations of the task which is naturally theirs. I freely admit the hardship to the pauper, and would willingly grant such reasonable delays as would enable him to communicate with his relations, and solicit their assistance; but, while granting this, I should impress him with the conviction, that my decision was irrevocable, and I should anticipate the best results to the community from the example which had been afforded in his case, hard though it may be.[58]

By the end of the 1870s the Board was clearly pleased with Campbell and M'Neill's efforts. Parish administration, it said, had become more 'efficient'. Nevertheless the Board felt there could be no relaxing of 'sound principles'; if each applicants's claim was fully investigated and then 'tested' a further reduction in pauperism was possible.[59]

What can be said of the Victorian Scottish welfare system? First, as Johnston stated, 1845 had been an important landmark: the State had accepted that Scottish society was no longer based on agriculture, but on industry and a free market economy. Some intervention was necessary. Second, although this had been accepted, once middle-class Scotland recovered from the traumas of the 1840s they continued to oppose either Edinburgh or London directing and developing policy. The way forward was through charitable action. Third, a strict demarcation between the Poor Law, Public Health and the care of the insane had been created – and the Poor Law was about the control of pauperism. Finally, once the Board's principal officers had been replaced, it too accepted the importance of voluntary effort. The unemployed, the 'profligate', the 'dissolute' and even many of the sick, those who in the narrowest of senses had no legal claim on State support, were outside the Poor Law's concern.

NOTES
1. Johnston, T., *The History of the Working Classes in Scotland.* (Glasgow, 1929) p.275.
2. Evidence and Statistical Memorandii of Maxwell, J. T. (13.5.07), to *Royal Commission on the Poor Laws, Scottish Evidence. Cd. 4978 (P.P. 1910 Vol. XLVI).*
3. Evidence of MacPherson, E. S. (6.5.07), to *Poor Law Commission, ibid.*
4. Evidence of Walker, W. S. (15.1.70), to *Civil Departments (Scotland) Committee. C. 64 (P.P. 1870 Vol. XVIII);* see also, evidence

of Gordon, E. S. (ex-Conservative Lord Advocate) (31.7.70), to *Report of the Royal Commission on the Sanitary Laws. C. 281 (P.P. 1871 Vol. XXXV).*

5. Evidence (20.4.70), to *Select Committee on the Poor Law (Scotland), 1869. (P.P. 1868-9 Vol. IX).*

6. Board of Supervision Minutes, 31.12.72, SRO HH 23.15.

7. Henley, J. J., *Report on the Boarding-Out of Pauper Children in Scotland. (P.P. 1870 Vol. LVIII);* Skelton, J., *Report as to the Boarded-Out Pauper Children in Scotland. C. 1382 (P.P. 1875 Vol. XXXII)* (in the Board of Supervision's Annual Report, 1874-5); Peterkin, W. A., *Report to the Board of Supervision on the System of Boarding Pauper Children in Private Dwellings. C. 7140 (P.P. 1893-4 Vol. XLIV);* evidence of M'Neill, M. (20.2.95), to *Departmental Committee on Poor Law Schools. C. 8027-I (P.P. 1896 Vol. XLIV);* Glasgow City Parochial Board, *Report on the Boarding-Out of Orphan and Deserted Children and Insane.* (Glasgow, 1872).

8. Sect. 60 *Poor Law (Scotland) Amendement Act. Ch. 83. (8 & 9 Vict. 1845).*

9. *Annual Report of the Board of Supervision, 1846. (P.P. 1847 Vol. XXVIII)* p.xiv.

10. Circular as to Poorhouses (2.2.50), in *Annual Report of the Board of Supervision, 1850. (P.P. 1851 Vol. XXVI)* App.(A.) No.1, p.1.

11. *ibid.* p.2.

12. For a fuller discussion of the appeals system, see Chapter 8.

13. *Report of the Royal Commission on the Poor Law (Scotland). (P.P. 1844 Vols. XX-XXV);* see also comments in Stark, W., *Considerations of the Affairs of the Poor* (Edinburgh, 1824); Monnypenny, D., *Remarks on the Poor Laws in Scotland* (Edinburgh, 1834); Glasgow City Parish, *Parochial Law* (Glasgow, 1885); Smart, W., History of the Scots Poor Law prior to 1845, in *Report of the Royal Commission on the Poor Laws (Scotland) 1909. C. 4922 (P.P. 1909 Vol. XXXVIII);* Graham, J. E., *The History of the Poor Law of Scotland* (Edinburgh, 1921); Cormack, A. A., *Poor Relief in Scotland* (Aberdeen, 1923); Hamilton. T., *Poor Relief in South Ayrshire* (Edinburgh, 1942).

14. Alison, A., *The Principles of Population and their Connection to Human Happiness* (Edinburgh, 1840) Vol. 1, pp.9-10.

15. *ibid.* Vol. 2, pp.229-30.

16. Alison, W. A., *Observations on the Management of the Poor in Scotland* (Edinburgh, 1840); Alison, S. S., *Report on the Sanitary Condition and General Economy of the Town of Tranent N.P.*, after 1840); Alison A., *Autobiography of Sir A. Alison* (Edinburgh, 1883).

17. See, for instance, Chalmers, T., *On the Sufficiency of the Parochial System, without a Poor Rate, for the Right Management of the Poor.* Glasgow, 1841).

18. *Sect. 68, op. cit.;* see also, Second Reading of Poor Law Bill (2.4.45), *Hansard 78 (Third Series),* pp.1399-418; for comment, Chapter XVIII, Glasgow City Parish, *op. cit.;* Smith, J. G., *A Digest of the Laws of Scotland relating to the Poor, the Public Health and other Matters managed by Parochial Boards* (Edinburgh, 1878) p.193; Lamond, R. P., *The Scottish Poor Laws* (Glasgow, 1893).

19. See, for instance, comments by Gorbals and City Boards, Glasgow City Parochial Board Minutes, 25.1.48 and 18.8.48, *SRA*

D-HEW 1.1.

20. Board of Supervision Minutes, 10.12.46 and 7.1.47, *SRO HH 23.2.*
21. Circular as to Outdoor Relief to Able-Bodied Poor (3.8.48), in *Annual Report of the Board of Supervision, 1848. (P.P. 1849 Vol. XXV)* App.(A.) No.8, pp.11-13.
22. *Lindsay v McTear, 1 Macq. 155, 1852.*
23. *Pertie v Meek, 1859, 21 D 614.*
24. Draft of Letter to Lanark, Board of Supervision Minutes, 14.11.61, *SRO HH 23.9; Return of Able-Bodied Poor. . . Occasional Relief. (P.P. 1865 Vol. XLVIII)*
25. Isdale v Jack, 4M (H.L.) p.1; for a criticism see, MacKay, G. A., *The Practice of the Scottish Poor Law* (Edinburgh, 1907) p.49.
26. Letters of Lords Colonsay (Duncan McNeill) and Belhaven, in Draft of Bill to enable Parochial Boards to relieve Destitute Able-Bodied (17.4.66), *SRO AD 56.254.1.*
27. Circular and Minute Respecting Able-Bodied Persons out of Employment (12.12.78), in *Annual Report of the Board of Supervision, 1878-9. C. 2416 (P.P. 1878-9 Vol. XXX)* App.(A.) No.7, p.16.
28. See Appendix 2.
29. *Sect. 68, op. cit..*
30. History of Poor Law Medical Relief since 1845, in *Departmental Committee on Poor Law Medical Relief (Scotland). Cd. 2008 (P.P. 1904 Vol. XXXIII); Return of Parish Medical Officers (Scotland). (P.P. 1905 Vol. LXVIII)*
31. Report on. . . Model Designs for Poorhouses (6.12.47), in *Annual Report of the Board of Supervision, 1847-48. (P.P. 1848 Vol. XXXIII)* App.(B.) No.4, pp.224-7; Circular as to Poorhouses, *op. cit.*
32. Lindsay, W. L., *A General History of the Murray Royal Institution, Perth* (Perth, 1878); Tuke. D. H., *Chapters in the History of the Insane. . .* (London, 1882); Easterbrook, C. C., *The Chronicle of the Crichton Royal* (Dumfries, 1940)
33. Halliday, A., *A Letter to Lord Binning* (Edinburgh, 1818) and *A General View of the Present State of Lunatics* (London, 1928); Browne, W. A. F., *What Asylums were, are, and ought to be* (Edinburgh, 1837); evidence of McNeill to House of Commons Committee (1848), quoted by Walker, *Civil Departments Committee, op. cit..*
34. *The Royal Commission on Lunacy (Scotland). (P.P. 1857 Vol. V); Lunacy (Scotland) Act. Ch. 71 (20 & 21st. Vict. 1857).*
35. Recent Changes in the Modes of Administering Scotch Asylums, in *The Annual Report of the Board of Lunacy, 1880. C. 3023 (P.P. 1881 Vol. XLVIII);* Evidence of Spence, T. C. W. (23.2.06), in *The Royal Commission on the Care and Control of the Feeble-Minded, Scottish Evidence. Cd. 4217 (P.P. 1908 Vol. XXXIV).* Although the family of the insane would face the usual Poor Law means test (see chapter 8), its name would not be entered in the Poor Roll or face any political disability. Spence argued that this had been done because, 'the cost of providing for an insane member of a family is beyond the means of a working man, and that the isolation of an insane wife or child is compulsorily effected rather in the interests of the community than of the husband or father'.
36. See for instance, Letter from Alison, W. P. to McNeill (14.4.56),

in Public Health Bills, *SRO AD 56.276.1.*

37. Public Health Bills, *ibid. 276.2;* Board of Supervision Minutes, 22.11.66, *SRO HH 26.1.*

38. Evidence of Gordon and Walker, W. S. (31.3.70), to *Royal Commission on the Sanitary Laws, op cit.;* Introduction, Skelton, J. *The Handbook of Public Health* (Edinburgh, 1892).

39. Sect. 39, *Public Health (Scotland) Act. Ch. 101 (30 & 31 Vict. 1867).*

40. See Appendices 2A and 2B.

41. *Parish Trusts (Scotland) (No.1), Parish Trusts (Scotland) (No.2) and Burgh Trusts (Scotland). (P.P. 1905 Vol. LXVIII);* Kay, A. C. and Tonybee, H. V., Report on Endowed Voluntary Charities in Certain Places, and the Administrative Relations of Charity and the Poor Law, in *Royal Commission on the Poor Law. Cd. 4593 (P.P. 1909 Vol. XV).*

42. Hatch, *Life Story of William Quarrier* (Glasgow, 1900).

43. Kay and Tonybee, *op. cit.;* Kerr, H. L., *The Path of Social Progress* (Edinburgh, 1912).

44. Evidence (20.4.70), to *Select Committee on the Poor Law, op. cit.*

45. Evidence (2.7.50), to *Select Committee of the House of Lords on the Laws relating to Parochial Assessments, 1850. (P.P. 1850 Vol. XVI).*

46. Evidence (13.4.69), to *Select Committee on the Poor Law, op. cit..*

47. See for instance, Paisley Parochial Board Minutes, 19.6.67, *Paisley Public Library 57.7.29.*

48. Obituary (10.3.19), *Scotsman.* p.4; see also, Half-Yearly Report (March 1889), in *Annual Report of the Board of Supervision, 1888-9. C. 5815 (P.P. 1889 Vol. XXXVI)* App.(A.) No.4, p.8; Letter to Board (26.8.90), in Salaries of Board of Supervision Inspectors, *SRO HH 1.915.*

49. Board of Supervision Minutes, 12.10.68, *SRO HH 23.13.*

50. Minutes, 14.1.69, *ibid..*

51. Minutes, 18.11.69, *ibid..*

52. Half-Yearly Report (March 1870), in *Annual Report of the Board of Supervision, 1870. (P.P. 1871 Vol. XXVII)* App.(A.) No.4, p.23.

53. Edinburgh City Parochial Board Minutes, 16.4.66, *Edinburgh District Archives.*

54. Chalmers Association for Information on Important Social Questions Conference, 1869 (Edinburgh, 1869-70).

55. Recommendation 45, in *Report of the Select Committee on the Poor Law (Scotland). (P.P. 1870 Vol. XI).*

56. Half-Yearly Report by Visiting Officer (June 1872), in *Annual Report of the Board of Supervision, 1872. C.681 (P.P. 1873 Vol. XXIX)* App.(A.) No.4, p.23.

57. Half-Yearly Report by Visiting Officer (June 1873), in *Annual Report of the Board of Supervision, 1873. C. 898 (P.P. 1874 Vol. XXVI)* App.(A.) No.5, p.17.

58. Half-Yearly Report (June 1872), in *op. cit.* pp.24-5.

59. *Annual Report of the Board of Supervision, 1877-8. C. 2166 (P.P. 1878 Vol. XXXVIII)* p.xiv; see also, Circular Letter as to the Use of the Poorhouse as a Test (28.1.78), in App.(A.) No.4, pp.18-9; Milne, D. M., *Scotch Poorhouses and English Workhouses* (Edinburgh, 1873); evidence of M'Neill, M. (15.3.93), to *Royal Commission on the Aged Poor. C. 7684-II (P.P. 1895 Vol. XIV).*

3

CONTROLLING URBAN CONGESTION, 1880-99

Writing in 1894, Robert Barclay, the Board's Superintendent for the South-West, expressed some concern over an increase in pauperism.[1] The area had 1431 more paupers than in 1893, the largest increase his area had recorded for over thirty years. Lanarkshire seemed particularly affected. Barclay went on to comment:

> This is, no doubt, attributable in one way to the depression of trade, and also to the fact that two of the largest Poorhouses in Glasgow were full, and the Poorhouse test was therefore inapplicable. The County of Ayr shows an increase of upwards of 4 per cent. over the preceding year, and the significance of this increase is intensified by the fact that it follows a period of decreasing pauperism.

His colleague, Kenneth Mackenzie, the Superintendent for the South Highlands, expressed similar concern, but noted that virtually all the increase had occurred in Dundee.[2] He remarked, 'Such an increase has led me to make particular investigation there recently, and I am satisfied that the cause is the serious depression in the jute trade, from which that city is suffering.' In fact, although the Superintendents were not to know it, pauperism had reached its lowest point. By 1900 the numbers on relief throughout Scotland had increased to 85,850, some 5,396 up on the decade. The increase was most marked in the urban and industrial areas.

The rise in pauperism noted by the Superintendents, could not be attributed to a single group of claimants. All had increased in number. But there were three – the 'disabled' casual labourer, the chronically sick and children – whose numbers seemed to be rising faster than others and who, during the 1890s, attracted considerable comment from parish administrators, the Board and charity organisations. This chapter is concerned with the altered policy for these groups, for it was over them that the sharpest debates about welfare – its philosophy and administration – occurred. But first it is necessary to look at the wider issue of Scottish politics. This was to have an important bearing not only on the control of parochial administration, but also on the concept of welfare.

In 1885 the franchise was extended to about 60 per cent of the adult male population. At the same time, partly as a move to head off Home

Rule and partly to facilitate the passage of domestic legislation, a Parliamentary Office for a Scottish Secretary was created. The Lord Advocate was no longer the *de facto* head of Scottish Administration. Although the new Office was rather parsimoniously staffed, it did herald an important change in the way Scotland was governed.[3] The Scottish Office was a political, not a legal department, and the Scottish Secretary was soon involved in welfare, making statements on both the Poor Law and on Public Health.[4] But of course, although he was responsible for the Board to Parliament, he was not in control of what it did. The Board and for that matter the parish, was ultimately responsible to the courts – what they judged to be adequate poor relief.

In 1883 the Philosophical Society of Glasgow sent a memorandum to the Home Office on the need for parochial reform.[5] Their members (many were from the medical profession) no longer had any faith in the large-property owner implementing public health measures. Although the Conservative Government in 1887 recognised that some reform was necessary, Lord Lothian, the Scottish Secretary, was against too radical a change. In his Local Government Bill the parochial boards were to be retained, with all their functions. All he proposed was the replacement of the old Commissioners of Supply with directly elected county councils. It was only after considerable press comment that the Government agreed to further change, and in an amendment it proposed that the local boards should lose their public health functions to newly created district councils, a separate 'sub committee' of the county. Although this move was welcomed, when the Bill was eventually debated, MPs from both sides of the House remained critical – a local health service had not been guaranteed. Led by the Liberal Member for West Aberdeenshire, Dr Farquharson, and the Conservative Member for Wigton, Mark Stewart, sufficient pressure was applied for the Government to agree an important concession: each county not only had to appoint a medical officer of health, but they could not dismiss him without Board approval.[6]

When the Liberals returned to office in 1892, the new Scottish Secretary, Sir George Trevelyan, pressed ahead with further reform. The Board was firmly told to reduce the property qualification of parochial board members. Trevelyan wanted the same franchise for parish and county.[7] The Board agreed, although not happy about the prospect of broader representation, and the qualification was reduced from £20 to £5. But Trevelyan also wanted to reform the Board itself; he wanted to make it more accountable to Parliament. As he told one public health deputation:

> What we want are men who are paid to give their whole time and to be always on the spot, always able to carry out the necessities of administration. If I had to remodel the Board, I think I should be more inclined to do so upon the lines which the Local Govern-

ment Board in Ireland is at present constituted – to bring it strongly into relation with the office of Secretary for Scotland, so that there might be some body who might be to blame for delay or for vexations or lax administration.[8]

He also had one other reform in mind. For the range of health duties the Board had to perform, a part-time medical officer was not sufficient.[9] So despite considerable Conservative opposition a new Local Government Act was passed. The Board of Supervision was abolished and replaced by a Local Government Board, with the Scottish Secretary as President, his Permanent Secretary, the Solicitor-General, a chairman, a legal member (who had to be an advocate) and a medical member (who had to hold a public health diploma or have five years experience as a public health officer). The latter three, as Trevelyan told the Commons, were to be the Scottish Secretary's 'inner circle' of administrative officers, salaried, full-time and resident in Edinburgh. To complement these moves, Trevelyan also proposed a complete reform of parochial administration. The local boards were to be replaced by popularly elected parish councils. That, he hoped, would introduce a much broader element into welfare provision, more 'representative' of the needs to be met.[10]

Outwardly these changes seemed to herald a dramatic turn in national and local government: Trevelyan was emphatic that the Scottish Secretary was not just a member of the Board, but actually determined policy.[11] However he re-appointed the old Board's chairman, John Skelton, a Conservative, as the new chairman. Although Skelton's appointment was matched by the appointment of a Liberal, James Patten-Mac-Dougall, as the legal member, Patten-MacDougall was no radical. He was known to favour Poor Law reform, but only to make its administration more 'humane'.[12] Moreover Trevelyan had not been able to secure Dr Russell, Glasgow's Medical Officer of Health – the outstanding leader of the public health lobby – as the Board's medical member. Russell did not want to leave Glasgow. Instead he had to appoint Dr McLintock, the Medical Officer for Lanarkshire. Although able, McLintock had less public experience and had little knowledge of the Poor Law.[13] McLintock, once appointed, also faced another problem: he was given no separate medical department. All the extra staff that Trevelyan had been able to secure had been specifically employed to deal with the new local government audit.[14] It meant poorhouse inspection was, as before, the responsibility of the general superintendents.

The 1880s and 1890s had therefore witnessed a considerable change in the administration of welfare. It was more democratic, more political and, for the first time, had a medical voice amongst the policy-makers. The importance of these changes can now be discussed in three specific areas. The first concerns the unemployed and the growing number of casual labourers seeking relief.

Throughout the 1870s and 1880s, the Board, in an attempt to control the 'disabled' casual labourer, had encouraged poorhouses to develop a more rigorous system of 'tests'. Stone-breaking, bone-crushing, rope-teasing, sack-making and firewood splitting were all introduced.[15] The Board had even been prepared to stretch the law. In the early 1870s it had permitted a number of the larger poorhouses to detain the 'ins and outers' (those who entered, left and then re-entered) for up to seventy-two hours.[16] This, it felt, would both repel the 'doubtful claimant' and improve pauper 'discipline'. The law permitted only twenty-four hours' detention. Glasgow, Dundee and Paisley all took advantage of this, with Barony going further by building and equipping a special detention ward.[17]

Despite these moves, the 'disabled' casual labourer continued to apply. This was soon noticed and a number of parish officials suggested part of the difficulty lay with poorhouse management.[18] First, they felt administrative control operated in favour of the able-bodied. Once certified as 'disabled', however minor the ailment, the lack of any systematic medical follow-up ensured that the claimant's case would not be reviewed. This was particularly so in poorhouses where there was no resident doctor – and that was most. Second, they pointed out that, unlike England, Scotland had no real tradition of 'test' yards. (English workhouses had developed quite an elaborate system to put the able-bodied to work.) Indeed, only a few of the more recently constructed poorhouses allowed complete segregation and the immediate concern had always been to separate the sick from the non-sick. Third, because most boards were cost-conscious, pauper labour was always at a premium. Hence good workers were pulled out of 'test' work to assist in ward duties or in the grounds. But they also recognised that there had been an important change in the labour market: an increasing number of 'middle-aged men with weak constitutions' could find little or no permanent employment. Some, they accepted, were bound to end up applying for poor relief. By the early 1890s, it seemed obvious that parish administration had to alter: 'test' yards and seventy-two hour detention could not cope.

The problems of urban distress had not affected only parochial boards. In 1888 the Glasgow Police Authority reported a steady increase in the number of habitual offenders, vagrants and beggars and urged some action.[19] Fines and imprisonment had had little impact in reducing their numbers. It suggested that the Burgh Police and Public Health Bill, then being discussed in Parliament, should be amended to allow the courts to commit this group to poorhouses for up to two years. There they could be usefully 'retrained'. Although the Bill was withdrawn, Glasgow Presbytery, which at that time was investigating housing conditions, took up the issue and on the suggestion of Barony's Inspector of Poor,

James Motion, agreed to visit German labour colonies.[20] Although differences in the legal code made it difficult to adopt the German scheme exactly – its core was compulsion – the Presbytery was sufficiently impressed to recommend something similar for the Scottish unemployed. It might prevent them 'sinking into degradation'.

The new movement was further strengthened in 1893 when the adverse winter weather exacerbated a trade depression. The Liberal Scottish Secretary, Sir George Trevelyan, asked the Board what schemes were being adopted to alleviate the situation.[21] In England, the Government had moved to ensure that the Poor Law granted assistance. A little later Trevelyan again pressed the Board, but his time he asked what it thought about taking 'similar action'.[22] Although Trevelyan was told that the law in Scotland was different, he continued to insist that the Government had to be seen doing something, and the Board agreed that one of its General Superintendents, Robert Barclay, should undertake a survey of local relief measures. After visiting and receiving reports throughout Scotland, Barclay revealed that the traditional methods of relief had been initiated.[23] Some 10 per cent of the population in the larger industrial centres had been or were still receiving assistance from the town council and organised charity. In Glasgow, he was able to report on the Charity Organisation Society's efforts in detail:

> During the year work was offered to 491 men, of whom 294 accepted it. These attended 7 044 times, and the wages paid to them amounted to £438.6s.8d., being an average of 1s.3d. per man daily. The men are employed from 9.30 till 5 o'clock, one hour being allowed for dinner. Every man is, as far as possible, put on piece. 503 853 bundles of firewood, and 79 203 composition firelighters were made. These being sold at the regular trade prices, realised £808.2s.10d.

At Leith he noted the Report of the Association for Improving the Condition of the Poor:

> During the year ending November 1893, temporary employment was found for 230 persons. This number is a small proportion indeed of the unemployed, but in its extent and quality the record is satisfactory in every way. Aid in food, &c. was given to 1,235 persons. This number is greatly in excess of any former year. With reference to this branch of the work the committee say they are satisfied that this department prevents actual starvation in households during times of pressure, but they do not think that this work does what they hoped – raise or stimulate – it merely tides over. Nor do they consider themselves capable of meeting the difficulty by giving, finding, or making work. Therefore this distribution of food, under the pressing need of bad times, must continue, as the best to be done under the circumstances, to meet want.

The situation in Leith was not unique. Barclay noted that in many areas the numbers seeking assistance had been so great that relief work had been abandoned in favour of direct financial assistance. Although this report, and another in 1894 for the Select Committee on the Distress from Unemployment, confirmed that parishes were still adhering to the 1878 circular, one observer, Glasgow's Lord Provost, reported an important change in its impact on the Poor Law. Workers he said, 'who from infirmity or of temperament, are always the first to be dismissed' were now applying for relief.[24] Indeed the Glasgow poorhouses had become so full that they were forced to board out many of the aged and infirm.

Barclay felt sufficiently impressed by their privation – the unemployed had received markedly less in allowances than the ordinary poor – to note that many had called for the relaxation of the 1866 ruling. He commented:

> While the present system of voluntary action on the part of municipal bodies and private societies cannot be said to have failed, it has been suggested to me that an alteration of the law is desirable. They propose that the parochial board should be empowered in special instances to grant relief from the poor rate to the ablebodied, upon a representation to the Board of Supervision.

Reaction to this suggestion was almost uniformly hostile. The *Poor Law Magazine*, although it accepted the report, remained firm against altering the law.[25] It continued to believe that much of the distress was due to the worker himself and commented: 'the class of persons who come most prominently to the front as unemployed applicants for relief, are not skilled tradesmen or the more respectable class of working men, but, . . . the inferior class of workmen, and those who through shiftlessness, imprudence or dissoluteness, are even in busy and prosperous times ever on the verge of destitution.' What was required, the *Magazine* suggested, was further effort to reform the labourer's character. Only relief work would suffice, and as in Scotland the Poor Law had no tradition of providing it, some other method would have to be found.

Most parochial boards too, dismissed the idea of assisting the ablebodied. It was important, as one commentator said, to prevent the unemployed from being 'pauperised'.[26] What parishes remained interested in was the casual labourer. During the trade depression, James Motion, Barony's Inspector, had continued to press for the legislative changes the Police Authority had wanted.[27] But after Barclay's Report his views changed. It was obvious, he told a local meeting, that philanthropy had not been sufficient; its funding was inadequate and could only deal with those that 'came along'. What was required, was to take the Presbytery's suggestion of labour colonies and adapt it to Scottish conditions.[28] Local authorities, parishes, the police and C.O.S., he suggested should combine to ensure a properly funded and managed authority. The police, as in Germany, would 'sweep the streets' of vagrants, parishes would commit their 'in and outers' and local authorities would send others requiring training.

Whatever the problems associated with unemployment, then, the focus of concern continued to be on the issue of control. In 1892 a group of burghs met to discuss detention for the habitual offender but found the issue of compulsion difficult to resolve. Would it be 'legitimately and wisely applied'?[29] The next year, however, an English Committee reported that some steps to detain this group ought to be taken and the burghs immediately sent Trevelyan a memorandum urging similar action in Scotland. Sometime later, Trevelyan was pressed in Parliament on what he proposed and he replied that a Departmental Committee on Habitual Offenders, Inebriates, Beggars and Vagrants was to be established.[30] It was to review the existing legislation and assess whether increased powers of deterrence might lead to 'reformation'.

Headed by Motion, the Poor Law witnesses presented a strong case for increased detention. In his experience, inebriates, offenders and casual labourers were all drawn from the same class: those who refused to make any effort at self-support.[31] The seventy-two hour detention ought to be extended to at least a week. George Greig, the Inspector at Edinburgh said he held similar views, but argued that poorhouse detention was not enough.[32] What this group required was reformation and that should occur in purpose built institutions under a separate authority. Govan's teetotal Inspector, Andrew Mitchell was even more emphatic.[33] Nearly all his offender, vagrant and casual labourer applicants applied because of drink. The only solution, he felt, was judicial detention – in a 'workhouse' – under police supervision.

The Committee reported in April 1895.[34] Although it recognised that drunkeness and petty crime had increased, it felt that there had not been sufficient evidence to suggest a direct link between that and the increased pauperism, nor indeed unemployment. The Committee also expressed some concern over the loss of liberty many of the schemes had suggested. Its recommendations were therefore less than the Poor Law had wanted. Habitual offenders were to be committed to labour settlements run by the Secretary of State; those of weak 'intellect' were to be sent to separately administered poorhouses; the Inebriates Act was to be strengthened, and vagrants and juvenile offenders were to have greater statutory supervision. But the Committee also recognised the changing nature of urban distress and what Barclay had recommended. First of all, to meet any emergency, it suggested the local police should give over-night shelter to the unemployed, with the right to extract 'a labour equivalent'. (It was important to keep the 'honest' worker away from the pauper vagrant – those that used the poorhouse, or slept on the streets.) But for the longer term the Committee felt some better system of organising relief works was necessary. Local authorities ought to be given power to contribute directly to such schemes. The experience of the 1890s had shown charity could not deal with the vast numbers seeking assistance.

The Committee's political reception was not favourable. By the time it had reported, the Liberal Government was in difficulty and collapsed a few months later. Lord Balfour, the new Scottish Secretary, held different views on the role of the State in alleviating distress and the Committee's recommendations on unemployment were rejected. Balfour also had some doubts on providing the Poor Law with statutory powers of detention: it would mean overturning traditional principles. All he would agree to was a minor amendment of the Inebriates Act.[35]

Thus by the late 1890s, the thrust into the problem of urban distress had produced few tangible results. No new form of assistance to the unemployed had been granted. Trevelyan's attempt to bring Scotland into line with England had not been seriously pursued. Indeed unemployment, as an issue in itself, had hardly been touched; attention remained as firm as ever on the casual labourer, those who had caused the Poor Law an administrative problem. But parishes had found that what they wanted – essentially control, regulation and punishment – was politically unacceptable. Motion had been told as much by Glasgow's magistrates: in an economic depression how could you punish someone if there was no work?[36] Vagrancy, begging and drink were other issues.

Children under parish care could be divided into three groups; those who received relief at home with their parents, those inside a poorhouse, and those who (being orphans or deserted by their parents) were boarded out. In the latter group there was also a small number of children whose parents were in prison or in hospital.[37]

It was the boarding-out of otherwise healthy children that distinguished Scottish child care from English: English Guardians believed strongly that the workhouse offered greater control over a child's development. (Although some were prepared to build separate institutions, called 'barrack' homes, it still meant congregating large numbers together.) But in Scotland, removing children from the poorhouse to country farms, with the clothing, schooling and domestic life of any other child was justification in itself. As Mid-Calder's Inspector told the Board during one inquiry:

> The parish of St Cuthberts, Edinburgh, have had from 18 to 20 pauper children boarded in and near Mid-Calder village for upwards of 25 years. When the children came first, the boys wore uniform clothing of white moleskin, the girls of blue drugget, every article stamped, 'St Cuthbert's Poorhouse'. They were ashamed of it and of themselves, and the other children kept aloof from them, – they were looked upon as Pariahs, the stamp of pauper was upon them, and paupers they would have remained.

I requested the managers of St Cuthberts to remove either the children or the 'pauper stamp'. They adopted all my suggestions, and the stamp was removed. Next, the uniform clothing was altered to varieties, such as worn by the other children in the place. The hang-dog look of pauperism gradually disappeared from their faces – they saw themselves treated as other children, and soon became as others.[38]

The belief in foster care also extended to the General Superintendents. William Peterkin, reviewing the system in 1875, rejected English claims that the system was too liberal – parents could desert in the full knowledge of 'family' support – and argued:

It may certainly be doubted whether we should have had so great a reduction in the number of paupers, if all orphan and deserted pauper children had for the last thirty years been removed from home influences and familiarity with the struggles of life, and from the training and teaching of our parochial schools, to be shut up in poorhouses for ten years of a conscious existence, or until old enough to be sent out into the world, ignorant of all that is required to enable youth to cope with the vicissitudes and endure the hardships and bear the disappointments of actual life.[39]

Yet there remained one group of children parishes could not board out. The courts had ruled that the Poor Law could not 'violently sever domestic relationships'.[40] Hence even where a parish had deemed a parent 'worthless' and had granted indoor relief, apart from the normal poorhouse regulations over work, eating and sleeping, children could not be physically separated from their parents. Only if a parent consented to foster-care could a child be sent out of the poorhouse.

Throughout the 1860s and 70s the Board continued to maintain the strictness of the court's ruling. Thus in 1871, when Linlithgow asked for advice on whether it could separate a mother from her illegitimate children, it was told just how restrictive the law was: 'a parochial board cannot legally separate children from their mother without the mother's consent, unless they obtain the Sheriff's authority, – which would only be given in extreme cases'.[41] But over the next few years, as the policy of adequate but discriminatory relief was far more ruthlessly implemented and thousands of women with illegitimate children were offered only the poorhouse, a new problem arose. What would happen if the mother refused relief and there was no family to provide support? Could the parish legally take the children into care? The Board's reaction to this was seen in 1877 with the case of Mary Kelly.

Mary Kelly, who had been 'in and out' of the Wigtonshire Poorhouse on many occasions, was found in a field one night by a local Kirkcowan farmer. The Inspector of Poor immediately offered her outdoor relief and sent the appropriate notice to her parish of settlement. That parish, Mochrum, insisted she be sent back to the poorhouse – which she refused. She also refused to allow her children to be admitted. Kirk-cowan became worried over its responsibility and asked the Board for advice, especially as she was expecting another illegitimate child. Would the Inspector be liable to prosecution? The Board promptly reviewed the case, and admitted it had some difficulty in providing advice. Nevertheless it suggested:

> The Board, without professing to state what may be the law upon the subject, must express their opinion that the inspector, having offered relief in the poorhouse, incurs no criminal responsibility if she perversely refuses to accept the legal relief of the poorhouse offered to her, and chooses to go out an lie in the fields. As regards the children, the advice which the Board gives the inspector is, to endeavour to get them away from their mother, and carry them to the poorhouse, if he can do so quietly and peaceably.[42]

Although an inspector might not be criminally liable, parishes had very little power.

This and other cases caused the Board some concern, and by the time a Kircudbrightshire Board sought advice six years later, it took a different view.[43] The parish was told that it did have discretion to board out any child of someone who had accepted and continued to receive poorhouse relief. Children who remained in a poorhouse would obviously suffer a much greater danger of acquiring pauper habits and it was therefore in everyone's interest that the child was fostered. The parent could, of course, still demand the child back, but only to leave the poorhouse.

The problems associated with child care had also affected the larger parishes, but in Barony, as elsewhere, the parish faced an additional difficulty. With an increase in the number seeking relief, Barony had found its poorhouse (Barnhill) becoming overcrowded, especially during the winter. At the same time its adoption of the Board's policy – adequate but discriminatory relief – meant a far greater number of women with illegitimate children were offered only poorhouse relief. Most accepted the offer, left after a few weeks and then re-applied. Over this, of course, Barony could do little. By the end of 1882 with over three-quarters of the children admitted, being admitted with their parents, the parish decided some action was necessary.[44]

Nevertheless Barony was in a predicament. Additional poorhouse accommodation would involve considerable capital cost, but the alternative was to resort to past policy and allow 'immoral' mothers outdoor relief. The parish's difficulty was further complicated by the fact that it was nearly impossible to recruit sufficient numbers of Roman Catholic foster parents around Glasgow. (Although Barony had more Protestant orphans, rural areas had relatively fewer Catholic homes.) After considerable discussion two Board members, Mr Sellars and Dr Buchanan, proposed that 'influence be used to induce mothers to allow their children to be boarded out' and in early 1884 a new effort went into recruiting homes in the north-east.[45] By chance their problems were mentioned by one member, James Brand, to the Visiting Officer, Malcolm M'Neill, who to his amazement informed him that parishes did, in certain cases, have the right to foster children, even if a mother refused permission.[46]

Some members still had doubts over what had been suggested. Fostering they said, would relieve parents of the natural duty to provide for their offspring. If the parishes did not enforce this duty, parents would be free to continue their 'careers', producing perhaps even more children. Nevertheless Brand and the others persisted. Apart from the moral benefits to the child in a 'normal' home, they argued that the mother, once freed from the worries of child care, would be in a much better position to obtain regular employment. It was important to 'rescue' children from 'hereditary pauperism' – in the long run the numbers seeking relief would decline.

Barony asked M'Neill for clarification of the legal position. He replied:

> I have to inform you that, without pledging the Board, I gather the ground of the opinion referred to, to be that the pauper surrendering herself and her family into the hands of the Parochial Board to be maintained according to law, and their legal maintenance in the Poorhouse involving separation, she is not entitled to prescribe to the Board how their duty to her children is to be performed, and thus, if they think it is best for the children, the Board are at liberty to maintain them elsewhere than under the roof which sheltered her.[47]

A little later, at the beginning of November 1884, Barony agreed to a trial period of fostering children whose parents were in the poorhouse.[48] Thirty-two Catholic children, of whom some thirteen had mothers in Barnhill, were taken north. Although M'Neill had restricted his letter to children of parents in the poorhouse, Barony was quite clear that the new policy was intended to cover those whose parents subsequently left the institution. If they wanted their children back they would have to demonstrate an ability to maintain a 'home'. A number of parents soon objected to Barony's new policy and demanded their children, but the parish refused. One mother, Mary Hannay, persisted, demanding the address of her two boys, William and Hugh. She appealed to the Board, which, after consulting the Home Office, informed Barony:

> If, as would appear from your letters, the invariable practice of the Parochial Board is to refuse access to boarded out children to the parents and other near relatives, I am to state that the Board cannot approve of such a practice as an absolute rule without exceptions, and they are of opinion that it is not justified by the Law.
> In the case of children whose parents or other near relatives are

of the depraved or criminal classes, and where the contact of the relatives with the children would be manifestly injurious to the latter, the Parochial Board would probably be justified in keeping the children apart.

The question whether children should be kept altogether apart from their parents and relatives rests, in the first instance, with the Parochial Board. Each case should be considered by them on its merits, and the Board have no doubt that in disposing of such cases the Parochial Board will exercise a wise and humane discretion.[49]

Barony remained unmoved and not only refused to give addresses, but over the next decade fostered about fifty such children each year.[50]

This policy, however, was entirely confined to Poor Law children. It was still based on a belief that parishes were only responsible for those who applied for relief – the legal poor.[51] Others, whatever their condition, had no claim on their services. Indeed Barony remained suspicious of the newly created Prevention of Cruelty to Children Society, which in December 1884 opened its first shelter in Glasgow. A special committee was established to ensure the poorhouse accepted only paupers.[52]

Although Barony welcomed the 1889 Child Cruelty Act, which allowed easier prosecution of neglectful parents and the right to remove children from 'harmful' surroundings, it still recognised that really determined parents could regain their child.[53] Thus when a Bill was brought forward for England in 1891 which allowed a Board of Guardian to retain a child until a High Court deemed otherwise, the Inspector at Edinburgh, George Greig (with Barony support), successfully petitioned the Lord Advocate for its applicablity to Scotland. Now, no parent whose child had been chargeable could claim automatic access.[54] One parent who tried, Mrs Campbell, was told by Glasgow's Sheriff that only the Court of Session could competently decide the case.[55]

Throughout the early 1890s this policy was gradually adopted by other parishes.[56] Indeed most Poor Law witnesses to the Habitual Offenders Committee said they thought such action was useful and ought to be extended – as it was with the 1894 Child Cruelty Act. This Act widened the definition of 'neglect' and more importantly for the Poor Law, deemed the poorhouse a 'place of safety'.[57] Any thought that the Poor Law need not be involved was dispelled soon after by a widely reported Court case. A police constable had removed an assaulted child from its mother and had requested Stirling poorhouse to provide overnight care. This was done, but later the mother's parish of settlement, Perth, objected to re-imburing Stirling, saying the family was not eligible for poor relief. On appeal the Sheriff insisted the police had acted correctly. Although the case was not one of poverty – the mother was subsequently prosecuted for cruelty – parishes had a duty to meet a child's welfare.[58] The Poor Law was brought in even more direct contact with preventing abuse by the 1897 Infant Life Protection Act. The local inspector was made the Act's local agent.[59]

By the turn of the century, the Poor Law had therefore broken new ground in the care of children. Yet this new policy had not stemmed from any radical desire to extend Poor Law operations. Rather it had developed from the problem of extending the policy of adequate but discriminatory relief. Offering poorhouse relief to claimants deemed 'immoral' had created a number of administrative difficulties. Greater numbers of children had been accumulated in mixed and badly segregated poorhouses, and were often left to the mercy of inmate – pauper – labour. This had caused some concern about the 'heriditary' transmission of pauperism and as extra institutional accommodation involved a capital cost, parishes had been forced to make a choice: develop English style 'barrack' homes or to do something new. They decided the latter.[60]

The issue had not stopped there. Although the new provision had been intended for the indoor poor, parishes also had children on the outdoor roll. If the aim was to prevent pauperism, then a number of inspectors began to suggest that the policy could not be confined to poorhouse cases.[61] Although there were many parents on the outdoor roll who could not be offered the poorhouse – they were not 'profligate' or 'immoral' – their poverty, ill-health and housing did mean family life was difficult. In these cases, the inspectors admitted, parishes had some problem in not making judgements about the appropriateness of a particular home or of parental attitude. Once drawn into this debate, there arose another issue: that of drawing a distinction between those on the roll and those outside who had children – non-paupers. The inspectors knew that many non-pauper children lived in unsatisfactory homes, but established policy, and the law, meant no relief could be offered. At the turn of the century, then, these officials saw that the Poor Law faced a more fundamental issue: could parishes legitimately intervene to 'regulate' the non-pauper? Would they, too, suffer the Poor Law stigma?

Until the 1870s there is little evidence of any marked change in institutional medical care. Most boards continued to rely on a local visiting doctor for the daily routine inspection, the performing of surgery and certifying inmates who were capable of work. Sick paupers, as previously, were looked after by their fellow inmates. But the arrival of safer surgery, the introduction of professional nursing and the expansion of voluntary hospitals all led to the public's expecting better medical attention.[62] At the same time the first phase of building lunatic asylums was being completed and each had resident medical officers and trained nurses.[63] By the 1870s, there was a growing discrepancy not only between statutory sectors, but between what claimants received as medical care in the poorhouse and what they might receive in a voluntary hospital.

This was soon noticed by Malcolm M'Neill, the Visiting Officer, who in his 1878 Report to the Board commented:

I have long been impressed with the anomalous condition of sick nursing in our poorhouses, which becomes year by year more strongly contrasted with that in some English establishments of the same character and in the various infirmaries scattered over Scotland, not to speak of the lunatic wards of the poorhouses themselves. It seems to be an undisputed principle of infirmary management that cases of disease capable of cure or alleviation are, irrespective of the character of the patients or the class from which they are drawn, worthy of the best attention which highly skilled advice and nursing can bestow.

He concluded:

It does not appear to me that the sick and the bedridden pauper has claims [which are] inferior, for the Infirmary patient is, in many instances in the receipt of charity, while the pauper is the recipient of a legal provision. In every poorhouse where there are sick or bedridden inmates there should certainly be trained nurses in the proportion of not less than one to every twenty patients, and the salaries of these nurses should be such as to secure persons of high class.[64]

In future, he argued, those in statutory care ought not to be in such an inferior position: it might be construed by the courts that parishes were not providing adequate maintenance. The Board backed his Report and the following year issued a Minute on the need to introduce trained sick nursing, with one nurse to every twenty patients, just as M'Neill had found operating in Liverpool.[65] Unfortunately few parishes adopted the suggestion. As the medical grant did not cover any expenditure for nursing, they would have had to meet the full cost. This clearly concerned the Board's Poor Law officials, for when the grant was doubled in 1882, one of the clerks suggested its extension to cover part of the nurses' salaries. This was eagerly taken up, and by 1890 fourteen parishes had adopted the scheme. Four years later, all the larger urban poorhouses, covering three-quarters of the sick, had trained nurses; by the early 1900s only twenty-two poorhouses, containing less than 10 per cent of the sick, had no nurse.[66]

Despite these developments poorhouse care continued to lag behind the voluntary hospital. Not only did the latter have better staffing, but they were beginning to employ more resident doctors and visiting specialists. They also had extensive and reputable training programmes for nurses. In an effort to maintain comparability and recruit enough of their own nurses, Glasgow, Barony, Govan and Dundee parishes similarly established 'training schools'. But, given the attractions of the

infirmaries – better pay and more surgical work – they found few willing
to remain once they had qualified.[67] Indeed so bad was the situation in
Edinburgh, that the parish was forced to reconsider its terms of service.
It agreed that no nurse would be used as a ward orderly and all would
have a share of surgical work.[68]

There was another aspect to poorhouse medical care. With the expansion of the voluntary hospital the majority of the poor, like everyone
else who had an acute illness, went there for treatment. As a result,
poorhouses began to accumulate cases the infirmaries did not want,
those who were chronically sick and infirm. But the development of
medicine for chronic illness was much less advanced; no poorhouse
ever employed consultants, built operating theatres or equipped special
laboratories. In fact, poorhouse medical facilities were fast becoming
the reverse of the voluntary hospital, crude and often makeshift. At
Craiglockhart, for instance, births, and even operations, were conducted
in the open ward.[69] The same was true at Craigleith, where its visiting
medical officer reported on the nature of his work:

> I have amputed a leg above the knee. I have done a hernia. Perhaps
> if I had a case of a man developing cancer of the tongue, I would
> not like to take that myself, because I had never removed a tongue;
> but if we got an operating room and a recovery room then we
> would not send him to the Infirmary. The last amputation I had
> was about two and a half years ago. Such cases, however, seem
> to come in little bursts; there will be nothing for a year or two,
> and then there will be two or three large operations. It not a pleas-
> ant thing to give chloroform in an ordinary ward, nor is it pleasant
> for other patients to hear the noise and disturbance. In the case
> of a major operation I ask a friendly surgeon to come with me,
> and we arrange between us to do the work. He comes and brings
> all his instruments and everything complete.[70]

Whatever the inadequacies of medical care, the introduction of
trained nursing did have one important effect: inmate labour was usually withdrawn from attending the sick. Henceforth the sick came totally
within the ambit of the medical profession, and few lay administrators
sought to influence the day-to-day running of the sick wards. Indeed
by the turn of the century the influence was beginning to be in the
other direction. Doctors were petitioning their parishes for separate
wards for those suffering from illnesses such as TB, VD and 'itch' complaints. They also pressed for the complete separation of children from
adults.

This more active care had wider implications. For many inmates there
was a thin borderline between sickness and health. Children and the
infirm often needed continuing attention: it seemed pointless to 'cure'
them in medical wards and send them back to the ordinary wards under
pauper care, only to find them reclassified as sick because of lack of

medical attention. These administrative inconsistencies were further underlined when outside specialists, under the Brabazon scheme, offered their services in needle-work, basket-weaving and reading to improve the patient's mental and physical well-being.[71] After considering the issue in 1895, Barony sought the Board's approval to extend nursing to other than the short-term patient.[72] The Board agreed that this was a good idea and allowed part of the nurses' salary to be set against the medical grant. Barony immediately extended trained nursing to the wards for children, the infirm and the mentally ill.

The increased awareness of matching medical care to individual needs also had an impact on diet. Since 1850 there had been no official alteration in what was sanctioned. It was still based on oatmeal, milk and small amounts of vegetables, meat and fish.[73] By the 1890s it bore little relationship to the urban worker's diet of wheaten bread, tea and potatoes. Moreover, while its originators stressed the value of milk and meat, later regulations and interpretations reduced the meat content in soup and substituted buttermilk for sweet or skimmed milk.[74] This had been thought necessary to improve poorhouse 'discipline': only good workers and the sick should receive meat.

During the early 1880s M'Neill had continued to urge poorhouse governors to maintain the policy of adequate but discriminatory relief and spent considerable time suggesting how they could improve conditions. To bolster this, in 1884, he asked the Board if he could examine the conditions in English workhouses.[75] In his report afterwards he seemed particularly impressed with the extra care being offered to children:

> It appeared from my inquiries that the amount of food issued to each English child is nearly double the quantity thought sufficient for less healthy children in this country, that its quality is better, and that much attention is devoted to securing such variety as to encourage appetite. Complaints have reached me of the inability of the children to consume their share of the poorhouse diet, and an argument against an increase is founded on this fact; but when the nature and unvarying sameness of the food are considered it is not wonderful, as, I think, that the appetites of delicate children should fail them. The English scale is unnecessarily high, but it is inconceivable that a Scotch child can be adequately nourished on one-half the quantity which is thought reasonable in the South.[76]

The Board at first hesitated to introduce any improvement, but then agreed that a more thorough inquiry should take place, and appointed Dr Bell and Dr Littlejohn to report on the issue.[77] Two years later, after visiting a number of poorhouses and voluntary hospitals, they agreed that the existing diet was inadequate to maintain a child's health. After recommending particular additions to each age group, they commented:

Indian Meal. – We are of opinion that the time has now arrived when the Board may safely dispense with the alternative use of Indian Meal, and should insist on Oatmeal being used in all cases, and we beg to recommend accordingly.

Buttermilk. – Again, the use of Buttermilk should be discontinued, and New Milk always used in Class E [Children over 5]. Buttermilk, we find, is of uncertain composition, and is not always easily obtained. From the perfection now arrived at in the making of butter, the residue is daily becoming poorer and less nutritious. While, therefore, buttermilk may be allowed to healthy adults, whose digestive power is stronger, we have ascertained that, in the case of young children, it either cannot be taken, or if it is, it interferes with the appetite of the child, and prevents the food from being consumed.

Variety in Soups. – Where broth is ordered, a variety should be allowed in the kind of soup. We found in several of the Poorhouses that a rotation of soups was in regular use, viz., broth, pea, and potato soup.[78]

The Board adopted the suggestions and duly issued a revised children's dietary.

Criticisms remained. Not all medical officers agreed that adult diets were sufficient. A number had complained that many inmates lost weight after admission, developed weak bladders and become anaemic.[79] Dr Aitchison of Craigleith decided to conduct his own survey and concluded that this was almost entirely due to what they ate. Although oatmeal and milk, he agreed, were the basis of a good diet, the continued preparation of watery oatmeal and the use of buttermilk, a laxative, led directly to the inmates' slow starvation. He recommended skimmed milk instead of buttermilk, meat in soup and a 'little suet pudding'. The Board quickly accepted his conclusions and a new dietary was issued in 1898.[80] But it refused to make the scales mandatory. It still felt there was a need for a gap between the ordinary workers' diet and those on Poor Relief.

As with relief to the able-bodied and to children, the period before 1900 had seen a gradual change in poorhouse medical care. Equity between the statutory and voluntary sectors, and the growing numbers of chronic patients pressurised parishes into reassessing the poorhouse's function. With improved medical attention and diets, it was no longer being viewed as a dumping ground for Scotland's 'moral' misfits. It was in the business of restoring people to full health. The question in 1900 was just how far that process should and could go.

How can the three issues discussed above be judged? First of all the period had seen the complete reform of national and local welfare administration. With the replacement of the Board of Supervision by the Local Government Board, welfare was no longer conceived in purely legal-bureaucratic terms. It was a political issue. But this reform, despite the inclusion of a medical member on the Board, had not lead to any radical change. A 'humane' Poor Law may well have been better for the poor, but it was still the Poor Law – the Board simply re-issued all the old circulars.[81] Linked with this, Poor Law policy itself had become more controversial. The policy of adequate but discriminatory relief had been established when the middle classes felt secure enough to force thousands off statutory support. However in the larger urban areas, after the 1880s, pauperism showed little decline; indeed the factors that contemporaries believed contributed to it – chronic under-employment, bad parenthood and disease – seemed equally or more prevalent. Initially parish reaction had been to elaborate traditional principles: detention for the casual labourer, greater moral classification within the poorhouse, stricter control of the outdoor roll. But their whole strategy ultimately meant controlling and punishing not just the pauper, but many ordinary workers. This seemed in conflict with the notion of a free and independent worker who, after 1894, could vote in parish elections. Even the Conservatives seemed wary of punitive intervention. Where would the line be drawn between offender, vagrant and honest worker? Who would decide? By 1900 the agenda for a much wider discussion and reassessment of welfare had been set.

NOTES
1. Barclay, R. B., General Superintendent of Poor, Half-Yearly Report to the Board of Supervision (July 1894), in *Annual Report of the Board of Supervision, 1893-4. C. 7515 (P.P. 1894 Vol. XLI)* App.(A.) No.4, p.10.
2. Mackenzie, K. J., General Superintendent of Poor, Half-Yearly Report to the Board of Supervision (July 1894), in *ibid.* No.5, p.13.
3. Scottish Office, Memorandum as to Local Government and Authorities in Scotland, in *Poor Law Commission. Cd. 5440 (P.P. 1911 Vol. LIV)*.
4. Scottish Office Outletters, Public Departments, *SRO HH 28.2.1*, 2.
5. Memorial of the Philosophical Society of Glasgow to Lord Roseberry, Under Secretary for Scotland (3.5.83), in *Sanitary Journal 1883-4*, pp.183-5; see also, Russell, J. B., Public Health and Pauperism, in *ibid. 1884-5*, pp.129-34; Simpson, A., The Administration of the Health Laws in Scotland, in *ibid.*, pp.193-8; The Local Government (Scotland) Bill, *SRO GD 40.16.6, 14, 22, 23, 59*.
6. Committee Stage, Local Government (Scotland) Bill (15.7.89), *Hansard 337 (Third Series)* p.466.
7. Board of Supervision Minutes, 29.12.92, *SRO HH 23.22*.
8. n.a. (1893-4), The Proposed Board of Health, in *Sanitary Journal*

XVII, p.27.
9. Reply to question from Cameron, Dr C. (Liberal, Glasgow College) (13.9.93), *Hansard 17 (Fourth Series)*, p.1102.
10. First Reading, Local Government (Scotland) Bill (27.4.94), *Hansard 23 (Fourth Series)*, pp.1613-36; Introduction, in MacDougall, J. P. and Dodds, J. M., *The Parish Council Guide for Scotland*. (Edinburgh, 1894).
11. Minute 25.1.95, Local Government Act, 1894, *SRO DD 5.439*; see also evidence of MacCrae, Sir G. (15.11.12) and Dodds, Sir J. M. (14.11.12), to *Royal Commission on the Civil Service, Third Report, Evidence. Cd. 6740 (P.P. 1913 Vol. XVIII)*; and evidence of Lamb, J. and Lord Alness to Committee on Scottish Administration, *SRO HH 45.62, 65*.
12. n.a. (1904), James Patten-MacDougall, in *County and Municipal Record III* p.64.
13. *Poor Law Magazine 1901*, p.609.
14. Maxwell, in *op. cit.*
15. M'Neill, M., Visiting Officer, Half-Yearly Report to the Board of Supervision (April 1889), in *Annual Report of the Board of Supervision, 1888-9. C. 5815 (P.P. 1889 Vol. XXXVI)*App.(A.) No.4, p.8.
16. *Annual Report of the Board of Supervision, 1870. C. 236 (P.P. 1871 Vol. XXVII)* p.xii.
17. Evidence of Motion, J. R. (7.5.95), to *The Third Report from the Select Committee on Distress from Want of Employment. (P.P. 1895 Vol. IX)*.
18. Dalgleish, W. Changes in Poorhouse Management, in *Poor Law Magazine 1891*, pp.393-9; Ross, Rev. H., The Able-Bodied Poor in Scotland, in *ibid. 1897*, pp.353-63; Pringle, J. C., On the effects of Employment or assistance given to the Unemployed since 1886. . . , in *Poor Law Commission. Cd. 5076 (P.P. 1910 Vol. LII)*.
19. Barony Parochial Board Minutes, 10.9.88, *SRA D-HEW 2.2*.
20. The Presbytery of Glasgow, *Report of the Commission on the Housing of the Poor*. (Glasgow, 1891); Association for Improving the Condition of the Poor (Glasgow), *Report on Labour Colonies*. (Glasgow, 1892).
21. Board of Supervision Minutes, 15.6.93, *SRO HH 23.22*.
22. Minutes, 12.10.93 and 7.12.93, *op. cit.*
23. *Report by the Board of Supervision on the Measures taken by Local Authorities for the Relief of Able-Bodied Unemployment. C. 7410 (P.P. 1894 Vol. LXX)* The Report was dated 10.2.94.
24. Evidence of Bell, J. (7.5.95), to *Select Committee on Distress from Want of Employment, op. cit.*
25. n.a., Literary Notice, in *Poor Law Magazine 1894*, pp.511-4 and, n.a., The Unemployed, in *ibid.*, pp.515-26.
26. n.a., Relief of the Unemployed, in *ibid. 1893*, pp.41-3.
27. Motion, J. R., Tramps and Vagrants, in *ibid.*, pp.569-78. (Paper read to Society of Inspectors of Poor, October 1893.)
28. Motion, Notes on the Scottish Poor Law, Unemployment and Labour Colonies, in *ibid. 1895*, pp.177-92. (Re-print of a paper read to Glasgow's Philosophical Society, November 1894.)
29. n.a., The Treatment of Habitual Criminals and Inebriates, in *ibid. 1892*, p.230-6.
30. Questions from Paul, E. S. (Liberal, Edinburgh South) (5.4.93), *Hansard 22 (Fourth Series)*, p.1435 and (15.6.93), in *ibid. 25*,

p.1221. The Chairman was Dr Cameron.

31. Evidence (13.11.94), to *Departmental Committee on Habitual Offenders, Vagrants, Beggars, Inebriates and Juvenile Delinquents. C. 7763 (P.P. 1895 Vol. XXXVII).*

32. Evidence (28.11.94), to *ibid.*

33. Evidence (19.12.94), to *ibid.*

34. Report (25.4.95), to *ibid.*

35. *Report of the Inspector for Scotland under the Inebriates Acts, 1908. Cd. 4682 (P.P. 1909 Vol. XXIV); Departmental Committee on the Law Relating to Inebriates and their Detention. . . Cd. 4766 (P.P. 1909 Vol XXVI).* A small labour colony was established by a group of Glasgow philanthopists at Ruthwell, Dumfriesshire, but its admission policy was voluntary.

36. Barony Parochial Board Minutes, 8.11.93, *op. cit.*

37. Skelton, *Report as to Boarded-out Pauper Children, op cit.*

38. *ibid.* p.5.

39. Peterkin, W. A., General Superintendent of Poor, Northern (Highland) District, Half-Yearly Report to the Board of Supervision (May 1875), in *ibid.* App.(A.) No.2, p.65.

40. Barbour v Adamson 30 May 1853, *Macq. 376. 25th Jurist 419.*

41. Board Minutes, 30.3.71, *SRO HH 23.15.*

42. Letters and Minute respecting the Case of Mary Kelly and Children, in *Annual Report of the Board of Supervision, 1876-7. C. 1884 (P.P. 1876-7 Vol. XXXVII)* App.(A.) No.4, pp.12-13.

43. Letter to Kirkpatrick-Durham Parochial Board, 19.12.83, in *Departmental Committee on Habitual Offenders. . . op. cit..* Appendix XXXV. It should be noted that the Board's Legal Members had not been consulted.

44. Barony Parochial Board Minutes, 2.10.82, 5.2., 2.4. and 6.8.83, *op. cit.*

45. Minutes, 15.10.83, *ibid.*

46. Minutes, 16.6.84, *ibid.*

47. Letter of 29.8.84, in Minutes, 22.9.84, *ibid.*

48. Minutes, 3.11.84, *ibid.*

49. Board of Supervision Minutes, 20.5.85, *SRO HH 23.20.*

50. Barony Parochial Board Minutes, 14.5.94, *op. cit.*; also Motion, Notes on the Scottish Poor Law. . . , *op. cit. For a discussion of Barony's problems see, statement of Gifford, J. (28.4.85), to Pearson, D. A. (ed.) Conference on Charity and the Poor Law.* (Glasgow, 1885).

51. Black, W.G., *A Handbook of Scottish Parochial Law.* (Edinburgh, 1893).

52. Barony Parochial Board Minutes, 29.12.84, *ibid.*

53. *Prevention of Cruelty to, and Protection of, Children Act. Ch. 44 (52 & 53 Vict. 1889).*

54. *Custody of Children Act. Ch. 3 (54 Vict. 1891);* see also evidence of Greig, G. (28.11.94), to *Departmental Committee on Habitual Offenders. . . op. cit.* and (5.3.96), to *Departmental Committee on Reformatory and Industrial Schools. C. 8290 (P.P. 1897 Vol. XLII).*

55. Glasgow Barony Parish Council v Campbell (28.5.96), in *Poor Law Magazine 1896,* pp.371-5.

56. See for instance, Glasgow Parochial Board Minutes, 23.8.94, *SRA D-HEW 2.1;* see also Appendix 3.

57. *Prevention of Cruelty to Children (Amendment) Act. h. 27. (57 & 58 Vict. 1894).*

58. Stirling Parish Council v Perth Parish Council (3.5.98), in *Poor Law Magazine 1898*, pp.443-51. Technically the Sheriff ruled the Act permitted the parish of residence to defray any immediate expenditure from the Poor Rate. Perth, therefore, was not liable. In effect, what the Sheriff was saying was that, under the Act, a child's parent could not be automatically 'pauperised'. Subsequently the mother was prosecuted for cruelty.
59. *Infant Life Protection Act. Ch. 57 (60 & 61 Vict. 1897)*.
60. Motion, Notes on the Scottish Poor Law. . . , *op. cit.*; Change, W., Children Under the Poor Law, in *ibid. 1899*, pp.513-18.
61. Patterson, J., The Disposal of Neglected Children, in *ibid. 1903*, pp.240-6 and Pressley, W., Children Separated from the Parents by the Authority of the Parish Council, in *ibid.*, pp.521-4.
62. See Appendix 2A.
63. Recent Changes in the Modes of Administering Scotch Asylums, in *op. cit.*
64. M'Neill, Half-Yearly Report to the Board of Supervision, (May 1878), in *Annual Report of the Board of Supervision, 1877-8. C. 2166 (P.P. 1878 Vol. XXXVIII)* p.13.
65. Circular on Sick Nursing in Poorhouses (31.7.79), in *Annual Report of the Board of Supervision, 1878-9. C. 2416 (P.P. 1878-9 Vol. XXX)* App.(A.) No.14, p.28.
66. (1) Memorandum as to the Nursing of Sick Poor in Scotland and (2) List of Poorhouses having Trained Nurses, in *The Departmental Committee on the Nursing of the Sick Poor. Cd. 1366 (P.P. 1902 Vol. XXXIX)* Appendix XXIV.
67. Evidence of M'Neill and Barclay (4.2.02), to *ibid.*; see also, evidence of Johnston, J. M.'c (Medical Officer, Glasgow City Poorhouse) (1.10.02), to *Departmental Committee on Medical Relief, op. cit.*
68. Edinburgh Parish Council Minutes, 9.5.99, *EPLER qYHV 251.*
69. Minutes, 8.12.97, *ibid.*
70. Evidence of Aitchison, R.S. (15.1.03), to *Departmental Committee on Medical Relief, op. cit.*
71. Edinburgh Parish Council Minutes, 18.12.97, *op. cit.*; Glasgow Parish Council Minutes, 17.9.97, *SRA D-HEW 1.2*; Barony Parish Council Minutes, 23.9.96, *op. cit.*
72. Barony Parish Council Minutes, 9.10.95, *ibid.*; *Poor Law Magazine 1897*, pp.554; and *ibid. 1902*, pp.44 and 46.
73. Barony Parish Council Minutes, 23.10.95, *op. cit.*
74. Circular on the Diet of Inmates in Poorhouses (18.11.69), in *Annual Report of the Board of Supervision, 1870. (P.P. 1870 Vol. XXVII)* App.(A.) No.1, p.1.
75. Board Minutes, 6.11.84, *SRO HH 23.20.*
76. M'Neill, Half-Yearly Report to the Board of Supervision (June 1885), in *Annual Report of Board of Supervision, 1884-5. C. 4559 (P.P. 1884-5 Vol. XXXIV)* App.(A.) No.3, p.15.
77. Board Minutes, 15.10.85, *op. cit..*
78. Report by Drs Bell and Littlejohn on the Dietaries of Children in Poorhouses (31.12.87), in *Annual Report of the Board of Supervision, 1888. C. 5550 (P.P. 1888 Vol. L)* App.(A.) No.8. p.18. Bell was President of the Royal College of Surgeons. Littlejohn was Medical Officer of Health, Edinburgh and the Board's part-time Medical Officer.
79. Aitchison, R. S., *Effects of Diets upon Kidneys.* (Edinburgh,

1896); n.a., The Poorhouse, in *Poor Law Magazine 1896*, pp.449-62.

80. Circular as to Dietary in Poorhouses (2.2.98), in *Annual Report of the Local Government Board, 1898. C. 9273 (P.P. 1899 Vol. XXXVIII)* App.(A.) No.5, pp.8-12.

81. Circular on Poor Law Administration (30.10.85), in *Annual Report of the Local Government Board, 1895-6. C. 8219 (P.P. Vol. XXXVIII)* App.(A.) No.5, pp.8-12.

4
PAUPERISM AND SOCIAL NEED:
THE NATIONAL DEBATE, 1900-14

The decade after 1890 had witnessed growing doubts by many councillors and officials about the validity of the Poor Law's established strategy in combating 'pauperism'. The re-examination of policy had pushed the philosophy of moral discrimination to its apparent limit, without effecting any further decline in the numbers that sought relief. In fact the very opposite occurred. During this period, the first tentative experiments in linking individual care to social welfare had been made, and there was a growing awareness that much more information was needed about the social and personal circumstances of claimants. Without a thorough examination of these circumstances, it would be impossible both to understand the complexities of poverty and to persuade the apathetic or sceptical electorate that something should be done. At the same time, the growing sophistication of 'social knowledge', seen in the evidence of charity organisers, the medical profession and others to the various commissions began to undermine the legitimacy of many traditional policies and practices. Moreover, these commissions were no longer one-off occassions or afterthoughts of schemes already approved; they were an integrated series, each one refining the instruments of social inquiry and setting an agenda for further studies.

It became steadily more apparent that capitalist growth did not always lead to individual betterment. The mature industrial economy of Scotland offered its evidence: urban over-crowding, labour market congestion, a low standard of public health, and self-generating poverty. The advocates of a free economy had assumed that it would facilitate the development of talents and advantages; this was not the case for the majority of the urban poor. The pressing question was how to cope with these new and apparently overwhelming problems. With the Labour Party only nascent, political life was dominated by the capitalist ethos and the virtues of economic progress. The critical task, therefore, was to remould social policy in a manner that would harmonise the individual with the on-going economic changes. In order to begin that remoulding, some more open discussion would be necessary and the period witnessed one of the most intense debates about the appropriate method of achieving this goal.

There were three important issues in this debate: first, how could an individual's social development be conceived; second, what was, or ought to be the individual's relationship to statutory welfare; and third, how should Government assist the pursuit and development of policy. The more traditional principles had begun by suggesting that if man was a 'free moral agent', any statutory assistance was an admission of the failure to be self-supporting. The operation of public institutions would reduce individual initiative, retard the proper development of talents and lead to inefficient allocation of resources. Any individual, with the full knowledge that public institutions would not arbitrarily intervene in his day-to-day existence, could allocate resources for himself in a much more efficient and rational manner. By implication, the role of both central and local government had to be minor and carry only residual powers to prevent an absolute breakdown in public order. Local government, because it was nearer the actual operation of welfare, was better placed than central government both to allocate whatever resources were available and to determine policy. In that way the philosophical ethos of the system would be maintained.

By contrast the new knowledge being elaborated through the inquiries of the 1890s and early 1900s was beginning to open up a radically different perspective. First it argued that the pecuniary nature of parish administration had sustained too restrictive a view of welfare. A leading advocate of this new philosophy, Dr Leslie MacKenzie, specifically criticised Poor Law administrators for their continued attachment to a philosophy of discrimination and public stigma. He claimed that, 'superficially, the Poor Law appears to have been instituted just to provide for those that could not provide for themselves; yet in the course of its evolution, it has come to be shunned rather than sought by many of those that have an unquestionable claim to its powers'.[1] But he also felt that blaming the individual for his or her poverty, as the Poor Law did, was fallacious. It hid a real understanding of how a person developed. As he had earlier told the Physical Training Commission:

> What is popularly regarded as the degeneration of the slums is largely a 'generational' degeneration, and depends not on hereditary disposition, but on environment. When the infections have been eliminated, when the malnutrition diseases have been eliminated, when, either by altering the environment or transplanting the children, the organism has become free to respond to the stimuli of light, air, and suitable food, it will be found that much of what has been taken for hereditary or transmissible degeneration is really confined to the individual generation. The scope for improvement by better nurture is almost unlimited.[2]

MacKenzie's philosophy meant one thing: the individual was a social being whose abilities and desires needed the active encouragement of public institutions. Only in this way, he argued, could the broad mass of individuals see their talents, abilities and needs free of the pernicious effects of capitalism. This was seen most succintly in his evidence to the Poor Law Commission. He told them that he 'did not take the ordinary view that everything done by the public authority necessarily takes something away from the person that is benefited', in fact it was the very opposite, 'what one needs to create is the feeling that that is the instrument for doing the work. . . to realise [him]self more fully'.[3] Social welfare could and would enable the individual to overcome the structural and environmental problems of a more advanced industrial economy.

In essence, this new philosophy, although reflecting the Alisonian desire to ensure that the working classes benefited from 'positively' created institutions, was stressing a very different role for Government agencies. To ensure the working classes' sense of participation in and belonging to industrial society, Government, especially national Government, ought to be prepared to offer them a new deal. That deal involved far greater centralised support and direction in the evolution and control of local policy. By elaborating certain national criteria of welfare far more explicitly than in the past, inequality could be reduced and a new sense of fairness amongst the less fortunate generated. If this happened then the newly enfranchised working classes, many of whom had clearly not shared in the general benefits of capitalism, would see that economic progress led to social and individual betterment. That in turn would strengthen the legitimacy of the existing mode of production.

The remainder of this chapter will be devoted to a closer examination of the way the issues between the two opposing lobbies – the upholders of the traditional Poor Law and those influenced by contemporary social inquiry – were resolved. It will concentrate first on three national events: the creation in 1901 of a Board medical inspectorate, the appointment in 1905 of a radical Scottish Secretary, and the establishment in 1905 of a Poor Law Royal Commission. It will then go on to discuss a number of debates at the national level. The process of change within local administration will be narrated in the next chapter.

The first of these three significant events, the appointment of Dr Leslie MacKenzie as full-time Medical Inspector, marked a change in the role of central government officers. The Society of Medical Officers had pressed for the creation of this post for over a decade.[4] However Lord Salisbury's Conservative Government did not embark very readily on any kind of social experiment, and with an equally entrenched Scottish Secretary, Lord Balfour, all attempts to discuss the issue were firmly suppressed. Nevertheless, beginning with the Supply Debates of 1898, some back-bench Liberal MPs began to openly attack Scotland's system of welfare for the first time.[5] Over the next two years the intensity of these attacks increased, until finally during the 1900 Debates, the MPs complained bitterly that the General Superintendents were unable to monitor health conditions in the Highlands.[6] It was time, they said, for Scotland, like England and Ireland, to have professionally trained medical inspectors who could impress on local authorities the need for change. The Lord Advocate, Graham Murray, was somewhat taken aback and replied, 'that the inspectors should be medical men is a suggestion that would not be read with favour. The Board have to perform other duties besides medical duties.' Although the 1894 Act allowed the appointment of an inspector, the Government could not see a need.

Yet pressure was maintained and, when the Board itself claimed its resources were more than fully stretched, Balfour was forced to relent and MacKenzie's post was hurriedly created.[7] To avoid creating a post parallel to, and therefore in conflict with, the General Superintendents', MacKenzie was told he would not have any 'general inspection' duties. Instead, MacKenzie, a fully qualified local government health official, was to devote less time to 'ordinary' administration and more to investigative work. If Balfour had intended the role to be a subordinate one, fully contained by other officials, then he had not taken into account either its propaganda element, or MacKenzie's particular character. MacKenzie, a one-time pupil of Alexander Bain – the Liberal and progressive Professor of Logic at Aberdeen – was not slow to demonstrate his intense concern over Scotland's health record.[8]

An early hint of his attitude occurred with the establishment in March 1902 of the Royal Commission on Physical Training. At the end of 1898, after some criticism from the Army about the comparatively poor physique of Scottish boys, the Education Department initiated a series of discussions on physical training between themselves, the School Boards and the Army.[9] It soon became obvious that there were many inter-related issues of education, physical fitness and the recruitment of soldiers, and the Department pressed Balfour to establish an Inquiry. Balfour, equally alarmed at the prospect of a decline in enlistments, agreed and informed his Cabinet colleagues that 'it is certain that the modern conditions of town life discourage many of the poorest children from any proper exercise'.[10] With Scotland's high emigration rate which drew away 'the brightest and the fittest', the failure of many schools to provide physical training, he said, had grave consequences for the maintenance of imperial power.

Nevertheless moral outrage at the likelihood of imperial decline, as the Commission knew, was not going to be sufficient to persuade the electorate that something had to be done. So MacKenzie and Professor Hay of Aberdeen were appointed special investigators to undertake a survey of school children in Edinburgh and Aberdeen.[11] Both surveys revealed how inferior the position of slum children was: one third of the children MacKenzie examined were suffering deprivation. But he went further than supplying information: he stated that physical education by itself would be futile unless accompanied by a better diet and by school medical inspection.

The implications of the surveys were not lost on the Commission. Although composed mainly of Conservatives, it recommended that school boards provided facilities for voluntary agencies to feed school children. If there were no local agencies, then school boards were themselves to provide the meals. Those parents who could not pay were to be deemed 'paupers'.[12] To one medical reviewer, the agenda had been set for a much closer examination of the issue of physical fitness and the State's role in providing assistance.[13]

With this alteration in perspective, MacKenzie was soon in action urging the necessity for school boards to medically inspect children. In a series of lectures and publications, he dismissed out of hand the ideology of laissez-faire and a restricted role for the State.[14] To him, this ideology, epitomised by the work of Herbert Spencer, was too ill-conceived for the 'practical' work of a medical officer. Once the State provided free and compulsory education, teachers, parents and medical officers had to know if children were unfit for schooling. As he told one health conference in 1903:

> If it be the case that the ranks of the mentally and physical ineffi-
> cient among adults are largely, if not chiefly, recruited from those
> that have had a bad start in life, the case for a scrutiny of the child
> and his conditions are overwhelmingly urgent. The inspection of
> children at school will not solve all the difficulties; it cannot cover
> the whole ground; it cannot secure to all a better start; but at least
> it will reveal some of the preventable causes of inefficiency.[15]

But MacKenzie also believed that parental responsibilities had to be balanced against the State's obligation to prepare a child for the world. Only then could it demand economically useful citizens. This more functional view of the relationship between social welfare, the State and the citizen certainly did not go unchallenged, but his later studies, one for the Edinburgh Charity Organisation Society on the health of schoolchildren and another more exhaustive one for Glasgow's School Board on the relationship between physical development and housing conditions, continued to underline the call for a re-examination of policy.[16]

MacKenzie's approach did not go unnoticed by the Board's Poor Law Branch. Before 1904, General Superintendents had visited every parish once a year, checking for financial irregularities and informing officials about established policy. With the new audit procedures fully implemented and MacKenzie demonstrating the utility of investigative work, the Board agreed that a change in duties was necessary.[17] Superintendents were instructed to conduct more specialised investigations into the nature of distress and offer parishes 'practical' advice on improving the Poor Law's administration. Although parishes only saw a Board official every other year, this new procedure, coupled with the audit, meant a far closer control by the Board on policy and practice. The Board insisted it could gather as much knowledge of local circumstances as a parish.

This qualitative change in the role of central Government officials heralded an important shift in the way the Poor Law was implemented. But in 1905 this change, although acknowledged by the Board as necessary, had not been fully elaborated. Some critical questions remained: how far Government could 'search out' and 'correct' the cause of distress; how far it could demand an alteration in an individual's behaviour; and how far it could override local responsibility. The next event, the appointment of John Sinclair as the Liberal Scottish Secretary in December 1905, ensured that these questions would be examined by a radical administration.

Sinclair's appointment brought a new tone to the politics of welfare. Although the majority of Liberal MPs had not given social policy any great consideration in the years before 1906, Sinclair had indicated what changes he would prefer, drawing on his considerable experience in the field of welfare.[18] In the 1880s he had been involved in the activities of Toynbee Hall, campaigning against sweated labour and in favour of adult education. By the 1890s he was espousing the causes of Home Rule, local government reform, employers' liability, and land reform. His election as MP for Forfarshire in 1897 brought him into contact with Dundee, where he was soon involved in a housing commission which sought to relieve urban overcrowding by the development of 'garden cities'. While most of his energies between 1905 and 1912 went into agricultural and housing policy, his immediate task on accepting office was in educational reform and the amendment of the Conservatives' Unemployed Workman's Act.

Because of Labour pressure, the Liberals in their election manifesto had already committed themselves to extending assistance to the unemployed. But the commitment had been made grudgingly. Sinclair, like his Party, felt that the distress of the preceding few years had been the exception rather than the rule, and he saw no reason to make dramatic incursions into the free play of the labour market. The Conservatives' Act underwent minor amendment and Sinclair left it to the Board to pursue more liberal policies in its administration. In that way he felt more immediate assistance would be given to those in need.

Educational reform was different. He felt that the medical and social need of children, unlike unemployment relief, overrode any consideration of economic utility. His first Bill, although small in scope, heralded a change of direction: it allowed school boards to make special provision for the education of mentally defective children. Previously they had been dealt with by parishes and lunacy boards. This was followed by a series of Bills designed to permit the medical inspection and the provision of school meals. Sinclair's administration, therefore, was dominated by a belief in a free, but socially aware, economic system. To support this belief, Sinclair needed an acquiescent but competent administration. What he had inherited was a Board still acknowledged as deficient in medical expertise and still largely dominated by 19th-century conceptions of welfare.[19] This was a reflection both of the Board's ambivalent attitude towards the Poor Law, and the role of Government patronage in filling vacant posts.

When John Skelton retired from the Board in 1897, Lord Balfour had appointed its Secretary, Malcolm M'Neill as the new Chairman. It would have been customary to have appointed the Board's legal member, James Patten-MacDougall, but not only was M'Neill both an 'ardent Unionist' and an ex-superintendent of poor (thus re-emphasising the importance of the Poor Law in the Board's affairs), but Patten-MacDougall had been Legal Secretary to the Liberal Lord Advocate in 1892-4.[20] Indeed for a time he had been Secretary to the Scottish Liberal Association. At the end of 1904, J. B. Russell, the medical member, died and a few weeks later M'Neill retired. The Conservatives were in a predicament. The public health lobby were all agreed that MacKenzie was the most suitable replacement for Russell, and despite his obvious Liberal credentials, the appointment was duly made. The Chairmanship was another matter. Patten-MacDougall had served ten years and no one else had either his seniority or experience of administration. The Conservatives hesitated to bring in an outsider and, swallowing their political inclinations, made the appointment. To offset this move, Ewan MacPherson, the current Lord Advocate's Legal Secretary, and hence a Conservative, was appointed the Board's legal member. Not only was it the first time a Liberal had held the chairmanship of either the Board of Supervision or the Local Government Board, but it also meant that no one on the former had any direct experience of Poor Law administration. When in 1909 the Secretary, James Falconer-Stewart, another ex-superintendent, retired, and Abijah Murray, a staff clerk from the Public Health Branch (and known for his 'progressive' views) was appointed in his place, all the senior posts became held by non-Poor Law men.

The Conservatives, though not unused to patronage, had always been careful not to introduce too much political bias in the departments under their control. To them it had been important to keep some semblance of civil service neutrality. Sinclair had no such qualms. Patten-McDougall resigned his post in early 1909 (he became Deputy-Clerk Registrar for Scotland). It was not an opportunity to be missed and Sinclair, with the willing approval of Asquith, appointed Sir George MacCrae, the Liberal MP for East Edinburgh, to fill the post. MacCrae had no direct experience of welfare administration, but he was known as having 'advanced' Liberal views. A hatter by trade and a one-time Treasurer of Edinburgh City Council, he had successfully fought the

1899 East Edinburgh by-election on such issues as the housing of the working classes, old age pensions and the amelioration of social conditions.[21]. This startling appointment was matched the following year when Sir Thomas Mason, another Liberal, was made Chairman of the Board of Lunacy. Similar appointments soon followed. In 1911 James Leishman, an Edinburgh Liberal Councillor, was made Chairman of the the newly created Scottish Health Insurance Commission, and in 1913, the Liberal MP for Inverness-shire, Sir James Dewar, was made Chairman of the Highlands and Islands Medical Services Board.

Putting radicals in these key positions was only one half of the transformation that occurred in the administration of Scottish welfare. The most common complaint by administrators during this period had been that they were both over-worked and under-staffed.[22] In this they had some justification. If allowances are made for comparable functions and population differences, then the staffing of Scottish welfare administration was less than 75 per cent of that in England.

Between 1910 and 1913 – following the 1908 Children's Act, the 1909 Town and Country Planning Act and the Poor Law Commission's recommendations on the need for extra staff – the Board acquired an additional two assistant secretaries, two extra medical inspectors, a veterinary inspector, an engineering inspector, and architectural inspector and a lady inspector. Additional clerks were also appointed. These were sizeable increases, bringing staffing levels in Scotland to 90 per cent of the English level.

One of the last acts in Sinclair's administration surpassed even the enlargement of the Board. Throughout the summer of 1911, MPs had been debating the National Health Insurance Bill. By the autumn the final clauses were passing through the Committee stage. The original Bill had stipulated one Commission for the UK, but with Home Rule in the air, the prospect of welfare administration in Scotland being conducted from south of the border was not at all pleasing to back-bench Liberal sentiment. At a private meeting with Lloyd George, the Chancellor of the Exchequer, about thirty Liberals argued that there should be a separate Scottish Commission.[23] Scotland, they suggested, had special employment problems, like that of the crofters, and only a Commission 'near the seat of action' could hope to be effective. The Government appeared to have no strong feelings and by 171 votes to 89, with Labour and Conservative MPs providing most of the opposition, a separate Commission answerable to the Scottish Secretary was created.

At a stroke Scottish welfare administration quadrupled. Health insurance demanded a considerable bureaucracy; medical officers, regional inspectors and intelligence officers all had to be appointed. The contention that Scotland had special employment needs had yet another result. The Commission was allowed to recruit comparatively more staff than its English counterpart. If this new complement of staff is added to that of the Board's, then the number of Scottish welfare administrators was now equivalent to England's. There was one final twist to all these developments. The Commission demanded a high calibre of staff, and in 1919 when it was amalgamated with the Board to make way for the Board of Health, many of its officials found themselves being appointed to more senior positions than those in the old Board. It meant even fewer Poor Law officials in position of authority.[24]

By 1912 the face of Scottish welfare administration had completely altered. With no senior officials having detailed Poor Law experience, traditional philosophy and practice had been superseded by acknowledgement of the necessity for greater and more ameliorative intervention. The language these new administrators used was radically different from that most in the Poor Law had known. They no longer believed in a central administration using friendly advice and persuasion: welfare was not the prerogative solely of local politicians and officials; it was a national issue, demanding central government action.

No discussion of welfare in the years before 1914 could omit the Royal Commission on the Poor Laws. This Commission was established at the end of 1905 and reported in early 1909. The issues which led to its recommendations will be dealt with later, but in Scotland the desire for a Commission stemmed from one principal difficulty: the changing profile of Poor Law claimants. One of the first acts of the Commission in 1906 was to investigate the nature of Scottish pauperism and it found the traditional profile of recipients on the outdoor roll had altered very little.[25] Widows and the elderly continued to form the bulk of those assisted. The same, however, could not be said of indoor recipients; poorhouses, it reported, were rapidly filling up with more sick and more 'disabled' casual labourers. The greatest increase came from men aged fifty to sixty-five. What greatly alarmed the Commission was that these changes were most noticeable in the larger, urban areas. Pauperism in rural Scotland was actually declining. During the early 1900s, in fact, the Board had begun to realise that this issue, the increased use of the poorhouse by two quite separate groups, did mean some action was required if the Poor Law's basic structure was to be maintained. The first question that brought the issue to a head concerned the development of medical services.

When the 1889 Local Government Act had inadvertently 'stereotyped fixed' the distribution of the medical grant, the allowance for trained sick nursing became a fixed charge. As all the larger poorhouses had these nurses, they received the largest slice of the grant, and the Board was left with little extra cash to improve other areas of care. During 1902, therefore, two Bills were introduced to allow the Board to vary the distribution of the grant.[26] A number of parishes, however, objected to the lack of consultation and the Bills were withdrawn. Shortly afterwards, in an attempt to placate local opinion, the Board appointed a

Departmental Committee on Poor Law Medical Services. Its purpose, parishes were told, was to review the basis of the grant and to recommend whatever improvements in the quality and administration of medical services it thought necessary. The chairman was Patten-Mac-Dougall. The other members were Dr MacKenzie and R. B. Barclay, the General Superintendent who supervised poorhouses.

After hearing evidence from about two dozen witnesses and reviewing the history of medical relief, the Committee reported in March 1904. Its lengthy recommendations, written by Patten-MacDougall, included the need for more 'observation' wards for the suspected mentally ill; more operating theatres, the continued segregation of the sick into 'modern' medical categories, with more and better beds; an improved diet; an end to pauper nursing; a national nurses' training scheme and the promotion of the medical officer's authority. To ensure this would occur, the Committee also recommended an increase in the Board's power. Poorhouses were to be managed by statutory regulation.[27]

Despite the Committee's origins, the Report's reception was favourable. A Poor Law Magazine review, while concluding that its recommendations meant a reduction in local autonomy, felt that this was no more than the 'natural growth of administration'.[28] It was the only sure way to obtain an improvement in care. Medical reviews were also favourable.[29] They welcomed the prospect of better provision for the sick. Indeed there is no evidence of any parish raising any objections. Not only had a threshold in the Board's control of policy been crossed, but also the status of the sick poor had been raised: they should receive care similar to that given the voluntary patient.

The Committee's parliamentary reception was equally uneventful. Some Liberal MPs inquired about possible action, but were told the Government preferred to act through administrative procedures.[30] A year later, the Government had had time to reflect and announced that a Bill embodying certain aspects of its recommendations was being prepared.[31] Three months later the Poor Law Commission was established and all prospective legislation was shelved until it reported.

One reason why the Government had stalled on introducing legislation had been the sudden impact of the 1902-5 trade depression on the numbers applying for relief. Many more unemployed casual labourers pleading disablement had applied for and received assistance. Some parishes reported that others, though equally affected, could not bring themselves to apply personally, but instead forced those they had supported – their parents, brothers and sisters – to do so. By the summer of 1904, the Board had become so alarmed that it began its own internal survey of the distress. Others had also noticed and in Parliament, Alex Cross, the Liberal Unionist MP for Camlachie, asked the Government to establish a formal Inquiry into its causes.[32] In December the request was granted and an Inter-Departmental Committee was established, composed of the Board's four superintendents and one of its staff clerks. Its aim was to examine the relationship between the administration of relief in the areas known to be worst affected – the large towns – and the growth of pauperism.

Unfortunately for the Committee there was no obvious correlation between those parishes which it considered had the most defective administration and those that had the greatest increase in pauperism. Although Govan, Glasgow and Leith had the most marked increases, there was nothing to suggest their methods were in any way more lax than any other parish. But it also observed, 'that the greater part of the increase of pauperism during the past decade is due to the chargeablity of men. Having made special inquiry as to the social condition of the men who are thus swelling the poor roll, we are informed that a large majority come from model lodging-houses.'[33] It suggested a radical alteration in Scottish Poor Law provision:

> To deal satisfactorily with such paupers, for whom, in a measure the Scottish Poor Law does not provide, we recommend the estab-lishment of a "Workhouse" or "Labour Colony" in some shape or form. It would, we think, be to their own advantage and to the benefit of the community that they should be compelled to work and that certain restrictions, under proper safeguards, should be imposed on their liberty.

As all of this implied new legislation, the Committee recommended an immediate thirty-five point plan to tighten administrative procedures and allow for the greater scrutiny of an applicants's case. The parishes concerned did little to implement any of the recommendations.[34] They all felt their own style of administration was not sufficiently defective for the major restructuring the Committee thought necessary. Thus the Board's attempt to control the growth of pauperism had failed, and failed for two reasons. First, parishes had not fully recognised the Board's authority to determine policy. Second, by the time of the Com-mittee's report, March 1905, Scottish unemployment – for the first time since the 1840s – had become a sensitive political issue.

Before the Committee had been established, the Government had consistently refused to grant parishes extra power to deal with the grow-ing number of unemployed labourers who sought their assistance (see p. 81). On 10 January 1905, in one final bid to persuade the Government to act, Glasgow City and Parish Councils arranged a conference between town, parish and trade councils on future strategy.[35] The conference was a failure. A suggestion by some parishes that the unemployed should be committed to labour colonies immediately encountered the hostility of the trade union representatives. Keir Hardie, in particular, felt that unemployment relief required a much broader perspective. He argued that to use or amend the Vagrant and Inebriate Acts, or to introduce compulsory poorhouse detention as some had wanted, would greatly offend the vast majority of respectable workers. Only a State organised system – one that had no stigma attached – would satisfy him. With the intervention of these Labour representatives and the suspicion between parish and town councils regarding their respective roles, any hope for a consensus on future strategy evaporated. Instead the Conference was reduced to recommending that the Government establish a more general Poor Law inquiry.

Thus by the spring of 1905, both the Board and parish councils had reached a critical point in their conception of welfare and in the future direction of policy. The Board had realised that it should play a more directive role in the implementation of policy. But it had found that local practice together with the changing nature of claimant needs meant no new consensus could emerge. It was therefore left to others, with more radical opinion, to thrust the debate on to a totally different plane. In the spring and summer of 1905 that was most forcibly pursued in Parliament.

In April, Keir Hardie asked the Lord Advocate to repeal the restriction of relief to the able-bodied.[36] He refused. The Liberals then asked for the Unemployed Workman's Bill to be applied to Scotland.[37] This request was also refused. Undaunted, the Liberals demanded further changes to Poor Law policy: better allowances for widows, children and the elderly.[38]

Quite apart from the Poor Law debate, the Conservative Government's position in 1905 continued to deteriorate and with the prospect of an early general election, Arthur Balfour, the Prime Minister, sought ways to restore his Party's electoral fortunes. The Unemployed Workman's Bill for England was one way. (It was to provide temporary Government assistance for the unemployed.) Another was to announce a Royal Commission on the Poor Laws. On 2 August, after announcing the appointment of the Commission, Balfour was asked by Edmund Robertson, the Liberal MP for Dundee, if the Commission would also apply to Scotland.[39] The particular question had clearly not entered Balfour's head and he vaguely replied he was considering it. A week later he had, and announced there would be one Commission for England, Scotland and Ireland.[40]

The confusion about a Scottish Commission was nothing compared to that which occurred almost simultaneously on unemployment relief. On 4th August, a Friday, when most Scots MPs had gone north, a remaining all-Party group moved to include Scotland in the Unemployed Workman's Bill.[41] Glasgow, they argued, had been particularly affected by the trade depression and was no different from any other industrial town in England. However inadequate the Bill, they felt it would be iniquitous for similarly placed workmen to be denied statutory relief north of the border. There was no Scottish Minister present and the Government spokesman, somewhat dumbfounded, indicated that apart from the Highlands, there was no logical reason why it should not be extended. A re-draft was agreed and introduced the following Monday. The Scottish press was astounded. The Prime Minister, despite the furore, accepted that it had become a Government decision. He argued that public opinion was in favour of some remedial action and that the Bill, because it would last only three years, was not a fundamental alteration in the Law. Conservatives, particularly Lord Balfour, the ex-Scottish Secretary were not pleased. To them it was a drastic alteration in the philosophy of Scottish welfare: the unemployed now had a right to public assistance.

These three events – the appointment of a medical inspector, Sinclair's radical administration and the establishment of the Poor Law Commission – had created the impetus for change. These alone would not have had such a profound effect had it not been for an exhaustive debate on the nature of welfare that took place between the summer of 1903 and the spring of 1908. By then a new and more expansive philosophy, which was to dominate discussions until the 1940s had emerged. There were three crucial debates: on the feeding of necessitious children, on extending legal constraint to the 'feeble-minded', and on the relief of distress: all centred on the State's role in providing assistance.

The origins of the first, the feeding of schoolchildren, have already been indicated. The Physical Education Commission's Report was too contentious for it not to emerge as a political issue. Indeed, no debate about welfare since the reform of the Old Poor Law aroused so much acrimony and engendered so much energy, for which there were two essential reasons. The first concerned the nature of parental duties. The opponents of this measure, headed by Lord Balfour and Sir Henry Craik (Secretary to the Education Department until 1906 and then a Conservative MP), argued that for the State to feed even a poor parent's child would reduce the 'natural' responsibility that a parent ought to have for its own child. The intrusion of the State on these duties could only result in a further loss of self-respect by independent workers and an erosion of the effort to maintain themselves and their families. Without this continued effort, economic development would be retarded. Craik in particular argued that there was more to ill-health and malnutrition than a failure to provide food.[42] There was no doubt in his mind that the condition of children had improved since 1872, when his Department began the modern education system. He felt that, '. . . behind the minor difficulties of the lack of food there lay a far greater evil in the ignorance of sanitation and its laws, overcrowding, and social conditions in our great manufacturing centres which told against life and against social welfare more seriously.'[43] Neglect was far more serious than shortage of food, and it would be best overcome not by state relief but by education. This dissolution of the bond of parental responsibility,

Craik went on, was the sure road to the eventual destruction of a family-based society. The duties of citizenship implied the sustenance of one's own children and without this, then a parent would look only to his or her own egotistic needs. The State could only assume this responsibility if it was based on terms the vast majority would want to avoid: poor relief, political disenfranchisement and the prosecution for neglect. Thus the opposition felt that not only would this measure undermine the existing system of welfare, but also that it would lead to the destruction of a certain moral form of society.

The second reason was a more practical one. Craik and the others argued vehemently for a more restricted and pure view of education, one that did not take into consideration the physical and social well-being of a child. Education was about schooling and not about welfare. Any move from this would mean educational institutions not only duplicating but also extending the Poor Law's work. To the opponents of the State feeding schoolchildren, the answer lay in charitable effort and improved education. The alternative was the creation of a nation of 'paupers' and the economic waste of resources. Thus their arguments implied political discrimination, social stigma and public economic restraint.

The counter-attack was equally vehement. Dr MacKenzie's views have already been discussed (see p. 45 above) and the more radical MPs were quick to follow his line of reasoning. They pointed out the 'tragic' reports on human 'wastage' by many of the special surveys, especially in the larger cities.[44] They argued that charity was never enough; often too late, indiscriminate, and based not on social concern, but on the morality of pity. The philosophical basis of their argument was that financial support through educational welfare 'would afford a means of developing a sense of parental responsibility'.[45] If this meant breaking the legal cocoon surrounding the family and treating its members on an individual basis, then so be it. The State by providing support, not in a punitive manner, but as part of the right to citizenship, would actually prevent the social and moral collapse of the family. This in turn would stimulate economic growth and prevent the Labour Party, whose very nature was antithetical to capitalism, from securing a lasting electoral base amongst the newly enfranchised and propertyless working class.

The political tussle began with the Supply debate of 1903.[46]During the traditional Opposition attack on Government policy a Conservative MP and member of the Commission, Sir Mark Shaw-Stewart, commented that he hoped MPs would support the call for a school meals service and for medical inspection. The special surveys, he told them, had been 'full of warning'. A little later the issue was taken up a fellow English Conservative, Sir John Gorst, the maverick member for Cambridge University. He left the Commons in no doubt that he had been shocked by MacKenzie's Report and went on to say:

> What an awful idea it is that in so many of these schools a large minority if not a majority, of the children are habitually underfed and underclothed. How is it possible to raise an Imperial race if that is the general character of the children in a large number of our schools. . . if anything like that state of things existed in England, then the condition of our children is rotten, and ought to have the immediate attention of everyone who desired to see this country great and prosperous. It should be prescribed by Imperial authority that the children in all schools should have the required periodical medical examination.

Two Liberals, John Bryce (Aberdeen South) and Dr Farquarson (Aberdeenshire West) also urged some action, but it was left to another English Conservative, Major Seely (Isle of Wight) to underline the parliamentary concern. The race, he said, was 'degenerating': 'Who believed it possible that in one of the greatest cities in the kingdom one-third of the children attending the primary schools are so hungry that it is impossible to train them? That is a state of affairs that is a disgrace to civilisation.'

Although press comment, especially in *The Scotsman*, was favourable, the Government initially refused to make any comment. Nevertheless, MacKenzie was not prepared to lose sight of the issue. A few months later, to an astonished health conference, he stated: 'If the medical inspection of school children is to become a reality some new powers will certainly be necessary. And there is no good reason why these new powers should not be sought for and obtained.'[47] Although the Conference reaction was mixed – Glasgow's Professor of Medicine, J. Glaister, felt improved sanitation would yield better results – everyone noted that the speaker was a Government official.

In early 1904 the Government introduced its first Education Bill.[48] It provided powers of medical inspection, and a number of Liberals attempted to include the feeding of schoolchildren in its clauses. This and the whole Bill failed. A new Bill came the following year.[49] Deputations were organised, but still the Conservatives refused to include the necessary clauses. This Bill, too, failed. With the formation of the Liberal Government a scurry of activity followed. A Labour-proposed Education (Provision of Meals) Bill was followed by a similar Labour and Liberal Bill for Scotland.[50] It was soon in difficulty. Conservatives felt the cost of meals, if the parent was unable to pay, should be borne by the Poor Law. Those parents would then be like other paupers and be politically disenfranchised. The Lords, after Lord Balfour's interjection, left Scotland out of the Bill. He said not only was he against it, but so too were most Scottish public bodies. Undaunted, the Liberals introduced another Bill in 1907. Its key clause, number six, stated that there would be no limit on expenditure (English authorities were limited to a penny rate); that clothing could be provided; and that if cleanliness was lacking parents could be prosecuted for neglect. Although School Boards would initially provide assistance, the case, if not otherwise dealt with by voluntary effort, would be reported to the parish council who could then provide the necessary sustenance. No political disenfranchisement would follow. The Bill's proposers (Ramsay MacDonald and Sir George MacCrae) argued for equity between England and Scotland and stated that some parishes and the STUC were in favour. However, the Conservatives continued to oppose the measure, claiming that the administrative intricacies of the Bill made it unworkable. A similar Bill was introduced in 1908, but within a few days the Scottish Secretary had himself introduced a more comprehensive education measure. The Poor Law was excluded and the Bill encountered no real opposition. The Conservatives had accepted that public opinion had turned in favour of statutory support.

Section Four of the Act allowed for school medical attention. Section Three allowed school boards to feed all school children for a fee. Section Six, while outlining the duty of the Board to report verminous, ill-fed or inadequately clothed children to the Procurator-Fiscal for prosecution under the Children's Act, also stated that:

> ... if it shall be shown... that such parents or guardians are unable by reason of poverty or ill health to supply sufficient and proper food or clothing for the child, or give the child the necessary personal attention, the school board, if satisfied that the necessities of the case will not be provided for by voluntary agencies, shall make such provision for the child out of the school fund as they deem necessary.[51].

A Treasury grant was included.

By January 1909, the tenor of future policy had become clear. Circular 417 from the Education Department swept aside caution, stating that Section Six was intended to 'check systematic parental neglect' and the school boards should, if a child's appearance cast doubt on its well-being, give assistance without delay. Only then should an investigation and possible prosecution take place.

The second crucial area of debate in this period was mental welfare. No reader of contemporary documents can fail to notice the pride and sense of achievement that the Scottish system of mental welfare had created. The years preceding 1900 had witnessed an ever-growing number of people declared insane and legally confined for their own and society's protection.[52] Yet there were two problems which were beginning to cause the Board of Lunacy some concern. First, the means of controlling the insane were laid down in a coherent and definite system that was the envy of many who worked in related areas. Certification of insanity meant legal restraint, at which point power lay with local boards. Those in other welfare institutions who had few controls, and who felt that they could do little to prevent the 'generation' of poverty, saw the workings of mental welfare as a model. But of course, only those certifiable could be restrained and medical opinion and practice had excluded many whom some now regarded as insane. These included the habitual drunk, the vagrant, the mother with illegitimate children, the epileptic and those with venereal disease. For the Poor Law in particular, all attempts to extend the areas of control, save for the 1898 Inebriates Act, had been blocked.

Behind these administrative difficulties lay another and far greater issue; the mental degeneration of the population. By 1900 many in both Scotland and England (a leading campaigner was the Eugenics Society), had become vociferous about the need to preserve the purity of the race. To them the South African war had demonstrated that their fears were not groundless. Only by proper control of all those likely to lead to racial impurity could the Empire be safe. What they wanted was simple: the prohibition of marriage between those deemed 'feeble-minded', an extension of certifiable detention and a campaign to eradicate 'immoral' acts. The Board of Lunacy, in their view, ought to be actively engaged in social control.

By early 1900, the Board had become alarmed by these demands. Its anxieties were focused in 1903, when Glasgow's local Board had eagerly taken up an investigation by its medical officer which showed that most of the insane under its control were there because of drink.[53] The Board's own counter-investigation was deliberately crushing. The association, it said, was spurious because there was little evidence to suggest that a higher proportion of those who drank excessively were more likely to become insane than those who did not. Those who were both insane and alcoholic were far more likely to have had some pre-disposition to mental unsoundness. There was little to suggest the hereditary transmission of drinking habits through the generations. The Board concluded its investigation by stressing that, 'the evils which [alcoholics] are capable of inflicting upon a community are not therefore so widespread as they are sometimes erroneously represented to be'. To use the Board and the lunacy laws for moral reform was unlikely to lead to any great social improvement.

Nevertheless the Board knew that no matter how hard it tried to hold the line, medical knowledge had advanced since 1857, and many not certifiable ought to be 'protected' from the vagaries of life outside an asylum. It had after all approved Glasgow's observation wards in 1889 and had in 1898 given similar approval to Glasgow's Board providing for the education of imbecile children. What was needed was a new working consensus, with policies which would maintain the system's essential features yet cater for those who would benefit from care and protection.

The Government accepted that an inquiry was necessary and on 9 September 1904 a Royal Commission on the Care and Control of the Feeble-Minded was established. Its remit was,

> To consider the existing methods of dealing with idiots and epileptics and with imbeciles, feeble-minded or defective persons not certifiable under the Lunacy laws; and in view of the hardship or danger resulting to such persons and the community from insufficient provision for their care, training and control, to report as to the amendments in the law or other measures which should be adopted.

After some representations a Scottish Commissioner, J. C. Dunlop, the Superintendent of Statistics for the Registrar-General, was appointed the following March.

In Scotland the attack for increased powers of detention was led by two Poor Law witnesses, R. B. Barclay, the General Superintendent and James Motion, Glasgow's Inspector of Poor.[54] They began their evidence by suggesting that city life was full of temptation to immorality and went on to give graphic descriptions of prostitution, alcoholism and the heredity transmission of 'vice'. Barclay was quite emphatic as to what he had seen in poorhouses:

> There are women who have had several illegitimate children, and who are of low mental type and facile disposition. I may note a case where I had recently to examine a woman of this class. She is known to have had ten illegitimate children. She can neither read nor write. She could not tell me, counting on her fingers, how many children she had. In the same poorhouse there is a feeble-minded mute who has had seven illegitimate children. Another illegitimate woman has had ten illegitimate children; her eldest daughter is following in her footsteps, and two of the young children (twins) show signs of weakness. I may mention the case of a woman now in a small poorhouse suffering from venereal disease. She had an unforgiveable temper, and is destitute of any feelings of modesty. Her husband is also in this poorhouse, a mental and physical nonentity. My experience leads me to say that the class of woman who come to our poorhouses with more than one illegitimate child are generally of feeble mind.

Motion presented a similar case and went on to recount the following pauper 'careers':

> J. S., 36, labourer, single; fifteen re-applications; seven from Glasgow Green and George Square, 'Houseless', and eight times from Night Asylum. Certified stricture, four; bronchitis, three; cystitis, one; debility, one; dyspepsia, one; and able-bodied, five. Applied first in March, 1890, and has made over forty re-applications since.
> W. M., 45, labourer, single, fourteen re-applications; from Drygate Model, four; Night Asylum, four; Portugal Street, one; McAlpine

Street Model, one; and four times 'Houseless'. Certified catarrh, four; rheumatics, three; diarrhoea, two; and able-bodied, five; applied first in October, 1884, and has made one hundred and thirty-five re-applications up till 15th May, 1905.[55]

Even the legislation, they argued, was inadequate. The Inebriates Act was so restricted in its operation that few alcoholics had actually been restrained. What they and other Poor Law witnesses wanted was a new philosophy of intervention, one that did not demand parishes proving in Court that an individual was a danger to himself and the public. They presented a strong case. But it hid some essential weaknesses. First, the witnesses lacked the Board's professional and independent status. Few of them were qualified to give a medical definition of insanity or to discuss the nature of individual treatment. Second, it was difficult from their evidence to perceive a model of restraint compatable with the gradual extension of democracy. What they had suggested implied not only greater discrimination and stigma, but also the enhancement of an official's power to control the lives of ordinary citizens.

The Board exploited these weaknesses ruthlessly. One Deputy Commissioner felt that the total control of 'defective' children by preventing marriage was impossible by 'tolerable' legislation.[56] Another effectively destroyed the eugenics case by stating:

The duty of the State towards the subjects of mental unsoundness is purely ethical and is limited to securing their safety and well-being, and to protecting the citizen from any annoyance that may be caused by their unrestrained presence in society. I am aware that some evidence has been given before this Commission suggesting that mental enfeeblement being largely genetic in origin might be stamped out by preventing propagation on the part of all persons who are judged to be mentally enfeebled or disordered. If mental unsoundness were a foreign strain introduced into a community then it could possibly be extirpated in one of the several ways suggested, but it is merely a variety which so long as individuals are not at a dead level of mental endowment must always arise anew, it is useless to propose any such means for checking its production. The ground for universal registration and control is therefore untenable.[57]

The only excuse for the forcible control of a defective's life, he argued, was if they were somehow being maltreated and that had been conceded by the 1857 Act. To go further and demand the registration of all those sheltered in their own homes would be 'of the nature of an inquisition'. Rooting out mental instablity and hence vice, evil and for that matter 'pauperism', given the varying talents of human beings, was impossible . The sound and the sane were equally capable of producing enfeebled offspring. His message was clear. Control, to be effective, would have to be total and that was electorally unacceptable.

His colleague, the Board's Secretary went further and indicated the tenuous nature of the present administration. He told them:

Though insanity cannot be defined, its meaning and practice is at present fairly well understood both by medical superintendents of asylums and by general practitioners. To legislate so as to disturb that understanding would create general confusion of thought and would go far to destroy the foundation upon which the fabric of lunacy legislation may be said to rest, which is, that a person cannot be admitted to any asylum unless certified to be insane, and cannot be detained in any asylum after recovery has in the opinion of the medical superintendent or principal medical officer of the asylum, taken place. Such legislation would be an injury to the interests of those who are admittedly lunatics in the popular sense; and it would I believe, fail in its object, because whatever scientific theories may be held, and rightly held, with regard to the irresponsiblity and mental or moral deficiencies of certain persons not certifiable as lunatics, legislation which should attempt to deal with such persons as lunatics would not have public opinion with it. . . the breaking up or serious disturbance of the existing lunacy law would be too great a price to pay for partial and more or less experimental measure(s).[58]

This was stunning evidence. No Commission could fail to take note that if its recommendations were at all revolutionary or experimental, public opinion would soon be so disorientated as to what mental disorder was that confidence in the system would collapse. But the Board did have one other concern. Just as it viewed any punitive social experiment with suspicion, so too did it suspect the more liberal expansive philosophy expounded by Dr MacKenzie.

His evidence stressed the belief that increased powers of detention would turn poorhouses, asylums and labour colonies into prisons.[59] It would be much better he claimed, if there were a more thorough classification of the medical and mental state of these individuals. This could only be facilitated by instituting a new principle. Previously a pauper, and for that matter a lunatic, was regarded as a 'derelict to be housed until he died', but if there were going to be change, it would have to be through a philosophy that would make control politically acceptable. The only possible philosophy, he argued, was one in which an individual was 'regarded as a temporarily incapacitated citizen to be nursed into efficiency'. While the Board appreciated this liberal approach, a problem remained, that of convincing the public that officials would not have unlimited powers to seize or detain those they deemed in need of restraint.

When the Commission on the Feeble-Minded reported in 1908, it was met without interest.[60] The reason was obvious. It had chosen the ignore all radical suggestions and plumped for reforms that would do little to alter the existing system. The Commissioners' basic recommendation entailed keeping the mentally sick under one local authority. The Central Board was to have an increased powers over asylum management and there was to be an extension of the categories to be assisted. Terminologies were to be altered. Out went *asylum* and *lunatic* and in came *hospital* and *mental defective*. The Treasury was to provide an annual grant for the new group of mental defectives brought under care. All defective children were to be under the control of the local board. Epileptics not mentally defective were to have their own institutions, and local boards were to be given easier powers to admit voluntary patients. Save for the last two recommendations, all of this followed the traditional practice that mental welfare was dominated by legal protection. To the Commission, medical knowledge although growing, did not command the same authority as the Sheriff. For this reason the legal restraint of an individual, even if mentally disordered, had to be conducted through established conventions. Any experimentation in provision would have to come, not through overt manipulation by public bodies, but with a patient's voluntary co-operation. What the Report was suggesting, then, was a model of welfare concerned about improving an individual's 'efficiency' or 'powers'. Public institutions should be perceived not as coercive agents of social control, but as agencies for helping individuals recover their mental and physical functions.[61]

The third significant debate surrounded the Poor Law Commission's evidence. Although the Commission's handicaps are well known – its members had largely been chosen to reflect traditional principles, it collected much of its evidence from official sources (no pauper was ever summoned) and contained only one Scot, Patten-MacDougall – there can be little doubt that its members sincerely believed their deliberations would greatly influence the development of policy. What then was its critical contribution to welfare? In Scotland it is possible to distinguish three sets of evidence that had a significant influence on both the Commission's deliberations and the subsequent debate. The first was the result of one of the Commission's own special inquiries, Dr Parsons review of Poor Law child care.[62] His exhaustive inquiry, based largely on provision in the principal cities, indicated the existing system had failed to meet a child's wider social need. Poor Law officials, despite being concerned about children, had not completely grasped the 'modern' elements of care: that to fully develop a child's ability required constant medical and personal supervision.

In detail Parsons criticised the three forms of assistance that a child was likely to receive. First, for those on outdoor relief, he felt that there was no rational principle for deducting household or family income from benefit. It meant that claimants were highly dependent on the good-will of officials and councillors, which the 1905 Inter-Departmental Committee had admitted was often variable. Only Edinburgh and Glasgow had lady inspectors and even they were not able to supervise every child. The majority of the other officials, he said, in the absence of fixed scales of relief, had neither the qualification nor the experience to assess a child's medical need or the degree of parental care. At best all they could provide was 'fleeting supervision'. Second, for those that were boarded out, although he commended many of the foster homes, he similarly felt there was not enough parochial supervision. (Once a year visits seemed usual.) Too much was left to the guardian.

It was however, the third form, poorhouse assistance, that attracted his most vehement criticism. Poorhouses in his view had become both a transit camp for those on their way to guardians and a permanent home for those either too ill or too 'vicious' in character to be fostered. As a result Parsons found that many had been kept in the institution for years with little or no contact with the outside world. His review of Dundee was typical:

> The girls' rooms were bright and homely in appearance, with pictures and ornaments, and well supplied with toys. The boys' rooms were barer and had no pictures on the wall. The bedrooms were bright, and contained about 430 cubic feet per bed. The beds were lath bedsteads with straw mattresses. The girls had a paved yard, with swings, in which to play. The boys also had a playground, and chiefly played football. The children were well clothed, except that the boys had no underclothes except a cotton shirt. They had a wollen scarf to wear in winter when going to school. They were bathed weekly, and oftener, if necessary. The towels were changed twice a week, and no special face flannels and tooth-brushes were in common use. The children assist in keeping the rooms clean, and adult inmates, including a weak-minded girl, also help. When ill, the children are sent to the adult sick wards of the poorhouse. There is no dentist.
>
> It is noticeable that the children are a badly developed type: as in other poorhouses, it contains a number of children who cannot be boarded-out owing to mental or physical infirmity. The health appearance of the poorhouse children is slightly better than that of the out-relief children. The number of badly nourished children is about the same. It is obvious that the mental condition of the children is poor. The condition of the teeth, both as regards decay and cleanliness, was bad. There was a large percentage of uncorrected defective sight, and also a number of cases of conjunctivitis, two being serious cases requiring isolation. The calorific value of the diets is ample, but the same criticisms as to the lack of variety applies here as in the other institutions.

His Report concluded with a recommendation for better medical attention, the provision of dental and optical treatment, the establishment of receiving homes for those not boarded-out and a wider variation in diet.

Parsons's criticism was similar to the theory of social welfare expounded by the cos: the need for personally orientated care. But he had gone further, he had not associated that perspective with the discriminatory treatment normally linked to cos. Instead he had shown that traditional Poor Law practices did have contradictions. Treating 'each case on its merits' allowed the personal bias of officials and councillors to influence the alleviation of need. The Poor Law's focus on the more legal concepts (settlement, the liablity of relatives, etc.) diverted its attention from the recipients' need for personalised support. The provision of 'model' poorhouses could only be an adjunct to, not the replacement of, other forms of assistance.

The second significant contribution came from R. H. Tawney, at that time research assistant to one of the Commissioners, Professor Smart of Glasgow University.[63] It was not so much what he said – other witnesses and indeed other investigations had revealed the same facts – but how he said it. His evidence related to the research he had done in Glasgow on the relationship between unemployment, boy labour and the functioning of the labour market. The problem he had hoped to understand was how at a time when there was a shortage of skilled labour, there could be so much under-employment amongst certain workers. It was apparent to him and others that the newly-created distress committees were receiving applications not only from the 'veterans of industry' but also its 'raw recruits'. The answer seemed to lie in the operation of the labour market when the young lads were first recruited. The different types of hiring practice between skilled and unskilled led to an eventual segmentation of the market and the casualisation of many of the unskilled. Unless a working lad secured an apprenticeship at the right age, a year or so after leaving school, he was often doomed to a dead-end job. Many could on leaving school obtain comparatively well-paid jobs, such as van-delivery, but there was little prospect of securing any long term career. Employers admitted that boys were employed for their 'commercial utility', which put more crudely meant they were cheaper to employ than adults. Once they achieved 'manhood', the distribution of work within a firm between adults and boys meant they would be dismissed. Having little training, the majority would drift into irregular and ultimately badly paid employment – and that in turn would preclude then from providing for unemployment, sickness or other debilitating conditions.

A traditional Poor Law administrator would probably not have disagreed with this analysis.[64] But he would have laid the blame for the eventual condition of the casual labourer on the individual's free choice of occupation on leaving school. What Tawney did was to present his evidence in such a way that emphasised the environmental, extraneous and structural causes of the labourer's position. The labour market was not something that a boy of fourteen could manipulate for himself. Unless a lad had family or other connections with a skilled trade, then an apprenticeship was often no more than a pipe dream. Anyway few fourteen-year-olds with parents in low paid or unskilled jobs could afford not to take the relatively high economic reward that would boost a family's earnings. Moreover, no fourteen-year-old had the power to determine the pace and direction of 'commercial' change which, in 1907, seemed to be leading to more semi-skilled, unskilled and casual labour. There was little, if any, 'free choice'.

Dr Parsons' evidence had thus destroyed much of the validity of Poor law practice and suggested the kind of inter-personal social welfare necessary; Tawney's had shown that the causes of distress were located within the socio-economic system; Dr MacKenzie's, the third significant contribution, presented a detailed critique of existing (mainly medical) services and suggested a general administrative structure for the alleviation of need. If he had been anybody other than the medical member of the Board his evidence would probably have been dismissed out of hand as that of a crank. However so concerned was the Commission, especially Beatrice Webb, about his statements, that they had to recall him to give further evidence.[65]

He began his critique from an assumption that, 'so long as relief is given only on condition of destitution, it necessarily comes after the fact'.[66] It was important to note that the majority of those who applied for relief were already chronically sick and it was therefore extremely unlikely that any form of poorhouse treatment would restore them to independence and self-sufficiency. Even many of those on the outdoor roll, because destitution came as the first test, would, like the chronically sick, be beyond hope of making an effective contribution to the economy. He went on to say:

> With the Poor Law there is no effort at prevention. No account in advance is taken of poverty or social conditions, or industry, or seasonal depression or privation. The effort of the Poor Law services is to keep pauperism at the lowest level; to apply rigid tests, medical and labour to all applicants – to keep the amount of relief down to the level of bare subsistence. . . It follows that the Poor Law medical service can never become effectively preventive. But if it cannot become preventive of disease among the poor, and yet is not adequately supplemented by other preventive organisations, the Poor Law medical service will remain an expensive service for dealing with an unending and uncontrolled stream of derelict sick. . . I am satisfied that the vast masses of preventable diseases are untouched by any preventive service, public or private.

Changes were occurring, he said, notably the observation ward scheme and Glasgow's hospital policy, but the structure of local government with its small units of administration, its disproportional expense and its inefficient officials militated against the rapid and wholesale adoption of new and more positive programmes.

His criticism was not just aimed at the Poor Law; he attacked the whole unco-ordinated nature of medical provision. Voluntary hospitals, he argued, were under so much pressure that many, although ostensibly free, had been forced to make charges or institute a subscriber's list. Some were so overcrowded that they sent chronic cases to the poorhouse. This lack of co-ordination ultimately led to one thing – there could be no carefully planned policy to enhance the overall quality of care.[67] MacKenzie stated:

a) that the relations between voluntary hospitals and Poor Law hospitals in Scotland need readjustment; b) that the voluntary hospitals, as they are serving public needs, ought to receive public rate aid; c) that existing public hospitals, whether rate-aided or not, are insufficient to meet the wants of the destitute poor; d) that practice has shown the need for futher hospital accommodation for the non-destitute; e) that the 'destitution' test has failed to restrict the class of sick to the 'friendless impotent poor' or destitute sick.

The way towards a more efficient and economical service and one that would respond more positively to need, he argued, was to create a preventive system of medical care. In this system, commercial considerations would be secondary. A sickness test would replace a destitution test. All health matters would be divorced from the Poor Law and centred on a Public Health authority, which in its infancy had shown that it was capable, efficient, flexible and high in public prestige. Freed from the relief of poverty as its prime function, this new authority could actively work to reduce disease and restore individuals to the full health necessary to develop their abilities.

The importance of MacKenzie's evidence lies not only in its coming from a senior member of the central authority, but in that it was the first exposition of the wider problems of health and other care since the 1860s. MacKenzie had combined a radical philosophy of State intervention with the need to reform the whole structure of local government. He had indicated to the Commissioners that if they wanted to meet social need, they would have to recommend both an alteration in the relationship of a citizen to the State and in how welfare was administered. In one day's evidence he had destroyed the rationale, established by M'Neill, Campbell and Craufurd, less than forty years previously, for minimal State welfare. That a critical break had been made was seen just a few months later, when for the first time, MacKenzie spoke openly about the future of health care. To an international education conference,

he commented: 'The current and traditional views of public health concern themselves primarily and exclusively with the environment; the
individual person is secondary. But the movement towards the better
care of individuals shows that the era of environmental hygiene is now
passing into the era of personal hygiene.'[68] New and sweeping developments were occurring in public conceptions of health and the Poor Law,
he stressed, could not escape from a re-examination of its role, purpose
and philosophy.

The debate and eventual disagreement within the Commission about
Poor Law reform has been documented elsewhere. It is, however, essential to grasp the almost total acceptance by the Minority and the grudging
acknowledgement by the Majority of Parsons', Tawney's and MacKenzie's evidence. Traditional philosophy was too well ingrained in the
Majority for them to turn into welfare radicals, but they did recognise
that the existing Poor Law practices had serious faults. To them, poverty
was still grounded in a moral defect of character which, without the
regulation of some social institution would destroy 'man's capacity for
self-management'.[69] The Majority's guiding philosophy – constant
supervision and 'friendly' advice – nevertheless was one that would
place the relationship between public official and recipient on a new
footing. This, unlike the established Poor Law philosophy, was to be a
total relationship. Voluntary agencies were to be directly linked to new
public assistance authorities which, with compulsory detention available for those deemed socially 'at risk', meant only those who avoided
all contact would escape 'the process of personal reform'. To achieve
this the Majority put forward five basic proposals; an increase in the
Board's powers to regulate parish activity; the reform of local government (urban parishes to be amalgamated with burghs and county
authorities to manage poorhouses); an improvement in the quality of
assistance (officials to be trained); the linking of assistance to any necessitous circumstance; and the integration of public assistance with local
charitable activities.[70]

The Minority, by contrast, began from a philosophy that saw the
wasting of human ability as a social evil and destitution as the inevitable
result of the social environment. The Minority also believed that they
had uncovered a broad evolutionary trend in social asssitance which
superseded the character of Poor Relief. The Public Health Authority,
the School Board, the Unemployed Relief Committee and the District
Lunacy Board all bore testament to more specialised and more preventive methods of care. It was now time, the Minority argued, to logically
finalise that process by attaching the principle of prevention to public
assistance. If needs were met when they first arose, then the demoralisation normally associated with destitution would be avoided. With
their deeply held views on social waste, they thought it essential to
have a series of welfare institutions that would 'search out', detain and

rehabilitate all those potential 'victims'. No one was to escape from this process, otherwise like some infectious disease, they would be a danger to public order.

Although both Reports offered substantial alterations to the philosophy and practice of welfare, they had their defects. The Majority, unlike the Commission on the Feeble-Minded, had not sufficiently grasped that the relationship between public servant and recipient was not one of alms-giver to a 'down and out'. The alms-giver had no power to change behaviour. If the conditions of relief were unacceptable, then the 'down and out' could seek some other less punitive donor. Although the Majority Commissioners did not demand the 'searching out' which the Minority wanted, their scheme of assistance implied an involuntary relationship (there would be no appeal), and allowed little, if any, countervailing power in the hands of the recipient. The Minority, for their part, by insisting on power to 'search out' and mitigate all social need, failed to realise their recommendations would ultimately create a never-ending multitude of public officials who would have little restraint on what they did. In neither Report had a formula to balance the protection of citizens' liberty with their right to receive some form of assistance been discovered. The Majority had cloaked their concept of 'care' in the terminology of the 19th century – stigma, moral discrimination and paternalistic, middle class rule – and the Minority their concern about a person's social development in the illiberality of a mechanistic bureaucracy. In a period when parish councils had been forced to become more accountable to a wider based franchise and when many of those entitled to vote were on the borderline of eligibility, the Commissioners had failed to acknowledge that the method of relief as much as its ethic was the central political issue. Neither Report was electorally acceptable. The working classes, as one Labour reviewer suggested, were far more interested in concrete rights, like those obtainable through insurance – ones that would guarantee a minimum of intervention in how they conducted their lives.[71] As a result, in the 1910 parish elections Labour rejected the Majority Report and gave the Minority Report only a cautious welcome.

The Commission's Reports caused almost immediate shock, alarm and dismay amongst parishes, seen most clearly in the *Poor Law Magazine*. The initial review was hostile.[72] It condemned the Minority Report as impractical, the work of social 'missionaries', and the Majority as the work of 'impervious Englishmen', deluded by theories of charity. However the next review, perhaps sensing the Minority had important political allies, stressed that Beatrice Webb was not a communist or anarchist out to destroy private property, but rather she was an 'evolutionist' who was deeply concerned about the Poor Law's apparent failure to prevent poverty.[73] The reviewer thought that some of what had been suggested, though not the abolition of parish councils, was necessary if the Poor Law was to retain popular support. Reflecting this, later reviews began to acknowledge that there had been a shift of thought, and although sternly defending the Poor Law suggested that some re-assessment of its function was necessary.[74] This need for change was underlined when the *Glasgow Herald* itself suggested the Minority's views on efficiency and economy were worth 'serious consideration'.[75] But the most authoritative Poor Law review came in 1911, with the joint Report of the Arbitration Committee of Edinburgh, Glasgow and Govan Parish Councils and the Society of Inspectors of Poor.[76] Save for the integration of parish councils, town councils and voluntary agencies, the Majority Report was approved.

By 1912 therefore, parishes had come to some sort of agreement that change was necessary. Grudgingly, they had also recognised that there needed to be a re-definition of welfare. The unmistakable acknowledgement of this came the following year, during the Royal Commission on Housing examinations, when the views of Glasgow's Inspector of Poor were ferociously demolished by Dr MacKenzie, one of the Commissioners.

> Q. You say, 'It is not so much the insanitary condition of the City as the kind of people who live in it. The insanitary slums arise from the way these people live, principally in congested districts where common-lodging houses are situated'. Do you mean that statement about insanitary slums arising from the way these people live to be quite general, or are you confining it to the type of slum that arises from misuse of houses? Do you go the length of saying that all slums are due to the tenants?
> A. In so far as that type of people come before my notice. . .
> Q. We are perpetually told by people that the whole condition of a house depends on the person in it. We know that the person in it is important, but what I want to make quite clear is that there are masses of houses in Glasgow, as no doubt in other great cities, where the structure and position and site and everything else are so radically bad that it does not matter what kind of tenant you have in it, the place ought to be swept out of existence?
> A. Clearly. . .
> Q. So that it is not entirely the fault of these people that they are like that?
> A. No.[77]

A year later, the Inspector's view had crystallised.[78] Welfare was not only about providing spiritual and moral education, it was also about the greater support of need. That meant the use of more and better trained 'social workers'.

The philosophy of welfare had come a long way since 1900. Administrative radicalism had focused the debate both on the need for greater amounts of individualised support and a national direction of provision.

72PAUPERISM AND SOCIAL NEED: THE NATIONAL DEBATE

The waste of human ability – the result of environmental conditioning – could be overcome by redesigning welfare institutions to fulfil a more positive and purposive role. Yet in 1914 the implementation of this policy had barely begun. To understand why this was the case and the difficulties it caused, it is now necessary to turn to the development of local policy in the years between 1900 and 1914.

NOTES

1. MacKenzie, W. L., *Mothers and Children: The Carnegie Trust Report on Physical Welfare (Scotland)* (Dunfermline, 1917) p.115.
2. Evidence given on 5.6.02, in *Royal Commission on Physical Training (Scotland). (Cd. 1508 (P.P. 1903 Vol. XXX).*
3. Evidence given on 28.5.07 and 12.6.07, *op cit.*
4. Munro, *op. cit.*
5. Especially Caldwell, J. (Mid-Lanark) (1.7.98), *Hansard 60 (Fourth Series)*, pp.809-98.
6. Especially Weir, J. (Rossshire) (6.7.00), *ibid. 85*, pp.801-92; for a note on Balfour's conservatism, see Lady Balfour, *Lord Balfour of Burleigh* (London, 1924); and Scottish Office staffing difficulties in Dodds, *op. cit.*
7. Evidence of MacKenzie, to *Physical Training Commission, op. cit.*; n.a. (1900-1), The Appointment of Dr MacKenzie, in *The Sanitary Journal of Scotland 7 (New Series)*, pp.517-9.
8. (1899), The Prevention of Tuberculosis, in *ibid. 6*, pp.551-600; (1900), Review of the Royal Institute of Public Health Annual Conference, Aberdeen, in *ibid. 7*, pp.295-301; (1900), On Heredity in Disease, in *The Scottish Medical and Surgical Journal 6*, pp.322-7.
9. Letter (23.12.98) from General Chapman, Commander of the Scottish District to the Master of the Merchant Company Schools, *SRO ED 7.1.11.*
10. *SRO ED 7.1.23.*
11. Report on the Physical Examination of 600 Edinburgh Schoolchildren, in *Royal Commission on Physical Training (Scotland). Cd. 1507 (P.P. 1903 Vol. XXX)*; MacKenzie was in fact appointed after Hay withdrew from conducting the Edinburgh survey. He had been Hay's assistant some time previously.
12. Recommendation 7.
13. Douglas, W. B. (1903), Report of the Royal Commission on Physical Training, in *The Scottish Medical and Surgical Journal 13*, pp.83-90.
14. *The Medical Inspection of Schoolchildren* (Edinburgh, 1904); *The Health of the Schoolchild* (London, 1906) (Being a Collection of Lectures, 1903-5).
15. (1903), Medical Inspection of Schools and Schoolchildren. . . , in *The County and Municipal Record 1*, pp.486-90. (Paper read to the Sanitary Association Congress, Perth, August 1903).
16. *Report on the Physical Condition of 1400 School Children. . . Edinburgh.* (Edinburgh, 1906); *The Physical Condition of Children Attending. . . Schools. . . for Glasgow. Cd. 3637 (P.P. 1907*

Vol. LXV).

17. Evidence of Penney, W. (13.5.07) and Stuart, Alex. (14.5.07), to *Poor Law Commission, op. cit.*

18. Lady Pentland, *Memoir of Lord Pentland* (London, 1928); *The Scotsman's* husting reports indicate only George MacCrae (East Edinburgh) explicitly mentioned reforming the Poor Law, others like J. Dewar (West Aberdeenshire) mentioned the inadequacy of charity to meet need, but were vague on what statutory aid they would like.

19. Supply Debate (22.6.05), especially Robert Munro-Ferguson (Liberal, Leith) *Hansard 147 (Fourth Series)* pp.1407-8.

20. Report (1904), in *The County and Municipal Record III*, p.64; Report (1904-5), in *ibid. IV*, p.101. `

21. Report (5.5.09) and Husting Reports (13.6.99, 16.6.99, 17.6.99 and 24.6.99), in *Scotsman;* for background of senior officials, see *Civil Service Appointment Returns. (P.P. 1912-3 Vol. LVI)*

22. Dodds, *op. cit.;* MacKenzie, *Poor Law Commission, op. cit.*

23. National Insurance Bill, Committee Stage (13.11.11), *Hansard 31 (Fifth Series)*, p.52.

24. Board of Health Staff, *SRO HH 1.471.*

25. Memorandum on the Census of Paupers (Scotland), 31 March 1906, in *Poor Law Commission, op cit.*

26. First Reading (4.2.02) *The Local Government (Scotland) Amendment Bill;* First Reading (21.2.02) *The Local Government (Scotland) Amendment (No. 2) Bill.*

27. *The Departmental Committee, op. cit;* Examination of Nurses – Origins and History, *SRO HH 2.15, 2.16.*

28. *Poor Law Magazine 1904*, pp.293-9.

29. n.a. (1904), Poor Law Medical Relief, in *Scottish Medical and Surgical Journal 15*, pp.47-51; Leader, in *British Medical Journal 1924(1)*, p.1029.

30. Questions from Munro-Ferguson, Tenant, H. J. (Berwickshire) and Haldane, H. B.(Haddingtonshire) (6.4.04), *Hansard 135 (Fourth Series)*, pp.783, 800 and 920; Minute of Board (11.4.04), *SRO HH 56.19.*

31. Question from Munro-Ferguson (8.5.05), *op. cit. 145*, p.1108; First Reading (7.6.05) *The Poor Law (Scotland) Bill.*

32. Question (13.7.04), *op. cit. 137*, p.1461. Cross had good contacts with Glasgow Parish.

33. *The Report on the Methods of Administering Poor Relief in Certain Large Town Parishes of Scotland. Cd. 2524 (P.P. 1905 Vol. LXVII)* p.xxv.

34. For instance, Leith Parish Council Minutes, 30.10.05, *EPLER qYHV 243L* Edinburgh Parish Council Minutes, 22.9.05, *op. cit.;* Glasgow Parish Council Minutes, 2.8.05, *GMLGR B514.79;* Govan Parish Council Minutes, 11.10.05, *GMLGR G.352.04143;* Dundee Parish Council Minutes, 28.11.05, *TRA TC.PCM.9.*

35. *Poor Law Magazine 1905*, p.57.

36. Question (10.4.05), in *op. cit. 144*, p.999.

37. Questions from Findlay, Alex. (Lanark N.E.) (14.4.05) and Black, Alex. (Banffshire) (3.5.05), in *ibid. 145*, pp.201 and 821.

38. Supply Debate (22.6.05), *ibid. 147*, pp.1404-24.

39. Question, *ibid. 150*, p.1349.

40. Question from Buchanan, T. R. (Liberal, East Perthshire) (8.8.05), *ibid. 151*, p.638.

41. Joseph Dobbie (Liberal, Ayr) was the first to speak, *ibid. 151*, p.299; also pp.396 and 419; Lords Debate, (8.8.05), pp.572-769.
42. Second Reading, Education (Provision of Meals) Scotland Bill (13.12.06), *ibid. 167 (Fifth Series)*, p.772.
43. Second Reading, Education (Provision of Meals) Scotland Bill (1.3.07), *ibid. 170*, p.378.
44. See for instance, Charles Douglas (Liberal, Lanark N.E.) quoting Dundee Social Union's *Report on Housing and Industrial Conditions* (Dundee, 1905) (8.5.05), *ibid. 145 (Fourth Series)*, p.1158.
45. MacNamara, T. J., (Liberal, N. Camberwell), a Scot sitting for an English seat (1.3.07), *ibid. 170 (Fifth Series)*, p.383.
46. Supply Debates (18.6.03), *Hansard 123 (Fourth Series)*, pp.1345-1399; reported (19.6.03), in *Scotsman* and *Glasgow Herald*.
47. Medical Inspection of Schools and Schoolchildren. . . , *op. cit.*; note also his comments to the Congress of the Royal Sanitary Institute the following summer: 'They [the medical inspectors] were not prepared to say what the organisation of this movement might be, but he thought that when they had got the actually established facts they would find that the ordinary administration of the public health and the School Boards themselves would be compelled not to leave these children alone', Discussion on the Hygeine of Schoolchildren (1904-5), in *Journal of the Royal Sanitary Institute 25*, pp.942-3.
48. The First Reading was on 28 March, the Second on 2 May and it was withdrawn on 8 August.
49. The First Reading was on 8 May and it was withdrawn on 7 August.
50. Necessitous Schoolchildren – A Historical Memorandum, *SRO ED 7.7.7*; see also *The Report of the Select Committee on the Education (Provision of Meals) (Scotland) Bill. (P.P. 1906 Vol. VIII).*
51. *Education (Scotland) Act 1908. Ch. 63 (8 Edw. 7.).*
52. Review of Lunacy Legislation since 1857, in *Annual Report of the General Board of Lunacy. Cd. 7404 (P.P. 1914 Vol. XLI).*
53. Glasgow Parish Council Minutes (District Board of Lunacy), 27.4.03 and 1.10.03, *op. cit.*; see also Wallace, A., Drink in Relation to Pauperism and Lunacy, in *Poor Law Magazine 1903*, pp.72-86 and 306-8.
54. Evidence (2.3.06), to *Commission on the Care and Control of Feeble-Minded (Scottish Evidence). Cd. 4217 (P.P. 1908 Vol. XXXVII)* ; see also evidence of Motion, (25.5.05), to The Departmental Committee on Vagrancy. *Cd. 2891 (P.P. 1906 Vol. CIII).*
55. See also, Pauperism and Vagrancy, in *Poor Law Magazine 1904*, pp.41-54.
56. Evidence of MacPherson, Dr C. (23.2.06), to *op. cit.*
57. Evidence of MacPherson, Dr J. (23.2.06), to *ibid.*
58. Evidence of Spence, T. C. W. (23.2.06), to *ibid.*
59. Evidence (11.6.06), to *ibid.*
60. *The Royal Commission on the Care and Control of the Feeble-Minded (Scottish Report). Cd. 4202 (P.P. 1908 Vol. XXXIV*; see comment in *Poor Law Magazine 1913*, p.341.
61. The Mental Deficiency and Lunacy (Scotland) Act. Ch. 38 (3 & 4 Geo. V. 1913; The Powers and Duties of the Various Authorities under the Act, in *The Annual Report of the General Board of Control for Scotland, 1914. Cd. 7944 (P.P. 1916 Vol. XXVII).*

62. Parsons, T. C., The Condition of Children who are in Receipt of the Various Forms of Poor Relief in Certain Parishes in Scotland, in *Poor Law Commission. Cd. 5075 (P.P. 1910 Vol. LII)*. Parsons was Medical Superintendent of Fulham Workhouse Infirmary.
63. Evidence (16.3.08), to *Poor Law Commission (Unemployment Evidence). Cd. 5068 (P.P. 1910 Vol. XLIX)*.
64. See for instance, evidence of Ellis, C. C. (The Board's Clerk responsible for the Unemployed Workman's Act) (14.1.08), to *ibid.*
65. See, letter to J. Burns (President of English Local Government Board) (11.5.07), in McKenzie, N., *Letters of S. and B. Webb, Vol II*. (Cambridge, 1978) p.254.
66. *op. cit.*
67. See discussion on Edinburgh Medical Charities in Kay, A. C. and Tonybee, H. V., *Report on Endowed and Voluntary Charities in Certain Places... Cd. 4594 (P.P. 1910 Vol. XV)*
68. (1906-7), The Medical Inspection of Schoolchildren, in *The County and Municipal Record IX*, pp.447-8. (Being a synopsis of Paper read to the Second International Congress on School Hygiene, London, August 1907).
69. Webb, S. and B., *English Poor Law Policy*. (London, 1929) p.350, who quote Prof. B. Bosanquet, a member of the Majority.
70. *Report of the Royal Commission on the Poor Law... for Scotland. Cd. 4922 (P.P. 1909 Vol. XXXVIII)*.
71. Norman, C. H., The Quality of Mercy, and Manifesto of Labour (19.11.10 and 3.12.10), in *Forward* pp.5 and 6.
72. Brown, R. S., Review of Poor Law Commission, in *Poor Law Magazine 1909*, pp.333-45.
73. n.a., Review of Poor Law Commission, in *ibid. 1910*, pp.36-47.
74. Reviews by Lang, R.B., Barrowman, D., Pressley, W. (all Inspectors of Poor) and Cunningham, J. (Chairman of Glasgow Parish Council), in *ibid., 1910, 1910, 1911, 1912*, pp.145-72, 307-11, 49-54, 245-63.
75. Leader (5.11.10), in *Glasgow Herald*, p.6.
76. *Poor Law Magazine 1911*, pp.188-206.
77. Evidence (30.10.13), to *Royal Commission on Housing in Scotland (Evidence)*. (London, 1920).
78. Lecture to the Glasgow School of Social Studies, in *Poor Law Magazine 1914*, pp.142-53 and 177-87.

5

MORAL REFORM, SOCIAL CONTROL
AND PARISH COUNCILS, 1900-14

Chapter Four has indicated the national debate about the development of welfare in the period from 1900-14. All considerations of this debate had had to recognise that the implementation of Poor Law policy ultimately rested on the decisions and actions of local politicians and officials. What, then, were the local reactions? How far did parishes alter their perspective on the development of statutory services, the position of individuals within that service, and the role of central and local government? How did they view existing policies to regulate family conduct, to develop public legal restraint and to improve the relief of distress? Only through an understanding of these questions will it be possible to appreciate how far the Poor Law was capable of reform and how far it actually was reformed. The first part of this chapter will therefore look at the relationship between philosophy and policies, leaving a discussion on policies and practice for the second part. But no account of developments can take place in isolation from the general political, social and economic changes that were taking place and the more important of these for welfare development will also be discussed.

The 1894 Local Government Act, within the limitations of the 1884 franchise, had seen the democratisation of parish councils. Considerable numbers of working men and a smaller number of women could now vote and become councillors. Yet although inspectors of poor felt that this had made parishes more 'representative', where they did keep lists of occupations, the majority of councillors, it seems, still came from the middle classes.[1]) Even in a mining parish like Bothwell, only a quarter of the Council was composed of working men.[2] The reason to the inspectors seemed simple: everyone was still prepared to accept the philosophy of adequate but discriminatory relief. There was no reason why the working class should not accept middle class respresentatives monopolising its administration.

In the early part of the decade, therefore, political power lay in the hands of the middle classes. Within that group, a number of councillors had evolved a much more distinctive philosophy: they specifically wanted to fashion the Poor Law into an active instrument of social improvement. This new philosophy can best be illustrated by the views of James Brand, the Tory (and Catholic) Chairman of Glasgow Parish Council, 1898-1901. Although in each of the larger councils a similar re-orientation of thought was evident, this councillor more than any other presented the most cogent case for reform and provided it with a defensible middle class logic. Moreover, it was a logic that transcended traditional Conservative and Liberal Party boundaries. What Brand was arguing for in Glasgow, Liberal councillors were suggesting in Edinburgh. The same applied in Leith. In other parishes like Dundee and Govan it was the small group of philanthropically minded ladies with their concern for children, women and the sick who pushed the discussion away from past issues towards the new philosophy.[3]

Brand began from the principle of social concern: the evils of urban overcrowding and public ill-health were being compounded by higher levels of unemployment and poverty.[4] The Poor Law, with its organisational abilities and its rateable power, was an obvious means for reducing distress. Thus Brand believed the Poor Law should adopt policies that would actively mitigate poverty and alleviate social need. He was prepared to admit, in theory, that this was 'socialism'. but with the larger parishes' problems in containing and controlling the flow of claimants, the modern administrator could no longer rely on 'sound principles', he had to achieve the best possible results in a practical manner. The first practical step, therefore, meant ceasing to view needs from a purely legal perspective. The cocoon that had surrounded established practice prevented the Poor Law reaching the roots of 'pauperism', the social and moral circumstances of urban life. Taking the 'causes of pauperism into account' would be an important tool for discriminating amongst those that neglected to maintain their own and their family's support.

Secondly, the Poor Law, like those in other welfare agencies, should seek the advice of 'scientific' observers. Social and medical investigations could assist them to determine the existence and extent of the various social evils afflicting urban life. If the Poor Law ceased to be a welfare agency that only discriminated after an application had been made and instead became actively interested in the regulation of social conduct, then it would be necessary to differentiate between those who would be assisted, when they could be assisted and with what aim.

Embedded in this social concern was the deep belief in moral propriety. The wilful destruction of public order and the neglect of good social conduct needed to be checked. To Brand, those who destroyed the social order – the prostitute, the family deserter and the loafer – should be actively pursued by the statutory agencies. The Poor Law, in the interests of society and the individual's own development, should be given positive and punitive powers to prevent any breakdown in public order. Thus, although the existing economic order did have dysfuntions which statutory agencies had a duty to correct, Brand stressed that man was still able to make choices about whether to pursue a life of degeneracy or become a respectable citizen. The Poor Law's task was therefore twofold. On the one hand it was to punish far more rigorously those who sowed public disorder – the casual labourer, the drunkard and the neglectful parent – and to provide them with corrective training. On the other, it was to extend support more systematically to those who, through no fault of their own, had fallen foul of the economic system. Certain types of claimant – the widowed, the elderly and children requiring separation from their parents – ought to receive the care and treatment likely to restore them to full citizenhood.

Although small numbers of Labour representatives had been elected, four in Glasgow in 1901 (out of thirty-one) and two in Leith (out of eighteen), no parish in the early 1900s had a distinct Labour group. After the December elections of 1907, all of that was to change. Labour clearly had a new spirit of organisation and attracted a much wider ideological commitment.[5] At each successive election the Labour representation grew, particularly in the poorer urban areas like Leith and in the heavy industrial mining areas of Fife and Lanarkshire. Meeting in groups, they began to evolve a distinct set of policies. At Bothwell and Cambuslang, where they held about a quarter of the seats, they pressed for a flat rate payment of 5s. for all those aged over 70.[6] In Glasgow, they went further and argued for the introduction of a fixed scale of relief.[7] In Leith, where they held a third of the seats, they attacked the Poorhouse punishment cells and labour yards.[8]

These new councillors began their philosophy from a totally different standpoint from Brand's: public assistance was a right and not a charity. A free market economy had increased the inequalities of wealth and instilled a belief in them that the industrial system was one of heartless struggle.[9] Unemployment, low wages and ill-health were the result. Further, they argued that moralising about personal behaviour merely served to underpin the assumption that welfare could improve conduct by deterrence and pecuniary treatment. Until a Socialist State was reached, the aim of social policy was simple: full maintenance for those that had fallen foul of the economic system. Finally, although the break-up of the Poor Law was approved, any attempt to tie punitive conditions to the receipt of relief, as in the Minority Report, represented very peculiar socialism.

Labour had four specific proposals. First, in order to avoid favouritism, injustice and wide variations in treatment, there should be fixed scales of relief. Next, middle class moralising on how to bring up children should be abandoned for the assumption that the mother was the best and most natural trainer of her children. Third, only through the proper medical and social classification of the indoor poor could stigma and demoralisation be avoided. Separate homes and institutions for the aged, the sick, the child and the epileptic were therefore necessary. Fourth, the Poor Law, until it was abolished, should assist all necessitous cases, and that included the able-bodied. All funds for this service should come from the National Exchequer. None of these proposals, save for national funding, were particularly radical. What marked them as distinctive from all others was the commitment of the councillors. No one could doubt that they wanted more welfare, more quickly, and over a wider area than anybody else.

Thus the decade after 1900 witnessed not only the flowering of an assertive middle class philosophy of intervention, it also saw the emergence of a much more coherent and cohesive alternative doctrine, one that had its origins in the material needs of a less deferential working class. This was a time of challenge, a time when councillors and officials were forced to seek wider support for their policies and practices. If the 'reformist' councillors were to succeed in persuading other councillors and the electorate of their policies, then 20th-century welfare would take on a far more directive and punitive form. On the other hand, if they were to fail, then because the Poor Law had become so contaminated by its association with 'adequate but discriminatory' principles, it would be in immediate danger of dissolution – the working class would simply refuse to accept its legitimacy.

The remainder of this chapter will look at the implementation of the local policy in three particular areas: unemployment relief, medical care and child welfare. It was in these areas that the issues confronted in the national debate – namely, the relief of distress, the public restraint of action and the regulation of family conduct – were the most severely tested. But first the wider context of Scotland's economy and health has to be examined: these factors were an important influence on parish perceptions of policy development.

By 1900 the Scottish labour market had undergone a profound change. With new industries being established in the Midlands and the South of England, Scotland's reliance on coal-mining, ship-building and heavy engineering all meant one thing: a reduction in employment prospects. The effect of this alteration was soon witnessed in the greater numbers of unemployed labourers who flocked to the cities and larger towns, especially during the trade depressions of 1902-5 and 1907-9. These areas had three special attractions. First, there was the prospect of securing casual work. Second, cheap or free accommodation, from common lodging houses to alley-ways, was readily available. Third, there was a greater variety of public and charitable institutions to tap for doles and assistance.

Added to a deteriorating labour market were the problems associated with urban overcrowding. Scottish health indicators had showed little sign of improvement. Indeed from the early 1890s the incidence of some diseases, notably respiratory and diarrhoeal, actually increased. So too did the infant mortality rate. Moreover it was noted that the probability of death in the first month of infancy was as high in affluent areas as in poorer ones. Even more startling was the discovery that diptheria deaths were inversely related to bad housing: those who lived in the worst slums had a better chance of surviving than those who did not.[10]

All of this had a profound effect on the Poor Law. Many more sought relief. Govan, for instance, saw applications rising by over 80 per cent, with the greatest increase coming from unemployed (but 'disabled') men. In Edinburgh, poorhouse accommodation became so over-taxed that men were forced to sleep in the open corridors.[11] Every industrial parish noted the same, applications were increasing, with more and more casual labourers going 'in and out'. The problems that this caused 'orderly' administration was fully explained to Glasgow by its poorhouse Governor:

> The admission of 3286 men in one year [1903], who do not require medical treatment, does not support the idea that those who enter the poorhouse are old, infirm, and physically unfit for work. Minute examination of the figures referred to brings us in close touch with a very important social problem. From these figures we find that 55.5 per cent are unmarried; 20 per cent married, but, with very few exceptions, living apart from their wives; 24.5 per cent widowers; 92.5 per cent come from model lodging houses; 97 per cent admit being more or less addicted to drink, and 55.4 per cent have been in prison while 47.7 per cent are from 20 to 50 years of age.[12]

He concluded: 'Whether the remedy is to be obtained by persuasive or compulsory methods, or by both combined, it is not easy to decide. No treatment, whether kind or severe in such Institutions as this, will materially affect the conditions of living so described'.[12] Deterrence, this Governor argued, had failed: there was a limit to the stone-breaking or rope-teasing any poorhouse could do. What was required were new powers that somehow would control the flow of applicants.

One of the first reviews of the issue came at the end of 1898 when Professor Jones of Glasgow University, addressing a local conference, indicated that voluntary effort to maintain labour colonies was not sufficient. The number of unemployed was growing and he urged parish and town councils to 'take more seriously the frightful leakage that was going on and which would go on as industry becomes more organised'.[13] The general tenor of his statement did not go unheeded. Late in 1899 the three Inspectors of Poor for Edinburgh, Glasgow and Govan organised a conference on unemployment, vagrancy and alcoholism. In a memorandum after it, they recommended that parishes ought to have extra power to deal more effectively with the 'in and out' labourer.[14] In Glasgow, they argued, magistrates had been able to use the 1895 Local Police Act to commit vagrants to a poorhouse for seven days. Although the numbers in any one year remained small (less than a hundred) there was no reason, in their view, why the principle should not be more broadly applied. The following year, James Motion, Glasgow's new Inspector, made their position even clearer. In a separate memorandum to the Scottish Office, he indicated that Balfour's Inebriates Act was too weak to deal effectively with the problem parishes faced. (A committal required four drink-related convictions.) The legislation, he said, should state that:

> . . . any person who is known to be a drunkard, a vagrant, pauper, or any person who, by reason of his or her drunken, depraved, dissolute, and dissipated habits, is a burden upon the public rates, or is unable, by reason of such habits, of supporting himself or herself without recourse to begging, or relief from the rates. . . [should]. . . be confined in a poorhouse. . . for a period of not more than two years. . . .

By developing special measures like labour colonies (either attached to poorhouses or in the country), parishes might be able to re-instil the work ethic.

In early 1902, the three major parishes agreed to promote a Bill, similar to one passed in England, which would allow them power to detain those who had been repeatedly chargeable.[15] It soon ran into opposition. First of all Glasgow City raised objections. They were against detention without substantial judicial review. They were also against parishes maintaining labour colonies, which would indicate assistance to people other than habitual drunkards. After it became obvious that Lord Balfour, the Scottish Secretary, also objected – there had not been sufficient discussion – the Bill was withdrawn. Another was soon in preparation and this time found a greater welcome.[16] Virtually all other parishes approved its contents.[17] So too did Glasgow.[17] Even the Labour Party seemed favourable.[18] It allowed three months detention if a claimant had been chargeable three times in the previous six months.

Unfortunately for the three parishes, Lord Balfour's objection remained. As he later explained to the Poor Law Commission, unemployed labourers, whether they were model lodgers, habitual drunkards or past criminals, had never had a right to Poor Relief, even under the most punitive of conditions.[19] Giving parishes the power to detain paupers (the Bill also covered those who required but refused assistance) might lead to abuse and that, he said, would greatly affect 'the liberty of the subject'. The move was too radical.

Nevertheless the next year the parishes continued to press for some measure, but this time they sought to specify much more closely the group they would like to detain, the habitually drunk.[20] Although they were able to obtain assurances from Graham Murrary, the new Scottish Secretary, that he might consider amending the Inebriates Act, they discovered that Keir Hardie and the Labour Party had changed their opinion. They wanted a much broader form of assistance, and in 1905 Labour's new found political power was dominant.[21] Undaunted, the parishes continued with their campaign. In the following year they approached the Liberal Government. The Lord Advocate, Tom Shaw, agreed that some measure to deal with the 'chronic poor' was necessary, but with the Poor Law Commission already sitting, all he was prepared to concede was a Departmental review of the Inebriates Act.[22] By the time the review was completed, in 1909, Government interests lay elsewhere and the campaign finally petered out.

Before 1914, parish attempts to meet urban distress had failed. The use of their poorhouses by men on the fringe of the labour market continued to grow. Indeed by 1909 Glasgow received over 100 unemployed (but 'disabled') applications a day. What had gone wrong? Basically the parishes, still controlled by the middle classes, continued to focus their attention on the casual labourer. Indeed throughout this period Glasgow's Inspector remained adamant what the response should be. To one medical audience he stated:

> Although these ins and outs are not directly certifiable as feeble-minded, I am of the opinion, from their degraded habits and conduct, that their condition of mind renders them unamenable to ordinary principles of right and wrong. These people suffer very frequently from diseases brought about by their disgraceful, drunken and immoral conduct. My view is that such people who come upon the rates by preventable diseases due to their own misconduct should in some manner be punished for so doing. I also believe labour colonies would be of some use in stopping the flow of certain cases to the asylums, such as epileptics and other defectives.[23]

and to another:

> It has been clearly demonstrated that the great bulk of the so-called unemployed belong entirely to the unskilled labour classes, people, who even when trade is good, work only at uncertain times. If something could be done to stiffen these men morally and physically, the cry of the unemployed would very soon cease. Those who are willing and able to work should be sent to a labour colony, and any unfit for work compelled to go to the poorhouse, while those incorrigible beggars and vagrants who will not agree to either ought to be sent to jail till they submit.[24]

What Motion and the others had done, though, was to stray into a wider issue: how far a public authority could regulate and control the 'honest' worker. But as Keir Hardie told the parish representatives in 1905, the working classes wanted a new deal, one that did not involve either the restraint of an individual or discriminatory treatment. Work tests, poorhouse relief and labour colonies were no longer acceptable. Both the Conservative and Liberal Governments recognised what had happened and national policy in any event changed, first by the 1905 Unemployed Workmans Act and then in 1911 by Unemployment

Insurance.

If parishes had failed to evolve popularly supported policies for the unemployed, how had it fared for the sick and infirm? It has already been noted that the 1890s saw the emergence of a fully fledged public health system and the further extension of the voluntary hospital movement. Chapter Four has also indicated that the Board began to develop a much closer system of monitoring the statutory sector. Parishes had not been slow to acknowledge these movements and indeed by 1900 most poorhouses did have trained nurses. However there were two important developments which increased pressure on parishes and the first of these concerned the extension of hospital services.

In the voluntary sector virtually all hospitals began to undertake large scale improvements. Some were rebuilt (Glasgow Royal Infirmary), others had new wings added for children (Dundee), installed x-ray departments or better laboratory facilities (Dumfries), while still others developed new specialist provision like labour wards (Edinburgh Maternity) and a TB sanatorium (Edinburgh Victoria).[25] In the public health sector, the Board similarly pressed local authorities to develop their isolation hospitals, and indeed annual capital expenditure rose to well over £100 000. Thus the early years of the century witnessed an increase in both the number and the quality of the beds. Many more patients were treated.[26]

This general increase in medical investment added a second pressure. There were many doctors, especially in the Public Health Departments, willing and able, not only to examine trends in public health, but also what actually determined good health. The first moves came with the Paton investigations into working-class diet. Others then examined particular items of diet, like children's milk consumption. Later, specific medical problems like rickets and defective eyesight came under observation. By the middle of the decade, survey techniques had been sufficiently developed to allow heights and weights to be correlated with the degree of urban overcrowding.[27] But just as these surveys advanced medical science and investigatory techniques, they also had an impact on the Poor Law. Every major city and many towns had someone conducting a survey into local health care. Thus parishes found themselves in an invidious position. To ignore the reports might lead others to criticise them for a lack of understanding about urban congestion. In practice, of course, the 'reformist' councillors were only too willing to seize upon the new knowledge, because for them it was important to persuade the public that parishes were facing serious difficulties in containing distress. The key question then, was not any unwillingness to consider the results of the survey work, but in the nature of the medical topics that emerged. In the field of Poor Law institutional care, there were two which soon dominated discussion: the improvement in the quality of indoor life, and the development of more specialist medical services.

The first of these can be illustrated by looking at improvements in poorhouse diets. Chapter Three indicated that in the 1890s there had been some uncertainty about the value of the old 1850 diet. The Board however, had decided not to withdraw it and instead left parishes to decide for themselves whether or not to introduce the suggested improvements. Most kept to their old scale. At Leith, for instance, the parish specifically rejected any dietary alteration and told the Board it could not accept all working inmates receiving four ounces of boiled meat a day instead of the previously agreed three.[28] Only those in the firewood factory who completed 300 sticks a day should get the full allowance. Dundee had similar discussions and argued that everyone, including the inmates, was happy with the old diet. Unfortunately, soon after its decision, the poorhouse suffered an outbreak of scurvy.[29] One inmate, an epileptic, died. The Medical Officer hastily provided fresh meat, milk, raw cabbage and lime juice, a diet far in excess of the Board's old scale.

These scandals were soon eclipsed. In 1899 the Prison Board had commissioned an inquiry into prison diets and when their medical consultant, Dr J. C. Dunlop, undertook a comparison of institutional diets, he noted, 'Compared to the Scottish prison dietaries. . . poorhouse dietaries appear to be of smaller nutrient value. That this should be so is anomalous, as no reason can be advanced why rogues in prison should be better fed than the unfortunate paupers in the poorhouse'.[30] Two year later, after conducting a survey of parochial asylum diets he made more searching comments:

> The more frequent causes of monotony of feeding appear to be the excessive use of porridge and unvarying boiling of beef. Porridge and milk is doubtless splendid food, and its use should be encouraged in all institutions, but two exclusively porridge meals daily are on account of their monotony to be condemned. The unvarying boiling of beef is a fault that should be easily rectified. Tea is found to be the only condiment used habitually. This is as it should be, and it is now an essential part of all dietaries, and a very necessary part of the dietaries of persons under the depressing influences of asylum treatment. Loss of liberty must be depressing.[31]

Dunlop concluded his Report by stating that the daily asylum diet should include the minimum of four ounces of meat (pre-cooked) or an equivalent amount of fish, four ounces of fresh vegetables (excluding potatoes) with tea, cocoa and bread 'ad libitum'.

The next year Miss Elizabeth Haldane, sister to an eminent Oxford physiologist and to the Liberal MP for Haddington, informed the Medical Relief Committee of Dunlop's work. By her brother's calculations, she told them, all poorhouse diets were insufficient.[32] Their calorific content was only two-thirds of that suggested by the American nutritionist Atwater. The Committee was so shocked by these revelations that it immediately wrote to the Board recommending further investigation. A few months later the Board withdrew the old scale, and stated that all poorhouses had to provide a diet at least equivalent to that of the 1898 scale.[33]

These incidents – the outbreak of scurvy, the squabbling over an ounce of boiled meat and the lack of knowledge over recent scientific work – all added up to one thing: poorhouse provision lagged far behind that in other hospitals. Glasgow, recognised this when it opened its new Poor Law hospitals in 1904, and decided to break with tradition. Medical officers were given the sole right to determine the quantity and quality of diets.[34] Later, after an incident in which an inmate burnt himself through brewing his own tea (prohibited in the rules, but allowed in practice), all poorhouse diets were altered to permit food to be given 'ad libitum'. Greater variation was also allowed in soups, stews and puddings.[35]

Other parishes seemed less willing to make alterations. At Leith, Council business almost halted after Labour councillors refused to ratify a vote for dietary improvements.[36] To them it did not go far enough. Eventually modifications like Glasgow's were made, but for many medical officers there was little doubt that the nature of poorhouse diets, in comparison with voluntary hospitals remained dull and monotonous.[37] Moreover, inmates were still subject to a strict regime, moleskin clothing, monthly 'liberty' days, occasional entertainment and of course, work. Those that refused to accept the discipline, like some sixty each year at Leith, faced the loss of privileges – meat in their soup, tea, concerts and tobacco – or even the punishment cell.

One of the reasons why the Board had established the Medical Relief Committee had been to review poorhouse policy. In the preceding decade, the Board through its circulars had suggested that inmates ought to be classified far more rigorously by their medical conditions and then segregated into wards or different parts of the poorhouse. With the greater amounts of surgical work being undertaken by voluntary hospitals, the Board also began to suggest to parishes that they introduce more specialist care, if necessary in separate buildings, apart from the ordinary wards.

Classification, segregation, medical specialisation and new buildings – the Board knew these were eminent ideals; their implementation would be a lot harder. The majority of parishes had either only one poorhouse, or if they had two (through amalgamation), they had been built to house all types of inmate. Thus the Board found that rural parishes were virtually unable to respond to the new policy. Few had the capital resources to extend their buildings and the majority were too far from voluntary hospitals to be able to hire non-resident specialists. All a rural poorhouse could do was to impose some classification and attempt segregation. However where there were only two or three staff and a few dozen inmates, as in Dalkeith, keeping proper segregation was extremely difficult. Only when the 1908 Children's Act brought in more children did this Combination agree to a separate hospital block and specialist nurses.[38] Other medical improvements also suffered delays and obstructions. In 1906 the Board had pressed for separate towels and fresh bathwater for each inmate. Although the bathing apparatus was inadequate, nothing was done.[39] Suggestions for toothbrushes were also ignored.

The Board found difficulties also with larger parishes. Leith, for instance, told the Board that it had just completed building a new poorhouse (the last to be built in Scotland) and could not afford a resident medical officer.[40] In Edinburgh, where the parish was also the local Lunacy Board, councillors were too committed to building a new asylum at Gogarburn to contemplate any other capital programme. Proposals to build two homes, one for children and the other for epileptics were squashed. A later suggestion that the parish should create observation wards, like Glasgow, for the suspected mentally ill, was also turned down.[41] The parish was only prepared to improve segregation and introduce some specialist services.

In the early 1900s the Board saw TB as the major medical problem. It was not yet a disease covered by the Public Health authorities, and many of those afflicted ended in the poorhouse. Edinburgh alone catered for nearly two hundred a year. After a special report by the Royal College of Physicians, the parish agreed to provide specialist facilities: separate blue dishes, marked bed covers (P for phthisis), similarly marked clothing, pocket spittoons and extra diets (solid butcher meat, good soup and extra milk).[42] Open air sheds were also built. But this was as far as Edinburgh would go and it was very happy when the Board removed TB care to the local authority in 1906.

The catalyst for Edinburgh, and indeed all other large parishes, was the Poor Law Commission. After adverse press criticism (the Webbs had published a report on Craigleith), the councillors hastily agreed to provide a new operating theatre.[43] Within a few years an additional two resident medical officers, a resident surgeon, a visiting opthalmic surgeon, two clinical assistants and extra nurses were appointed. The establishment of an x-ray department, an observation hospital and a children's home were also agreed.[44] At the same time as the appointment of the Board's additional inspectors, the Commission's criticisms were closely reviewed. All calls by the resident medical officers for equipment and staff were immediately supported, and to emphasise the altered direction in policy, each large poorhouse was specially inspected.

Craiglockhart was visited by Dr Dewar and he issued a nineteen page memorandum on his observations.[45] He began by urging the end of pauper nursing; it was no longer appropriate for a modern hospital. He then went on to emphasise just how far voluntary hospitals had improved their medical care. It was time, he suggested, for the Poor Law to cease using the 19th century philosophy of 'less eligiblity' and instead accept that an extensive range of medical services were necessary if pauper needs were to be met. He told Edinburgh:

> The existence of illness, which in a poorhouse is often incurable and generally of a chronic and disabling nature, removes the question of eligiblity. Very exceptionally is sickness preferred to health; thus there is little or no fear that the attractions of a hospital, however great, will make persons desire to qualify for admission.
>
> But apart from that, the standards of decency and humanity which prevail today ordain that a public institution, especially a public hospital, must be a public example and worthy of imitation, and that its staff, its equipment, its routine procedures, and its administration must be determined by modern medical views and hygienic requirements, and be but little influenced by the humble status of the patients admitted to its wards.

This issue was perhaps most acutely felt by the men suffering from contagious diseases. Dewar commented specifically on the two wards provided:

> These are well-ventilated rooms, lit by windows on both sides, and with open fires; yet they did not favourably impress me. They are in charge of an inmate; their situation at the top of a long and steep stair makes them somewhat inaccessible. Thus it is not easy to keep the inmates of each ward apart, as I found one day on making a surprise visit. [One] ward has eight beds. Cases of scabies remain here for a few days; cases of foetid ulcer for a period, it may be, of several weeks. The 'House' Nurse visits this ward daily, issues medicines and lotions as required and applies dressings. The patients in these wards have no bed-cards, and do not seem to receive much attention. In short they are isolated to a superfluous and unfortunate degree.

Dundee, like Edinburgh, also sought to improve its specialist services. TB care was introduced and, after a General Superintendent commented adversely on expectant mothers delivering babies in the same room as other sick women, the parish agreed to a new maternity ward.[46] Observation wards were also agreed and the Dundee Social Union was permitted to introduce the Brabazon scheme (see p.xx). Requests by the resident Medical Officer for equipment, including a new operating room, were also met.[47] Nevertheless, Dundee received an equally condemnatory report by Dr Dewar.[48] He noted that straw mattresses and shake-down beds were still in use and complained that in one ward several babies were mixed with women suffering from 'nervous disorders'. The maternity ward, in a basement, was ill-lit and full of flies. But it was in his criticism of the operating theatre that his Report struck hard at the division between voluntary hospitals and poorhouses:

> The outstanding deficiency of the Hospital is in respect of the absence of a [proper] operating room. For more than one reason it is obviously impossible to send cases requiring operative treatment to the Dundee Royal Infirmary. Dr MacVicar, therefore, does all the surgical work. During the past sixteen months seventy-three operations were performed here. These are at present conducted in one of the two side rooms. In order to see for myself the exact conditions which prevailed, I paid a special visit when a major operation (excision of the knee-joint) and two minor operative procedures were to be performed. At the commencement, although the fire had been on for some time, the room felt cold, the temperature being 54 F. It rose gradually, reaching 66 F within the hour. The windows were closed, but a draught from a ventilator was noticeable. An open fire is, of course, undesirable where ether is used as an anaesthetic. The light is said to be better here than in the side room of ward 3, which is used for operation upon male patients. The light on the occasion in question was not defective, but it might be improved if the panes of yellow and cerise coloured glass were removed from the upper sections of the window and panes of colourless glass substituted. The floor is of good wood. The walls are rough and not well suited for an operation room. Artificial light is supplied by means of incandescent mantles. The operating table is a slab of wood fixed upon trestles. It seemed somewhat shaky, but not insecure. The space in the room is cramped.

Glasgow's difficulties were similar to Edinburgh's and Dundee's. Its two large poorhouses were both unsuitable and inadequate for more advanced medical work. One, the City, was falling down. The need for new accommodation had long been recognised and within a month of the amalgamated parish being formed, the council agreed to a review. It too concluded that the existing poorhouses prevented more modern treatment being followed. This they argued had a serious consequence: without the prospect of an early recovery, a pauper's return to work was greatly hindered. A further report was requested from their Resident Medical Officers, Dr William Core and Dr McCubbin Johnston.[49] It was equally critical and concluded:

> It must not be forgotten that the standard of health amongst poorhouse inmates is decidedly below that of the general population. They are constantly seeking, and many actually require medical advice, and a considerable proportion fall victims to acute illnesses requiring transference to Hospital. Further, a large

number of the infirm class are in such a weak state of health, many being bed-ridden, that Hospital treatment for them would be desirable. Should these poor helpless men and women who require as much care and nursing as more acute cases, be still consigned to the venal ministrations of pauper warders? . . . [Moreover] the surroundings of the destitute sick preclude the possibility of successful treatment. Many are deterred by the associations of the Poorhouse from seeking that relief which can be adequately given in Hospital only. Were outdoor medical relief of a more temporary character, and the parish Hospitals administered as such and not as Poorhouses, our results would be more satisfactory.

After further discussion a new strategy emerged, and plans for a general hospital and two smaller district ones were submitted. The former was to treat the chronically sick and the latter, situated in the poorer districts, were for acute cases. The proposal was quickly approved and the hospitals were formally opened in 1904.

Almost immediately the policy ran into difficulty, for two quite separate reasons. One was that the majority of councillors continued to mix moral and clinical judgements about treatment. During their discussions, they had argued that all but one group of children would be sent to the general hospital at Stobhill. The other group, the 'test' mother with young infants, would go to Barnhill. But in practice Glasgow's the relief committee (a single councillor on a rota basis, see p.xx) continued to use Barnhill for those who had a 'bad record of behaviour'.[50] Pleas by the medical officers that VD, skin and other diseases were acute illnesses had little impact.

A year after the hospitals had been opened, the parish was forced to conduct an inquiry and the Inspector was asked to review the difficulties the policy had encountered.[51] He reported:

After much consideration. . . I have failed to evolve any properly defined scheme which could be applicable in every case. With paupers repeatedly chargeable there is no difficulty; their characters are known only too well, both to the outdoor and indoor officials. Yet, within this class, it has to be said that many are most exemplary in their behaviour and amenable to the ordinary discipline of the institution. Are they to be ranked with the decent or with the disreputable class? Then in new cases, upon whose decision are each to be morally classified? They have to be sent to the poorhouse or hospital usually before there is any real inquiry as to their character. . . these difficulties become intensified if the inmates are also to be separated morally in the work apportioned to each. Such would mean the duplication of workshops, machinery, etc. . .

Having thus indicated the chief difficulties, I would venture to suggest that the principles, at least, might be obtained. By a graduated process of sub-classification, with extended privileges as to the employment, dietary, liberty days, and the reception of visitors to the deserving class, I am of the opinion that many of the objections to the more comprehensive scheme would be removed.

To begin this process the Inspector suggested that TB patients who had been repeatedly chargeable should be moved to Barnhill (irrespective of the fact that Stobhill had the specialist equipment for their care). All maternity cases were similarly to be sent and only after the birth would they be assessed for possible transference to hospital. Suspected epileptics were also to be sent to Barnhill. The effect of this kind of mixed moral and clinical judgement was seen in the number of admissions made: they remained static, at around 9 000 per annum. The majority of these remained as before, the chronically sick and infirm, those who had nowhere else to go.[52] Indeed, so few were the number of acute cases being treated that for a time the nurse training scheme was put at risk. Although the council subsequently toned down its moral classification and informed the medical officers that they would be allowed more clinical freedom, few extra sought the parish's care.[53]

The second problem was one of staffing. Soon after the hospital plan had been approved, the councillors agreed to end 'pauper' nursing.[54] Only trained nurses were to be employed. Subsequently they agreed to staff Stobhill with four resident medical officers and the Eastern and Western District Hospitals with three each.[55] Despite these improvements the parish found many doctors and nurses leaving. Although they were paid rates equivalent to that in the voluntary sector, there was not a sufficient variety of cases to further their careers.[56] As a result the quality of staff remained low. It was only after the Parsons Report had embarrassed the parish that the councillors were forced to act. A dentist, an opthalmic surgeon, a nurse with medico-psychological certificate (for the care of epileptics) and a visiting surgeon and physician were all appointed.[57] So too were additional nurses.

Glasgow had encountered the same problem as the other larger parishes. Once medical treatment had been recognised as an essential part of the Poor Law, there was a move away from established principles. Many had found the old philosophy died hard and it proved difficult for parishes to abandon discrimination. By the time the war broke out, the Board realised the contradiction. It had already told parishes that there could be no more new poorhouses.[58] Instead, only separate and specialist institutions would be allowed, ones that would eventually have to offer care 'on a level with the best voluntary infirmary'.[59] As for the unemployed, parishes had failed to evolve a suitably acceptable policy.

The 1890s had seen the steady growth in awareness of a pauper child's

Sir John McNeill, Chairman of the Board of Supervision, 1845-68.

Sir John Skelton, Secretary of the Board of Supervision, 1868-92 and Chairman of the Local Government Board, 1894-97.

W.A. Peterkin, General Superintendent of Poor, the Board of Supervision, 1865-92.

Sir Malcolm M'Neill, Chairman of the Local Government Board, 1897-1904.

J.R. Motion, Inspector of Poor, Glasgow Parish Council, 1898-1921.

James Kyd, Inspector of Poor, Dundee Parish Council, 1894-1906.

E.F. MacPherson,
Legal Member of the
Local Government
Board, 1904-19.

W.L. MacKenzie,
Medical Member of the
Local Government
Board, 1904-19.

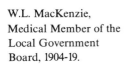

J. Patten-MacDougal,
Chairman of the Local
Government Board,
1904-09.

Robert Munro,
President of the Board
of Health, 1919-22.

Dr T.F. Dewar, Medical Inspector, the Local Government Board and the Board
of Health, 1910-28.

Sir George MacCrae, Chairman of the Local Government Board 1909-19.

Sir G. Collins, Secretary of State for Scotland, 1932-36.

needs. This, coupled with the new Child Cruelty and Infant Life Protection Acts, had lent support to those who felt the Poor Law should deal with any child from an unsatisfactory home. Gradually, therefore, the number of children separated from their parents increased, posing a major administrative problem. Many felt that these children, because of their 'unsatisfactory' homes, were both ill-nourished and physically unfit. That in turn meant there was little prospect of parishes being able to find foster-parents. Nobody would want them. This, then, was the crucial issue for those who wished the Poor Law to go beyond what had been done in the 1890s. It was no use intervening in a family's life if parishes were unable to develop more specialised and more child centred forms of care. The public were unlikely to accept any child, however ill-nourished, being sent to a poorhouse designed and managed for the control of 'paupers'.

By 1900, inspectors in the larger parishes were beginning to understand that this particular problem did require a reorientation in policy. Dundee's Inspector, James Kyd, was one of the first to recognise the issue and urged his council to introduce some form of probationary training in a separately established children's home. There children could spend time under more direct supervision.[60] The parish at first agreed but then put the issue in abeyance. The councillors thought other claimants, the casual labourer and the chronically sick, required the more urgent attention. Only in 1915 when the problems of improving the structure and provision of their poorhouse was solved did they agree to a separate home.[61]

Edinburgh was another parish which initially prevaricated. It had taken nearly a year of hard argument from the lady councillors to persuade the council to appoint a specialist nurse for Craiglockhart's children.[62] Even then the accommodation provided was no more than a corner of the women's sick ward. However, with the Paton Report on the inadequacies of working-class diet and MacKenzie's showing that 30 per cent of schoolchildren were undernourished, the parish felt compelled to act. Within a few months of the latter's Report, the council had conducted a survey of its own.[63] It found the group most vulnerable to deprivation were children whose 'drunken' parents had been struck off the roll for refusing poorhouse relief. In a complete reversal of traditional policy, the parish reviewed all the more recent cases and offered them outdoor relief under greater supervision; it was important, the parish said, to prevent any further fall into the degeneracy of 'drink, lunacy and vagrancy'.[64] Soon afterwards, a special feeding scheme under a newly appointed lady inspector, Miss Barclay, was established and by the end of 1904, four hundred pauper children were being fed at approved restaurants, a typical lunchtime diet being:

Monday	Broth, mince and potatoes or stoved potatoes.
Tuesday	Potato soup and suet pudding.
Wednesday	Broth or pea soup and meat sandwich.
Thursday	Potato soup and rice pudding.
Friday	Broth or pea soup and suet or rice pudding.
Saturday	Coffee and meat sandwich; now and then a pie.[65]

But hand in hand with this came a much harder attitude towards the parent. Those who had deserted their family were much more ruthlessly pursued. Posters with their full description appeared on public notice boards and a reward, of up to 20s. was offered to anyone who could supply information leading to their discovery.

All that had been done so far had cost very little. But Edinburgh's main problem was similar to Dundee's: the trade depression and the general increase in the chronically ill meant its poorhouses were fully taxed. A report by a number of councillors at the end of 1904 called for a separate children's home, but its cost on top of the other capital improvements ensured its narrow defeat.[66] Nothing more occurred until the Poor Law Commission's Report. With its specific recommendation that poorhouses should not be regarded as a 'suitable' place for children, Edinburgh, like other large parishes, became acutely embarrassed. Soon after its publication, the council agreed to build a separate home. The need for improved facilities was further underlined the following year by a special Board survey of Craigleith. Dr M'Vail, their lady inspector commented specifically on the medical arrangements:

Staff. – The staff in charge of the children consisting as it does of a single paid attendant without hospital experience whose only assistants are inmates of the Poorhouse, is in my opinion quite inadequate. The attendant, I am convinced, does her best, and care seems to be taken to choose as far as possible a good class of inmate to help her, but even so additional service is urgently required. For the care of young children it is very desirable to have a nurse with hospital experience.

Hospital Accommodation. – The Children's Hospital Ward is on the third floor. Many children requiring hospital treatment are well enough and indeed benefit greatly by being out of doors most of the day. It would be a great advantage if children could be given accommodation on the ground floor where their cots could be wheeled outside whenever practicable. Nearly twenty-nine per cent of deaths among children under five years admitted to Craigleith Poorhouse during the four years ended June 30th 1912 have been due to some form of tuberculosis, for which fresh air is, of course, a recognised form of treatment.

Feeding of Infants. – The cleansing and making up of feeding bottles should be undertaken by the paid staff, and should on no account be left to inmates. Up till now the inadequacy of the staff may sometimes have rendered such precautions impracticable. Of 326 admissions to the hospital ward of children under 5 years during the four year's period above mentioned, 70, or 21.4 per cent, were due to gastro intestinal disease.

Boarding-out from Poorhouse. – Before children are boarded out from the poorhouse, it is the rule to have them examined for certain conditions by the resident Medical Officer. No examination is made of the organs of special sense. It would, I think, be of considerable advantage if arrangements could be made to have the eyes, and throats of children examined and defects remedied before sending them to a country district.[67]

The parish agreed to employ additional nurses and an opthalmist. Dundee and Edinburgh had found child welfare a difficult issue to resolve. What of Glasgow?

At the end of 1898, when the old City and Barony parishes had been amalgamated, the new parish had about 350 children receiving institutional care. Half were classified as healthy, a third were infants and the remainder sick. In late 1900, under the guidance of Brand and James Motion, the Inspector, a new scheme for institutional child care was presented to the council.[68] First, they suggested all children should be under the supervision of trained nurses and be moved to a separate block at the new Stobhill General Hospital. Second, expectant mothers were to be sent to either the district hospitals or the poorhouse, depending on their character. Third, all poorhouse children who could not be sent to school were to be educated by a specially trained teacher. Finally, those requiring probationary or temporary care were to be taught simple tasks like sewing, gardening, tailoring and shoemaking. This would ensure they were educated in the proper attitude to work. The council accepted the proposals and they were duly implemented.

Over the next decade the parish continued to develop the scheme. This in part stemmed from its very success. More children were pulled into the poorhouse because outdoor officials felt that children could receive better care. More parents applied, the inspectors said, because they saw the availability of trained nurses and a children's doctor.[69] By 1910 the number of children in institutional care more than doubled. Yet this apparent success produced a number of problems. The poorhouse accommodation became over-taxed. As early as 1903, some children had to be boarded-out in convalescent homes in Rothesay and Lanark.[70] At the same time the Board raised objections to the parish using its Medical Grant to cover the nursing of healthy children.[71] Although the Board relented and allowed the Grant to cover the nursing of all children under two (whether sick or not), the basic problem of providing adequate accommodation remained.

By 1907, in response to this, a number of councillors proposed that the parish itself should establish a special convalescent home for the less physically fit.[72] But like Edinburgh and Dundee, the others baulked at the cost. The parish had just completed the building of three new hospitals. Instead, it was agreed that any such children should be sent on the Fresh Air Fortnight Scheme, a charity which took slum children on holiday down the Clyde. Nevertheless, the congestion grew and the following year the Inspector felt compelled to reiterate the call for a special home. This time, however, he introduced a new aspect to the policy. He stated quite categorically, 'the whole order and control of the house would be removed as far as possible from institutional life'.[73] The next year, with a belief that the new Children's Act would increase the numbers still further, the parish agreed to open a training school for girls at Dunoon.[74] There, under the supervision of a trained nurse, the girls would be introduced to domestic service.

The Poor Law Commission's Report added further impetus and the Inspector recommended that a home for those unlikely to be self-supporting ought to be established, as boarding out did not meet these particular children's needs. They required far greater professional care. There was little opposition and a Home at Dunclutha, Kirn was opened in 1911.[75] Amongst its rules, it allowed the children clean underclothing and stockings once a fortnight and a fresh bath with a separate towel once a week. Boys were taught gardening, joinery and other traditional male trades, while girls concentrated on more domestic chores. Recreational activities, like flag signalling, drilling, singing, dancing and learning first aid were also pursued.

Thus Glasgow, as far as institutional support for children was concerned had pursued child welfare beyond either Dundee and Edinburgh. In this it had crossed the divide between the passive control of 'neglected' or 'needful' children and asserted that much more than sustenance was required. But Glasgow found that that was not enough. The number requiring special assistance either through institutional care or by boarding out continued to grow. Stobhill alone received over 2 000 admissions a year. With a staggering 3 000 children on their roll, either in hospital or being fostered – well over double that of the 1890s – Glasgow, like Edinburgh, found many new social and medical needs required attention. Not only had the parish to consider extra staff, it also had to search far more vigorously for additional foster-parents, even as far as Orkney.

Yet Glasgow acknowledged that it was not simply a question of children who required separation from their parents. The same line of reasoning also applied to those whose parents, although honestly making an effort to maintain a 'moral' home, had difficulty in doing so satisfactorily. Thus the parish also sought to increase the amount of supervision available to those on the outdoor roll. In 1900 the Inspector conveyed his desire for institutional support, and also suggested 'that a lady with nursing experience be now included in the Department for special visitation and inspection of particular homes and children, where the services of a lady will be appreciated'.[76] Shortly afterwards a lady with a medico-psychological certificate, Miss Jeanie Thompson was appointed: the first qualified 'social worker' to be employed by a parish for the care of children. Two years later, a circular from the Board suggested that women with children, particularly widows, should have an increase in allowances to offset their need to undertake part-time work. The Board felt that this would reduce the amount of parental neglect inherent in the traditional practice of paying low benefits to those who could work. Glasgow was quick to establish a special roll and recruited another lady inspector for home visitation.[77] Despite this move, it was obvious to the council that the amount of time available for one official was far too limited for the number of cases – some 2 500. The Inspector was particularly concerned about widows with what he called 'depraved habits', who had no idea of cleanliness, the repair of clothing and the purchase and preparation of food. Unless additional support was given there could be no alternative but to separate the children and board them out. A leaflet was subsequently published for them and other mothers with hints about home management.[78] The parish also sought to enrol the services of the clergy and other voluntary agencies to provide more domestic support. This latter innovation apparently did not work and more thought was given to the issue.[79] Although the clergy were again contacted, it was agreed that the more senior inspectors should be involved in a closer review of each case.

Outside the principal cities, developing child welfare proved more hazardous. In Ayrshire, for instance, the parishes in the Kyle Combination consistently refused to consider the Board's request for separate accomodation and specialist services. Children remained under the care of adult paupers. Provision only changed when the poorhouse was engulfed in a public scandal over the death of an inmate. In the spring of 1906, when a number of children contracted measles, the Governor adopted the usual practice and isolated them in an attic room. A few days later its Medical Officer reported a 'painful and shocking event': the body of a young child had been found dead at 5 a.m., 'her face gnawed by rats'.[80] He added:

> The child was suffering from measles, but death was not anticipated from that cause. There is, however, a strong possiblity that death was due to natural causes, and that the gnawing took place post mortem. My reason for thinking this is – 1st – The small amount of blood to be seen on the bed clothing. 2nd – The position of the child's body when found. 3rd – The fact that neither the other children nor the attendant were awakened by its cries.

The Board immediately instituted an inquiry and sent Robert Barclay, its area Superintendent to make a full report. Afterwards Kyle was left in no doubt what had gone wrong:

That, when this outbreak of measles occurred there was no proper acommodation or nursing in the Poorhouse for the affected children, and no effort was made to have them removed elsewhere. Further, the Board are informed that the hearing of the nurse in attendance on these children is defective; they would specifically impress upon the House Committee that a woman afflicted with deafness is not a fit and suitable person to act as a nurse for young children.[81]

Although the Board's suggestions were eventually adopted, the Superintendent continued to report his concern.[82] Children still had to share baths and at mealtimes eat without knives or forks.

Parish involvement with child welfare was further extended by the new Children's Act. Although inspectors of poor had been designated the local agent for the 1897 Infant Life Protection Act, its weak powers meant that relatively few cases of 'baby farming' were prosecuted; both Leith and Glasgow had tried but without success.[83] The majority of foster-parents simply avoided having too many children in care at any one time. Edinburgh did not bother to officially appoint its Inspector as a Visitor until 1906.[84] All of that was to change with the 1908 Act.

The new Act increased the age limit for inspection to seven, included any child received by a foster-parent and stated that the 'brokerage' had to be completed in 48 hours.[85] The foster-parent's home then had to be inspected and approved by the parish. With the Board insisting on immediate implementation, the larger parishes quickly extended the duties of their children's inspectors to cover the new provisions.[86] Glasgow, after a year of using the existing staff, appointed an extra three lady officers. Other parishes usually appointed their own inspector, with an additional fee for every home that was monitored. From a few hundred registered in 1909, the numbers rose to nearly 5 000 in 1914, with home visits normally every three months. To ensure everyone understood the Act, the Board urged parishes to initiate prosecutions. The first was of an unfortunate Glasgow laundrymaid, whose failure to give the appropriate notice cost two months imprisonment.

The Child Cruelty Acts had also increased parish responsibilities. The onus had been on other agencies, however, notably the Society for the Prevention of Cruelty to Children, to initiate action. Many parishes had wavered on whether or not to undertake a more strenuous 'policing role' of their own. To assist and provide long-term care might have resulted in an auditor's objection; it would have run counter to the principle of no relief to the able-bodied. The 1908 Act did not specifically overturn the principle, but it did say that the parish was 'to be active' in pursuing negligent parents. Moreover neglect was given an explicit and far wider meaning; it now covered incidents where a parent had failed to provide for their children, or knowing that they could not provide, had failed to apply for assistance. The lack of proper clothing, forcing a child to beg or using the home as a brothel all came under the new definition of neglect. parishes had the legal and financial power to commit children to its own or another's care.

The Act heralded an important shift in policy and parishes reacted to it. With the approval of the procurator fiscals, they all began to initiate prosecutions. Early in 1910 Glasgow went one further and allowed assistant inspectors to take action on their own accord. The results of this new procedure was fully explained by the Inspector:

> The first case was brought before Sheriff Davidson on 24th February, when upon a deposition by the District Assistant Inspector, that he had found three children, whose mother was in receipt of parish Relief, in a naked, filthy and starving condition, and otherwise grossly neglected, he granted a warrant, committing all three to the care of the parish till they attain the age of sixteen years. There were grounds in this case for prosecuting the mother on a charge of cruelty, but in respect that her husband had only died a week before, and that she was in an advanced state of pregnancy, this charge was not proceeded with.
>
> The next case was brought before Sheriff Fyfe in 7th instant, when upon a deposition by Mr Watt [the assistant criminal officer], his Lordship granted an order committing three children to Stobhill. Their mother had been put on the Roll for drunkenness, and she refused to allow them to go to Stobhill, and disappeared from the address where she was residing. When found a week or two later, the children were in a starving and neglected condition, and the condition of the mother in no way improved.
>
> It is to be noted that this procedure has been a means of greatly improving the condition of neighbours of the parties from whom the children were removed. The mere fact that we can go to the Sheriff, and without further evidence than the sworn deposition of an Assistant Inspector, obtain a warrant to break into their house and remove neglected children, appears, even more than a prosecution, to be a powerful factor in bringing a certain class of people to a better understanding of their duty.[87]

At the same time any concern that a parish might have had over assisting non-pauper children was also dispelled. Early in 1910, an able-bodied man who had neglected his children was successfully prosecuted for failing to apply for Poor Relief. The Sheriff ignored the man's pleas that he could not obtain assistance other than by becoming a 'pauper'. What Barony had begun rather tentatively in the 1880s now had full legal backing. A parish could separate a child from a parent and have a Court Order restraining them until the parent's behaviour altered. There was an additional factor in this development: for those who had deserted their families, parishes could press for much more severe punishment, up to six months hard labour instead of only thirty days. They were not slow to do so. In Glasgow alone, the number of prosecutions increased from less than a hundred per annum to well over two hundred and fifty. A quarter received at least three months.[88] From 1900 to 1914 there had been a considerable change in parish attitude towards child welfare. But problems remained. One of them surrounded the propriety of assisting 'non-pauper' children. Even as late as 1913, one official could comment that it was interfering with God's Law: family relationships were inviolate.[89] Parishes, he felt, should revert to traditional policy: attaching stigma to pauperism, character reformation through poorhouse 'training' and reducing the role of the State. A second problem lay in the fact that many saw the 1908 Act as an adjunct to their powers of prosecution. They expected their officials to combine a welfare approach to child care with a much more punitive one against 'neglectful' and 'immoral' parents. Thus an inspector's attention remained focused on the legal aspects of control and given that the powers of the 1908 Act appeared analagous to the 'searching out' demanded by the Minority Report, it was little wonder that some felt their activities had done little to win public support.[90]

Thirdly and perhaps most importantly, the 'reformist' philosophy had shown itself to be contradictory. Not only was there still an attachment to established practices of discriminatory treatment, but there was also a continued difficulty of persuading other middle class councillors that the extra expenditure necessary was absolutely essential. Even in Glasgow, where new forms of provision had developed, the actual number of children requiring assistance far outmatched the quality of care. Faced with other seemingly more intransigent problems. like the casual labourer and the sick, parishes had not been able to give child welfare any priority. As a result no further significant development could occur and the structure of provision lay more or less ossified until it was formally decided to abandon the Poor Law in the 1940s.

NOTES
1. Wallace, A, The System of Relief in the Large Cities, in *Poor Law Magazine 1899*, pp.57-72; Evidence of Motion, Barclay, Hawden (Edinburgh) and Cochran (Glasgow), to *Poor Law Commission, op. cit.*
2. Bothwell Parish Council Minutes, 13.12.01, *SRA CO1.23.10.*
3. Evidence of Miss M. L. Walker on Dundee (17.6.07), in *Poor Law Commission, op. cit.*; Wallace, A. on Govan (6.11.02), in *Medical Relief Committee, op. cit.*.
4. Brand, J., Address to Poor Law Medical Officers, in *Poor Law Magazine 1896*, p.218; Address to Glasgow Poor Law Officers' Association, in *ibid. 1898*, p.173; Valedictory Address, in *ibid. 1902*, pp.1-12; evidence to *Poor Law Commission, op. cit.* Appendix XXII.

5. Reports from the Hustings (4.12.01, 7.12.04, 3.12.07 and 4.12.07, November and December, 1910 and 1913), and passim, in *Glasgow Herald* and *Scotsman*.

6. Bothwell Parish Council Minutes, 14.1.08 and Cambuslang Parish Council Minutes, 22.10.08, *SRA CO1.23.12 and CO1.25.12*.

7. See Chapter 8.

8. Leith Parish Council Minutes, 23.3 and 21.4.08, *EPLER qYHV 243L*.

9. Labour's philosophy and policy has been collated from the motions put forward to Glasgow, Edinburgh, Dundee, Bothwell, Cambulsang, Leith and Carmicheal Parish Councils, the evidence of Stewart, to *Poor Law Commission, op. cit.*; Norman, *op. cit.* and report of election manifestos 1910 and 1913, and passim, in *Forward*.

10. Chalmers, A. K., *The Health of Glasgow, 1818-1930* (Glasgow, 1930) p.191.

11. Report by Barclay, J. B., on Craiglockhart and Craigleith Poorhouses, 31.12. and 28.11.03, in Edinburgh Parish Council Minutes, 12.1.04, *op. cit.*; see also, J. J., A Plea for a New Poor Law, in *Poor Law Magazine 1904*, pp.253-62 and Appendix 4.

12. Report on Barnhill Poorhouse – Employment of Inmates, December 1903, in Glasgow Parish Council Minutes, 17.2.04. *op. cit.* The number in Glasgow's Institutions were:

	no. of admissions per year		nos. at 15th May	
	sick	ordinary	sick	ordinary
1899	7600	6500	401	1898
1904	9400	9700	1694	1988
1909	10900	11900	2470	1908
1913	9800	5800	2371	1510

13. *Poor Law Magazine 1899*, pp.53-6.

14. Edinburgh Parish Council Minutes, 10.11.99 and 14.1.01. *op. cit.*; also evidence of Motion, to *Departmental Committee on Vagrancy, op. cit.*; Lamond, R. P., Inebriates and the Inebriates Act, 1898, in *Poor Law Magazine 1900*, pp.171-8; Memorandum of Motion on, the Inebriates Act and Poor Law Detention, to the Scottish Office, 1901, in evidence (28.1.09), to *Departmental Committee on the Law Relating to Inebriates. Cd. 4767 (P.P. 1909 Vol. XXVI)*.

15. Edinburgh Parish Council Minutes, 14.3.02 and 30.5.02, *op. cit.*; also *Poor Law Magazine 1902*, pp.113-5 and 178-82; *The Detention of Poor Persons (Scotland) Bill, 1902*. First Reading, 24.7.02.

16. See, *Poor Law Magazine 1903*, pp.47-9.

17. Edinburgh Parish Council Minutes, 9.1.03, 1.5.03 and 2.10.03. *op. cit.; The Detention of Poor Persons (Scotland) Bill, 1903.* First Reading, 20.3.03.

18. Govan Parish Council Minutes, 29.1.03, *GMLGR G352.04143*.

19. Evidence (14.5.07), to *op. cit.*

20. Govan Parish Council Minutes, 11.1.04, *op. cit.*; also Memorandum by Edinburgh Parish Council on, The Inebriates Act and Poor Law Detention to the Secretary for Scotland, January 1904, in evidence of Kyd, J. (10.2.09), to *Inebriates Committee, op. cit.*

21. Letter of Scottish Office (4.11.04), in Govan Parish Council Minutes, 30.1.05, *op. cit.*

22. Meeting of 29.5.06, in *Poor Law Magazine 1906*, p.244.

23. Evidence to the Lunacy Commission, *op. cit.*
24. The Unskilled Labourer and the Vicious, in *Poor Law Magazine 1904*, pp.441-54; also, Transactions of the Scottish Sanitary Congress, September 1904, in *The County and Municipal Record III*, pp.451-2.
25. n.a., Edinburgh Medical Institutions, in *British Medical Journal 1927(1)*, pp.573-7 and, n.a., The Glasgow Hospital System, in *ibid. 1922(2)*, pp.884-8.
26. Evidence of MacKintosh, Dr D. J., (Glasgow Western Infirmary) (14.12.99), to *The Departmental Committee on Prisons (Scotland). Cd. 219 (P.P. 1900 Vol. XLII);* Johnston, Dr J. M'c., State Provision for the Care of the Destitute Sick, in *Medical Relief Committee. op. cit.*, Appendix III. Between 1894 and 1913 the number of inpatients treated by the major Glasgow voluntary hospitals doubled to 22,000 per annum, two-thirds of whom required surgical care.
27. Armour, M. (1904), Milk Depots for Infants, in *Journal of the Royal Sanitary Institute*, p.699-703; Foggie, W. E. (1905), Notes on Rickets in Dundee, in *Scottish Medical and Surgical Journal XVI*, pp.231-6; Pollock, W. B. I. (1905-6), The Eyesight of Schoolchildren; being a Record of the Examination of over 3,000 Schoolchildren, in *Proc. of the Royal Philosophical Society of Glasgow XXXVII*, pp.93-124; MacKenzie, W. L. and Foster, A., *The Physical Condition of Children Attending the Public School of the School Board of Glasgow. Cd. 3637 (P.P. 1907 Vol. LXV);* Kelynack, T. N., *Defective Children* (London, 1915).
28. Leith Parish Council Minutes, 12.3.98, 7.5., 27.5. and 29.5.02, *op. cit.*
29. Dundee Parish Council Minutes, 24.3.98, *TRA TC.PCM.3;* Sandeman, Dr L. S. Report on Scurvy, in *Medical Relief Committee, op. cit.* Appendix VI.
30. Dunlop, J. C. *Report on Prison Dietaries. C. 9514 (P.P. 1899 Vol. XLII)* p.127.
31. Dunlop, J. C. *Report on the Dietary of Pauper Lunatics. Cd. 955 (P.P. 1902 Vol. XLI)* p.96.
32. Memorandum on Indoor Relief – Diet, (1.12.02) in *op. cit.* Appendix XLIX.
33. Circular as to Poorhouse Diet. (6.2.03), in *Annual Report of the Local Government Board, 1903. Cd. 2001 (P.P. 1904 Vol. XXVIII)* App.(A.) No.5, pp.9-13.
34. Glasgow Parish Council Minutes, 15.2. and 20.5.04, *op. cit.* ; MacKay, G. A., *The Management and Construction of Poorhouses* (Edinburgh, 1908) pp.82-91 and 231-5 and Appendix 5.
35. Glasgow Parish Council Minutes, 15.6 and 23.11.10, *op. cit.*
36. Leith Parish Council Minutes, 27.12.10, 17.2.11 and 14.3.13, *op. cit.*
37. Watson, D. C., *Food and Feeding in Health and Disease* (Edinburgh, 1910) pp.546-7.
38. Dalkeith Combination Poorhouse Minutes, 17.12.09 and 24.4.10, *SRO CO.2. 99.2.*
39. 29.11.11 and 10.4.12, *ibid.*
40. Leith Parish Council Minutes, 4.5.08, *op. cit.*
41. Edinburgh Parish Council Minutes, 16.2., 14.4.06 and 1.12.08, *op. cit.*
42. Memorial by the Royal College of Physicians on the Treatment

of TB in Poorhouses (2.4.00), in Minutes, 21.5.00, see also 3.12.00 and 2.2.03, *ibid.*

43. Minutes, 15.3.09, 5.4.09 and 4.1.10, *ibid.*; also letter of Dr Holland (the London Hospital) (1.4.09), in *Scotsman*. p.9.
44. Minutes, 4.11., 28.11.11, 1.4.12, 29.1., 8.9.13 and 2.3.14, *op. cit.*
45. Report on Craiglockhart Poorhouse (1.6.12), in Minutes, 16.12.12, *ibid.*
46. Dundee Parish Council Minutes, 21.9.99, 28.10.01 and 27.7.02, *op. cit.*
47. Minutes, 26.1.03, 21.2.07 and 21.3.07, *ibid.*
48. Report on Dundee East Poorhouse (14.3.12), in Minutes, 21.3.12, *ibid.*
49. Report by the Medical Officers of the City and Barnhill Poorhouses regarding the Future Hospital Requirements of the Parish of Glasgow (29.5.99) and Report by the Special Committee of the Parish Council on Poorhouse and Hospital Accomodation (18.8.99), in Glasgow Parish Council Minutes, 1.9.99, see also 1.3.99, *op. cit.*
50. Memorandum on Barnhill Medical Officer's Classification, Minutes, 21.6.05 and 3.7.05, *ibid.*
51. Memorandums by Inspector and Clerk with Reference to the Disposal of Applicants for Indoor Relief, and the Classification thereof. . . , June and October 1905, in Minutes, 11.9. and 17.10.05, *ibid.*
52. Eastern District Hospital Medical Superintendent's Annual Report, 1908 and Memorandum by the Medical Superintendent on Classification, November 1908, in Minutes, 18.6.08 and 7.1.09, *ibid.*
53. Minutes, 22.1.09, *ibid.*; see also fn.12.
54. Minutes, 22.5.01, *ibid.*
55. Minutes, 19.10.03, *ibid.*
56. Mackintosh, D. J., *The Construction, Equipment and Management of a General Hospital* (Edinburgh, 1909).
57. Glasgow Parish Council Minutes, 27.2., 19.6., 23.8.12, 15.3. and 24.4.14. *op. cit.*
58. Letter dated 29.3.11, in Edinburgh Parish Council Minutes, 3.4.11, *op. cit.*
59. Letter dated 12.5.14, in Glasgow Parish Council Minutes, 14.5.14, *op. cit.*
60. Dundee Parish Council Minutes, 12.2.01, *TRA TC.PCM.6.*
61. Children on the Outdoor Roll, 12.9.01 and 29.5.15, *ibid.* and *ibid.20.*
62. Edinburgh Parish Council Minutes, 7.6.97, 8.12.97, and 16.6.98, *op. cit.*
63. Minutes, 14.12. and 21.12.03, *ibid.*
64. Minutes, 14.1.04, *ibid.*
65. Minutes, 8.2. and 3.3.05, *ibid.*
66. Minutes, 5.9.04 and 5.6.05, *ibid.* It had first been suggested by Barclay.
67. Report of 19.12.12, in Minutes, 6.1.13; see also 16.10.11, *ibid.*
68. Report on Indoor Accomodation, and Memorandum on Children who become Chargeable, Glasgow Parish Council Minutes, 1.9.99 and 19.10.00, *op. cit.*
69. MacGregor, A. S. M., *Public Health in Glasgow, 1905-46* (Edinburgh, 1966) Chapter 9, comment on discussion with Motion.

70. Memorandum by Inspector of Poor on the Children's Department of Stobhill Hospital, Glasgow Parish Council Minutes, 26.11.03; see also 18.8.03, *op. cit.*
71. Letters of 14.2 and 29.4.05, in Minutes, 24.2. and 12.5.05, *ibid.*
72. Memorandum by Inspector of Poor on Indoor Accomodation, Minutes, 19.4.07. *ibid.*
73. Report by Inspector of Poor on the Children's Department at Stobhill, Minutes, 18.8.08, *ibid.*
74. Memorandum by Inspector of Poor on Children in Parish Institutions, 25.2.09 in Minutes, 11.3.09; see also 16.2.09, *ibid.*
75. Memorandum by Inspector of Poor on Indoor Accomodation, 16.8.10, in Minutes, 25.8.10, and Memorandum on the Employment of Inmates at Dunclutha House, Kirn, in Minutes, 20.2.12 *ibid.*; Rules and Regulations of Dunclutha House, Kirn, in Glasgow Parish Council Miscellaneous Prints, 1912, *SRA T-PAR 1.19.*
76. Memorandum by Inspector of Poor on the Administration of Boarded-Out Children and Lunatics, Glasgow Parish Council Minutes, 22.10.00, *op. cit.*
77. Memorandum on Widows and Children (5.6.02), in *Annual Report of the Local Government Board, 1902. Cd. 1521 (P.P. 1903 Vol. XXIV)* App.(A.) No.5, pp.14-5; Glasgow Parish Council Minutes, 12.7.02, 22.1. and 7.8.03, *op. cit.*
78. Memorandum by Inspector of Poor on Widows and Children, Minutes, 19.12.05, *op. cit.*; Hints about the Management of the House and the Children, Glasgow Parish Council Miscellaneous Prints, 1905-6, *SRA T-PAR 1.4.*
79. Memorandum by Inspector of Poor on Women with Children, 15.5.09, in Glasgow Parish Council Minutes, 17.5.09; see also 30.10.08, *op. cit.*
80. Kyle Combination Poorhouse Minutes, 13.3.06, *ADA C03.65.2.1.4.*
81. Letter, 4.4.05, in Minutes, 12.4.06, *ibid.*
82. Reports by Barclay, the General Superintendent, 24.11.06 and 31.3.08, in Minutes, 8.1.07 and 26.5.08, *ibid.*
83. Lamond, R. P., Memorandum on the Children and Education Acts, 1908, *GMLGR G362.7*; Edinburgh Parish Council Minutes, 9.12.97, Leith Parish Council Minutes, 12.1.04 and 30.5.05, *op. cit.*
84. Edinburgh Parish Council Minutes, 21.5.06, *ibid.*
85. Memorandum by Inspector of Poor on the Children Act and Prosecutions, Glasgow Parish Council Minutes, 22.12.09, *op. cit.; The Children Act, Ch. 12 (8 Edw. 7. 1908).*
86. Report by Kyd J., Inspector of Poor, for the Children's Committee, 1909-10, Edinburgh Parish Council Minutes, 4.5.10, in *op. cit.* ; Leith Parish Council Minutes, 14.9.09, in *op. cit.;* Glasgow Parish Council Minutes, 1.3.10, *op. cit.* and Memorandum Regarding Procedures adopted by the Parish Council of Glasgow and its Inspector of Poor of the Children's Act, 1908. (1911), *GMLGR. G362.7;* Bothwell Parish Council Minutes, 14.10.09, *SRA CO1.23.13;* Uphall Parish Council Minutes, 3.6.09, *West Lothian District Library 1.1.2;* Beath Parish Council Minutes, 18.5.09, *Fife Regional Council Records 6.10.4.*
87. Supplementary Memorandum by Inspector of Poor on the Children's Act, 1908, June 1910, *GMLGR G362.7;* Glasgow and Govan

court cases in, *SRO SC. 36.7.22.*

88. Memorandum by Inspector of Poor on Wife Desertion; an Inquiry into its Causes, 1913, Glasgow Parish Council Miscellaneous Prints, 1913, *SRA T-PAR 1.22.*

89. n.a., The Child under the Poor Law, in *ibid 1913*, pp.93-110; see also W.S.A, Children under the Poor Law, in *Poor Law Magazine 1915*, pp.1-7.

90. n.a., The Working of the Children's Act in Glasgow, in *ibid 1914*, pp. 66-8; Motion, J. R., Children under the Poor Law, in *ibid.* pp. 142-53 and 177-82; Cunningham, J. J. (Chairman), The Child under the Poor Law, in Glasgow Parish Council Miscellaneous Prints, 1912, *SRA T-PAR 1.19.*

6

UNEMPLOYMENT AND PUBLIC ORDER, 1921-35

The pre-war debates and development of policy had left much about the nature and form of welfare to be decided. However one thing had been clear, punitive measures which sought to regulate and constrain behaviour were no longer acceptable. A popular democracy could not accept that its members, because of their poverty or social need, should be subject to the close regulation that had once been the hallmark of good Poor Law administration. If there was to be any investigation or legal restraint, then some new basis for the conduct of public authorities had to be found. After the war, which had cost the lives of so many ordinary working men and which had seen the emergence of a much stronger Labour movement, the issue of State action in welfare again returned to dominate the political debate.

An early example of this can be seen in the 1919 reform of the Board. Although the Government had stalled on any legislation to amend the Poor Law after 1909, Board members had made it clear they still wanted change. Sir George MacCrae, speaking in 1912, commented: 'If the unemployed, the aged, the sick, the feeble-minded, the vagrants, and, most important of all, the children, had been or would be removed from the operation of the Poor Law, then the doom of the Poor Law, as we now know it, was sealed.'[1] It was important, he said, to develop a system of welfare that could rehabilitate the poor into 'useful and self-support-ing members of society'. MacKenzie, similarly, in a number of speeches and writings continued to emphasise his preventive model of develop-ment.[2] Nevertheless the political will to implement any change seemed lacking, and it was not until the spring of 1917, when Lloyd George's Coalition Government was faced with maintaining war-time morale, that the issue was formally reviewed. As part of its post-war 'reconstruc-tion' plan, it proposed to create a Ministry of Health, a department that could put into practice much of the preventive work suggested by the Minority Report. At the same time the Government established a small committee under the Liberal MP, Sir Donald Maclean, to consider 'what steps should be taken to secure the better co-ordination of Public Assis-tance in England and Wales'. When it reported later in 1917, like the Minority Report, it recommended breaking up the Poor Law. All local government functions were to be concentrated under one authority (counties and county boroughs), which would have separate committees dealing with health care, children, the aged, the insane and the unemployed. With Robert Munro, the Scottish Secretary, having already agreed that its proposals would also apply to Scotland, the Government at last seemed to be supporting radical reform.[3]

Scottish opinion had also changed. In September 1917 the Society of Medical Officers announced its support for both a reformed Board and a local health service.[4] The existing system of administration, it said, split between Public Health, the Poor Law and National Insurance, was 'inadequate and inefficient'; it could neither unify or expand services. Their recommendation was followed by the Scottish Insurance Committee's (the lobby for approved societies under the 1911 National Insurance Act). It too argued for the establishment of a Health Ministry – 'if the country was to benefit in the widest sense from the enormous sacrifices it had made and was still making'.[5] The medical profession, for its part, at first seemed reluctant (it feared State control), but later in December, the Royal College of Physicians similarly agreed to support a reformed Ministry.[6] Under the Local Government Board the 'essential interest of health' had been 'obscured'. Further support came from the local authorities, and by March 1918 they had drafted a scheme to amalgamate the Board with the Health Insurance Commission – under the Scottish Secretary and a Parliamentary Under-Secretary.[7] With Liberal M Ps similarly pressing for action, a radical measure looked possible.[8] But as in England, parishes raised objections. The Parish Councils' Association urged the retention of a separate 'ad hoc' public assistance authority, one that would co-ordinate all income support services, and with the reservation of the insurance lobby and the medical profession over how much the local authority would control health services, Munro, like his English counterpart, was forced to retreat from any full-scale reform.[9] It was not until November, just after the Armistice, that the Government finally announced a new Health Bill.[10] Three months later, after an all-Party group of M Ps had met Munro, its Scottish application clauses were withdrawn and a separate Bill for Scotland announced.[11]

Munro's measure, like that of the English, did not seek to reform the Poor Law, nor did it propose any new medical services. All he would pledge was the possibility of a further bill to remove the responsibility for public assistance from health administration.[12] Instead the principle aim of the measure was to create a Health Board. Its second clause stated:

> It shall be the Duty of the Board. . . to take such steps as may be desirable to secure the effective carrying out and co-ordination of measures conducive to the health of the people, including measures for the prevention and cure of diseases, the initiation and direction of research, the treatment of physical and mental defects, the collection, preparation and publication of information and statistics, and the training of persons for health services.

The new Board was to amalgamate the Local Government Board, the

Highlands and Islands Medical Board and the National Health Insurance
Commission. It was also to transfer school medical inspection from the
Education Department. The Scottish Secretary was to be its President,
with a new Parliamentary Under-Secretary for Health as its Vice-Pres-
ident. Six others, drawn from the existing Boards, were also to be
appointed. (They were to include MacCrae, as Chairman, MacPherson
and MacKenzie and from the Health Insurance Commission, Sir James
Leishman, Dr. J. C. M'Vail and Muriel Ritson.)

The Bill encountered little parliamentary opposition. Sir Donald Maclean, for the Opposition, thought the Scottish measure could have been
more radical and moved positively to break up the Poor Law. With the
Scottish Central Government smaller than England's and with the Poor
Law having fewer statutory duties, the issues, he said, were less complicated. Adamson, the Labour leader, also thought the Bill was too limited
and argued for a 'bolder' line in establishing a separate Ministry of
Health with a reformed local authority. But although not as sweeping
as they and some others had wanted, the Act did mark an important
change in welfare philosophy. The Poor Law had been placed in a Board
with a preventive and health-orientated constitution.[13]

The impact of this rapidly changing political ethos was felt almost
immediately by parish officials. MacCrae, addressing a meeting of
parish councils, urged them to adopt 'a broad view' of what had
happened and change with 'the times'.[14] A few months later the Board
itself issued a new set of instructions, and parishes found the 'pauper'
had been renamed a 'poor person'.[15] The Government, it said, would
no longer support an active policy of discrimination.

That there had been a substantial shift in working-class opinion was
soon seen to be real. In November 1919 Labour captured ten parishes
and increased its representation on many more.[16] In each the new councillors set about putting party policy into practice, a policy which had
been re-emphasised by Adamson earlier that year. Addressing the same
meeting as MacCrae, he stressed that Labour still wanted radical reform.
The Poor Law he said:

> cannot be justified either through the ethics of Christian faith or
> of the general principle of the great moral law. The taint of
> pauperism inseparable from Poor Law relief; the small scale of
> payments which are altogether inadeqaute to relieve poverty; and
> the miserable associations of the Poorhouse system, have caused
> the iron to enter into the soul of Labour [and] the present system
> should be broken up and thrown on the scrap heap.[17]

To Labour only a welfare system based on 'the widest sense of medical
treatment' would suffice.

1919, then, seemed something of a watershed in welfare development.
Both the Coalition Government and Labour had agreed that one of the
'paramount' duties of the State was to promote the 'people's health'.

Yet as MacCrae had freely admitted to the parishes much of what had been suggested during the 'reconstruction' debates remained in abeyance. In reality the Board of Health Act was about rearranging the duties of central Government, not about the reform of local services. The Government had not been able to secure any agreement on abolishing the separate 'ad hoc' destitution authority (the parish), nor in fact, whether it should retain a means 'test'. Moreover, although the 1919 reform had given the Board a 'pro-active' constitution, there was no detail on how its statutory aims were to be implemented. The influence of parishes, the medical profession and the insurance lobby had been too great. Just how slender a consensus existed was seen when Munro assumed the Presidency of the Board; in the autumn of 1919 he halted any immediate discussion of Poor Law reform. Instead he referred the matter to his Consultative Council on Local Health Administration. By 1920, with the Government retrenching on public expenditure, it looked as if the enthusiasm for 'reconstruction' had waned.

The remainder of this book will look at how the debate over the Poor Law was finally resolved. Three particularly Scottish issues have been chosen: unemployment relief, the provision of hospitals and the public definition of poverty. It was these issues, more than any other, that underlined what the debate was about; the abolition of pecuniary and stigmatising care. The next two chapters will examine in greater detail the latter two issues. This chapter will concentrate on unemployment policy between 1921, when parishes began to assist the able-bodied, and 1935, when the majority of such claimants were finally transferred to the nationally financed Unemployment Assistance Board. All three illustrate that basic working class hostility to pauper provision remained and that no politically acceptable solution could emerge until this had been faced.

The Government during the war had gradually extended national insurance to virtually all industrial workers. But the problems associated with demobilised soldiers after 1918 had forced it to grant the temporary extension of unemployment benefit beyond the agreed thirteen weeks before the war. (This, the original 'dole', was to last until March 1921.) Yet, the Government had no coherent policy for dealing with more permanent unemployment. Indeed it based its 1920 Unemployment Insurance Act (which was also to replace the demobilisation scheme) on a 'balanced' fund, outgoings (15 shillings per worker, irrespective of family size) would be covered by low contributions and a minimum Treasury grant. The reason for this was simple: once industry had readjusted itself after wartime production, the Government assumed there would be a return to normal employment. Few, if any, would actually exhaust the new fifteen weeks of benefit. The contrary in fact occurred; the slump of 1920-22 was followed by the deeper problem of structural unemployment, particularly in the traditional industries of coal, steel and shipbuilding. By the summer of 1921, when many English unemployed had finally exhausted their entitlement to benefit (as an emergency, the Government in March had allowed workers to claim an additional sixteen weeks), or found it inadequate, they began to apply for and receive Poor Relief. (25 shillings for a married couple and 5 shillings for each child was a typical allowance.) But in Scotland, they could not.

At the end of the war, this lack of access to Poor Relief stood in contrast to other all-UK provision. National insurance, of course, covered both countries, so too did the child welfare schemes (run by the public health department), and the feeding of schoolchildren (run by the education authority).[18] It was a situation over which the Board felt some embarrassment, for through its arbitration decisions (permissable after the 1897 Poor Law Amendment Act), it had, in fact, begun to modify the 1866 House of Lords decision. The origin of this ruling began from two quite separate decisions, both on the issue of family desertion. In each of these cases the parish providing the relief, the parish where the claimant was residing, had sought to recover its costs from the claimant's parish of settlement. The latter had all rejected the claim, believing the pauper was not entitled to relief. The settlement of a pauper was determined by having at least five years continuous residence in one parish, or if that could not be established, by place of birth.

At Perth Sheriff Court, in November 1903, the Sheriff decided that a woman, Janet Clark, suffering from TB was entitled to immediate relief, even though the husband was able-bodied and living in a neighbouring parish.[19] The woman had in fact left her husband sometime previously to live with another man. He summed up his decision by saying that no husband need keep an adultress and that Rattray, the parish of residence, 'would have been open to a serious animadversion on the ground of neglect of duty had they not at once supplied relief to the pauper as they did'. A few days earlier, the Board had decided that two children who were kept by their grandmother and whose widowed father, Alex Garrow, had left for England were entitled to relief, even though Garrow was able-bodied.[20] The settlement parish should, it said, pursue him for re-imbursement of costs.

The *Poor Law Magazine* immediately recognised what had happened and commented:

> The general result would seem to be that relief may be given to the dependant of an able-bodied man. And this curious result follows that the dependant, irrespective of age or sex or status, is a pauper in his or her own right. That is a contradiction in terms, but it is an inevitable result. In none of these cases was the dependant who became chargeable actually residing with the able-bodied husband or parent; but that does not seem to affect the

principle, which no doubt, will soon be applied in cases where the parties live together.[21]

It was not to be proved wrong. In an arbitration case soon after, the Board agreed that three Forfar children, Catherine, Allen and Alex Wilkie, who left their father because of his cruelty and went to live with their grandparents, were entitled to relief.[22] It was up to Forfar to recover payment from the father. In another, three children had been deserted by their father and were left with grandparents.[23] This time the Board explicitly rejected pleas that the Poor Law should not interfere in domestic arrangements. In a third, a drunken woman, Elizabeth Stewart, was left in goal for a night while her child was boarded out by an inspector.[24] The father refused to re-imburse the parish. Pleas by the parish of settlement that he was able-bodied and that the matter should have dealt with by the Child Cruelty Act were also rejected by the Board. The inspector, the Board said, had no alternative.

Over the next few years similar cases occurred, but it was not until 1911 that the Board extended entitlement still further.[25] A woman, Helen Campbell, who had left her husband on account of his cruelty, applied for and received relief from the parish where she was currently residing, Dumbarton. The husband's parish of settlement, Houston, refused to reimburse Dumbarton. Houston argued that Campbell had offered to take her back, and in its pleas to the Board added, 'If every married woman, in a fit of temper, deserts her husband and chooses to throw herself on the parish, married life will turn out a failure, and a serious imposition on the rates will ensue.' The Board refused to accept this argument making reference to the Perth decision. But that decision was one where the woman had been living with another man. In this case the husband, denying cruelty, was willing to have his wife back.

A more dramatic decision was made in 1918. An 'immoral' woman, Helen Hamilton, who had left her husband, subsequently became ill.[26] Rutherglen, the parish of settlement informed Glasgow, where she had applied for relief, that she should be refused because although she was 'a bad wife', the husband was 'able and willing' to provide suport. This it did, but the woman came back a few days later with a Sheriff's order for interim relief. Accepting that the 'domestic arrangement' had failed, Glasgow sent her to its poorhouse. The Board agreed. It was up to Rutherglen to recover Glasgow's costs from the husband.

Thus by 1919 the Board's attitude towards able-bodied relief had shifted. It regarded the dependant of any able-bodied person as entitled to relief – in their own right – if there was an obvious and immediate need. The Board itself commented:

> Legally the able-bodied poor do not exist. But experience has shown the impossibility of adhering strictly to this legal qualification, and in practice it has been found necessary to interpret disablement in a very wide sense. Inspectors of Poor have been

instructed to excercise every discretion in dealing with applications for relief from persons who appear to be able-bodied. . . . To apply rigidly all the provisions of the Statutes would have been impossible, and we thus have gradually built. . . a body of practice that we think has done much to improve and humanise the law.[27] But of course in Scotland, whatever the Board's circulars and arbitration decisions, the able-bodied as a 'class' had no right to relief, and with the Government's decision in 1920 to restrict the national insurance system, the stage seemed set for some considerable debate over the future direction of policy. If the unemployed were not going to be wholly maintained by insurance and the Government was committed to 'improving' the nation's health, how were their needs to be met?

The issue began, innocuously, during the miners' strike of April-July 1921 (the miners were fighting wage reductions). On 12th April, a few days after the strike had begun, the miners' union branch at Auchinleck approached their parish for help in the feeding of children and other dependants.[28] The ratepayer council immediately asked the Board for clarification of its legal position: with nearly half the parish on strike, how much assistance could it give? A few days later, on the 19th, similar representations were received from the three Labour-controlled Fife parishes of Auchterderran, Beath and Ballingry.[29] Here, as in a number of places, the strike had taken an ugly turn, with looting and police baton-charges widely reported.[30] The same day the Board issued a circular to all mining areas. It said:

Parish councils have no legal authority to grant relief to able-bodied persons or their dependants. Relief can be competently afforded only to applicants who are both destitute and disabled. It will be obvious, however, that the parish councils, as authorities responsible for relieving destitution, cannot allow women and children to suffer undue hardship through lack of food. The policy which should be adopted by parish councils should be to refer applicants for relief on account of the strike to those administering any voluntary or other funds available for the relief of distress, but if no such funds exist, or if they are insufficient, or if they become exhausted, and absolute destitution threatens to cause physical injury to applicants or their dependants, parish councils may then afford such relief, as, in their discretion, they think necessary.[31]

On the surface, at least, this appeared as no more than a restatement of the 1878 circular: parishes could only anticipate 'disablement'. As a result, except for one parish, relief was restricted to either occasional cases or to those where a medical certificate had been obtained. The exception was Newbattle, a mining parish controlled by Labour, which thought it saw an opening for relief on a much wider scale.[32]

On the 22nd April the parish agreed to appoint a sub-committee to deal with any application from families suffering what it termed, 'undue hardship'. Two weeks later, after some discussion over whether the Auchinleck circular was legal, the parish confirmed its position. Nevertheless the Inspector remained unhappy over his own liability (some 227 families had been assisted at a cost of £275) and the following week, at another special meeting, he told the councillors that the Board had urged him 'to get a medical certificate for every applicant'. New-battle, however, still felt uncertain over the circular's wording; 'anticipatory disablement' seemed an elastic term, and it was agreed to seek further advice. On the 20th Alex Stuart, the area's General Superintendent, arrived and was immediately asked whether 'if the medical certificate stated the applicant was in good health, what was the legal position to grant relief'. Stuart replied there was none, but the parish could grant relief 'if the mother and children were in immediate danger of suffering from the lack of nourishment'. Newbattle thought that meant it could continue, but when the local press canvassed the possibility of the parish auditor issuing a surcharge, the councillors asked for another meeting. After being pressed on what the circular meant by 'destitution', Stuart was forced to admit that 'the Board had gone a little way from the strict legal position out of sympathy with the people who were suffering and had given the parish councils a loophole to relieve really destitute people approaching sickness.' If Newbattle's auditor did raise an objection, he went on, it could always produce the circular. The parish agreed to restrict relief to those who had a medical certificate.

Able-bodied distress due to a single strike was one thing but almost as soon as the Newbattle issue had been resolved the Board was finally caught up in the wider issue of mass unemployment. From the end of 1920 Scotland had yet again met a rising tide of unemployment with the traditional methods of relief, backed this time by National Insurance payments. Newspapers ran distress appeals. Local Authorities hastened public works. Firms went on short-time, organised their own relief funds and remitted rent on employee's homes. Savings were withdrawn and shopkeepers, especially the Co-op, extended credit.[33] But with the Government refusing to concede any more than the additional sixteen weeks 'uncovenanted' benefit until November (when they proposed another sixteen weeks), the depth and extent of the depression meant these methods proved insufficient. By the beginning of July, with over 250 000 (20 per cent) out of work, virtually all industrial parishes were reporting widespread and increasing distress. It was in the mining areas, with much post-strike unemployment, that the issue of State assistance finally broke.

At Wemyss (Methil and Buckhaven) on 21st July, the Labour controlled parish, after representations from the local unemployed and on reconsidering the April circular, agreed to leave it to its officials to devise a scheme of assistance.[34] A loan scheme, although entirely illegal, was instituted. On 31st July, the *Sunday Post* stated that Wemyss was giving unconditional relief on the Board's authority. Though incorrect, the Board was soon deluged with requests for similar authority from other hard-pressed inspectors.[35] On 3rd August, at Blantyre, after an urgent letter had been sent by the Inspector, the Labour parish read the following telegram:

> Relief may be given to able-bodied unemployed persons only in cases where absolute destitution threatens to cause physical injury to health. Such relief is not legal relief and therefore not claimable against parish of settlement. Where relief afforded ordinary Poor Law procedure should be followed and strict investigation of individual circumstances should be made. Letter follows.[36]

and enrolled 300 miners. Each family received 21 shillings. It was the first parish to agree on unconditional relief.

The following day the Board re-issued its Auchinleck circular and immediately the inspectors at Glasgow and Govan began providing assistance.[37] Indeed the pressure had been so great that half the cases in the Glasgow Sheriff Court were Poor Law appeals.[38] By mid-August, six other parishes had followed suit and some 2 000 were on relief. The Board, seriously alarmed, tried hard to explain that what they were doing was illegal. Bothwell on the 8th was told the Board's position remained firm and that, 'It is not intended that parish councils should relieve all unemployed workers. Relief should be granted only where it is quite clear that there is no other way of preventing distinct injury to the health of the applicant or their dependants.'[39] A letter the following day re-emphasised this point and added that it was 'definitely' not suggesting assistance except 'under the conditions and reservations expressed in the Auchinleck letter'. Even then, Bothwell was told, if a ratepayer raised a successful action, a surcharge would depend on how the parish had 'reasonably interpreted' the Board's circular.

But matters were moving outside its control. At Dundee, where 12 000 were due to have their additional national insurance 'stopped', the Town council asked Winston Churchill, their M P and Colonial Secretary, for assistance.[40] He expressed surprise that Poor Law practice in Scotland differed from England and immediately brought it to the Cabinet's attention on 19th August. The Cabinet, although seriously alarmed by an estimate of 500 000 likely to be out of insurance by October, nevertheless agreed with the Ministry of Labour that there could be no further extension of unemployment benefit. For those out of benefit the 'gap' until November would have to remain. Instead, as the English Board of Guardians were to be given extra borrowing facilities, and with Churchill arguing 'it was absurd that Scotland should suffer from such a disability', the Cabinet agreed, 'That the Secretary for Scotland should examine Poor Law Administration in Scotland with a view to seeing that the unemployed seeking Poor Law relief were not placed in a less favourable position than similar persons in England.'[41] Like Dundee's Town Clerk, the Board was aghast; both were expecting a new National Insurance Act.[42]

The Board did not immediately rescind the Auchinleck circular. Govan, for instance, when it asked for guidance, was not told that there had been a change in policy. The letter it received said simply:

> (1) Relief should not be given for the purpose of paying rents that are in arrears. (2) As far as possible, any relief given to able-bodied persons should be given in kind. (3) . . . Relief even in such cases should be given only after strict investigation has been made into their circumstances and the usual Poor Law procedure has been given effect to, e.g., reference of the applicant to the parish Medical Officer, etc., etc. . .[43]

In fact, the Board had told Munro it faced certain 'administrative difficulties' in implementing the Government's decision. The 1866 judgment, it said, had been explicit, there was little discretion to go beyond what parishes had already been advised. This was seemingly underlined, when at Airdrie Sheriff Court, in a widely reported case, an appeal by an unemployed ploughman was refused. The Sheriff, although sympathetic, said it was illegal.[44] The Board's difficulties were further highlighted by developments in Fife. Here the coalfield parishes of Auchterderran, Ballingry and Beath had at first agreed to provide assistance, but when a number of Ballingry's ratepayers threatened legal action, they withdrew.[45] It was only when a deputation of the Fife Miners' Union headed by Walter Adamson, their General Secretary, approached the Board on the 2nd September, that more positive action was taken.[46] The Lord Advocate, Tom Morison, immediately issued a memorandum in which he stated that:

> Although, under existing law, poor relief cannot be competently afforded to applicants who are able-bodied, it is a matter of common knowledge that where unemployment causes destitution, it consequences are such as seriously to undermine the health of individuals affected, and speedily to produce in them a condition of physical disablement. It follows that if steps are not taken to alleviate the distress, serious claims for poor relief will soon emerge in respect of disablement which the parish council would be bound to recognise. . . in the absence of any [voluntary funds], it might in the circumstances be expedient as being less costly to the parish in the end if the council were to provide immediate relief. . . The amount of relief to be given would be such as the parish council in their discretion thought necessary, and they would also consider whether it should be given in money or kind.

and that when their accounts were audited, '. . . the Board will give due consideration to the terms of this memorandum in regards to any action taken in accordance therewith.'[47]

The possibility of any retraction from this position was quickly dispelled by serious rioting on the 6th in Dundee.[48] There the parish had continued to prevaricate on the granting of relief. During three days of disturbances, the parish offices were sacked and with the unemployed chanting the 'Red Flag', the city centre was looted. The Board immediately sent a Superintendent, C. C. Ellis to urge the parish to give assistance. At the same time, on the 7th, Munro informed the Cabinet of Scottish developments. Many ratepayers, he said, were objecting to its previous decision, 'they thought it was an intolerable burden', and suggested either a grant for local authority relief works or the Treasury to bear a proportion of parish expenditure. Later that day the Cabinet met again, and after further discussion, ignored his pleas and agreed to assimilate English and Scottish Poor Law policy.[49] To placate Scottish opinion, at the insistence of the Board, it also agreed parishes would be protected against ratepayer action by an Act of Indemnity. It was left to the Prime Minister and the Chancellor of the Exchequer to hold further discussions on the future of unemployment relief.

Throughout September 1921 both the Board and the Ministry of Labour continued to receive weekly reports on developments. On the 9th, some 2 000 Edinburgh unemployed marched through Princes Street to the Board itself and then to the parish council, which, unlike Dundee, immediately agreed to assist.[50] On the 16th, at Airdrie, a deputation of the unemployed was told that the Bank was refusing further loans unless the Government provided security. The Board quickly persuaded the Bank that it would. A more serious disturbance occurred at Aberdeen where on the 20th, as some 5 000 marched on the parish, a riot broke out. Glasgow also saw large demonstrations, with the Special Branch reporting that John McLean and other 'communists' had infiltrated the more moderate Trades Council unemployed workers' committee. Similar events did not escape the smaller parishes. At Uphall, 'hundreds', headed by a pipe-band, marched on the council.[51] At neighbouring Kirkliston, after a demonstration, the parish hastily agreed with their demands and seemed pleased when 'the men took the scale and came back stating agreement'.[52] Others, although less hesitant, nevertheless remained unhappy. Bothwell sent the Lord Advocate's memorandum back and asked for it to be signed.[53] The Board refused, saying it was 'an official pronouncement'. So too did Ardrossan, although privately the Inspector told the Board, 'though appalled at the outlook from a ratepayer's point of view I believe this council are with you'.[54]

At the beginning of October the Cabinet again discussed the issue of unemployment.[55] With Churchill still pressing for regularising the Scottish position, a small committee under Munro was established to review the unemployment benefit scheme. A few days later, the Cabinet agreed with its recommendations. A new Insurance Act was to be passed granting to the unemployed allowances for their wives (5 shillings) and children (1 shilling), and just as importantly continuing 'uncovenanted' allowances beyond the insured fifteen weeks. At the same time it was agreed to broaden the Act of Indemnity. As a temporary measure, parishes were to assist the unemployed who either had no benefit or whose benefit was insufficient. Although Scotland was not to receive any preferential treatment – the Treasury thought the Board's reports on parish bankruptcy had been 'alarmist' – extensive Government loans were also to be made available. Despite considerable parish opposition, the Poor Law Emergency Provisions (Scotland) Act came into force on 10th November.[56] It was to last until May 1922 and was retrospectively dated from 19th April.

1921, therefore, had witnessed a dramatic shift in Poor Law policy. But as the Board itself conceded, the Poor Law Emergency Provisions Act was no carefully planned Government initiative. Nor was it the logical outcome of the Maclean recommendations. No one, save perhaps the Treasury, really wanted the unemployed on Poor Relief. How had it come about? Firstly, although Munro made no mention of Scotland when the Cabinet agreed that the Board of Guardians could assist strikers in England, the Board was clearly concerned over the mining community's welfare. The Auchinleck circular may have looked like a restatement of 1878, but in practice, as Stuart had told Newbattle, the Board expected parishes to use discretion and be flexible. Secondly, as soon as the Cabinet agreed that there could be no extension of unemployment benefit and that Scotland should have no special consideration, the unemployed were bound to look to the parish – they had nowhere else to go. Finally and interestingly, what had occurred had not come about through any orchestrated campaign. Neither the Labour Party nor the national unions had become involved until well after Churchill's intervention.[57] Indeed Adamson had not intervened until his own Union asked him to lead a deputation and, like his fellow Labour MPS, he remained opposed to workers receiving 'pauper' benefit. In most places, all that happened was the inspector or parish met the unemployed, discussed the issue and agreed a scale. With a Government entrenched in financial orthodoxy and with the prospect of widespread rioting, it was, as one Labour MP said, the only thing they could do – the Scottish worker 'would not starve willingly'.[58]

But 1921 represented another kind of shift. The last lingering hope of post-war 'reconstruction', the implementation of a liberal and 'progressive' welfare system, had gone. In its place was something very different. With cut-backs and financial entrenchment everywhere, those unemployed out of benefit, or whose benefit was inadequate, had been abandoned to a destitution authority. The Government, instead of abolishing the Poor Law, had re-invigorated it. In Scotland, where the Poor Law had no real tradition and no policy towards the unemployed, the first thing the Board set out to do was to establish some national policy.

By the middle of September, the Board's weekly reports told it that the majority of industrial parishes had agreed to assist. 10 000 were already on the Poor Roll and some 60 000 were expected by the end of October.[59] That created a new problem for parishes: they all offered widely differing scales of assistance. In Dundee a family with three children would receive 33 shillings, in Edinburgh it was 40 shillings, and in Glasgow only 27 shillings and 6 pence. By the middle of September a number of parishes became alarmed at the confusion this was causing and asked the Board to issue guidance on what was 'adequate'. The Board refused – the relief given was still technically 'illegal' – but it did agree to call a 'representative' conference of the larger parishes. After much discussion the parishes reached agreement on what they thought was an appropriate scale of assistance: 12 shillings and 6 pence for an applicant, 10 shillings for the wife and 3 shillings and 6 pence for each child. They also agreed to a full household means test. The next day on the 24th, the Board issued a circular embodying the recommendations and added, (1) That the amount of relief given should be enough but not more than enough to provide necessary sustentation in the strictest sense of the phrase, and (2) That the amount should be distinctly less than the wages that the recipient could earn if engaged on relief work.'[60] It meant that a family with three children, with no other income, would receive 33 shillings a week.[61]

Only two parishes openly challenged the September agreement: Falkirk and Larbert. Both Labour-controlled, they found that the unemployed expected the Board's notion of adequacy to be challenged. At first Falkirk refused to consider any alteration. Its Chairman told one deputation that the parish had 'to consider the law as it was' and in its view the September agreement was a national scale.[62] Nearby Larbert was less hesitant, and with over 400 out of work agreed to implement the Labour Party's scale, 30 shillings for a married couple and 5 shillings for each child. The Board's reaction was immediate. A few days later, a General Superintendent appeared and said it would not approve any application for a Government loan unless the parish adhered to the September agreement.[63] This, however, enraged the local unemployed committee, and the following week at a mass meeting in Falkirk Town Hall they urged Falkirk not to betray what Larbert was doing.[64] The parish Chairman immediately changed his mind and announced that the new Act had freed Falkirk from Board control. The Government was not going to meet any of the cost of relief and so, he said, it was up to parishes themselves to decide what necessity meant. Within a week Falkirk had increased allowances by about 30 per cent.[65] Nevertheless the Board continued to press Larbert. At the beginning of December it was told that although the Board 'was tolerant of the parish baiting the Government', increased allowances could not be accepted if it 'sank the ratepayers'.[66] But Larbert's industrial position improved and by January, with only 66 on the roll, it no longer required a Government loan.[67] Falkirk's position was different. With nearly 500 unemployed receiving assistance, its bank had become alarmed. The Board's Superintendent, C. C. Ellis, was sent to make a special inquiry after which the Secretary wrote:

> . . . The [Board] would remind the council that the 'agreed' scale was the outcome of the deliberations of officers and councillors of a wide experience in the administration of relief. No complaints have been received by the Board from recipients of relief in parishes where the 'agreed' scale had been adopted. . . The Board would point out it is the duty of the parish council to see that the aliments being paid are in no way excessive, in short, that they conform to the two principles laid down in their Circular of 24th September last. . . I am also to point out that extravagant relief is illegal and liable to be surcharged. In the circumstances I am directed to intimate that the Board cannot agree to the parish council continuing to pay the able-bodied unemployed on the scale now obtaining. . .[68]

Although the parish at a special meeting tried to impress on Sir George MacCrae, the Board's Chairman, that it had been 'democratically elected' and its 'intervention was arbitrary', MacCrae remained adamant. The cost of living had declined and the loan Falkirk was seeking would not be approved.[69] By March the revolt was over.

The Board's difficulties with Labour-controlled parishes was not over. At Blantyre, the left-wing council, fresh from its vindication of unemployment relief, pressed for the further elaboration of what constituted need. During October it not only modified its means test, but also decided to subvent the wages of full and part-time workers which were below the September scale.[70] Everyone, the parish said, should have the same basic income, irrespective of status. The Board was clearly caught off-guard. Its initial reply was to state the question was 'one of difficult and far reaching importance'.[71] But a week later its attitude hardened. The new unemployment benefit regulations allowed for payments for part-time work and it urged the parish not to 'embark on the course proposed'.[72] Another letter soon followed in which it stated that only in very exceptional cases of ill-health could a parish provide temporary relief to the dependants of an employed person.[73] Blantyre, nevertheless, refused to reverse its decision, the Chairman, William M'Anulty, explained:

> What man was entitled to more money for going about through unemployment compared to a man who was employed, and who could not even earn sufficient to bring him up to the pauper-standard. There was no argument in it. He for one was going to sink or swim by the decision they had already come to.[74]

The parish arranged a deputation to see MacCrae and in a subsequent letter the Board's position was fully explained.[75] For those who were in full-time employment, the Board argued that it would not only 'be unsound to relieve such cases because it would be subsidising wages', but under the 1921 Act, it was illegal. Nevertheless the Board recognised that part-time work placed it in a more difficult position. Under the Act, Blantyre was told:

> An applicant must be destitute and must be unemployed and unable to obtain employment. Before dealing with his application the parish must determine in the first place whether the amount he is actually earning, together with any household income, is sufficient for the maintenance of himself and his family. If it is not they should in the first instance refer him to the Employment Exchange with a view to his obtaining Unemployment Benefit and dependants' allowances in respect of the days during which he is not employed. In a large number of these cases he should be able to obtain these, and these together with his wages and the assistance he will obtain from the Local Authority under the Maternity and Child Welfare Schemes and the Education Authority, should be sufficient for his maintenance.
>
> In cases where Unemployment Benefit is unavailable and the parish council are satisfied that a man partially employed has not enough to maintain himself and his family they must consider whether for the days in which he is not working he is unemployed in the sense of the Act. If they are satisfied on this point as well as on the fact of his being destitute, it will be competent for them to grant relief in respect of the days of unemployment, the amount of such relief being calculated in accordance with the scale.

Faced with the Board insistence that a full means test be applied, that the September scale was a maximum and that wage subvention could only occur in the most extreme of cases, on 5th January the Labour members resigned.[76] The Chairman said they were not going to be 'ruled by the Board'. It was the first time any council had resigned because of Government policy.

In 1921 there remained one other problem for the Board. The September scale had operated on the basis of a maximum and in the belief that the Education and Public Health Authorities would fully co-operate with parishes on individual cases. It quickly became apparent that these authorities, notably Lanarkshire and Glasgow, were not too keen to become involved in the relief of distress and parishes soon found the unemployed making application to them for extra clothing and diets.[77] The Board initially agreed that, on some suitable deduction from the weekly allowance, clothing could be given. But in December, when the implications of a more indiscriminate policy were realised, its policy hardened.[78] The Board argued first, that the September discussions had not contemplated any provision for clothing and second, that the cost of living had declined. In its final letter to one of the parishes that had pressed the issue, Govan, the Board concluded:

> In view of the difficult and dangerous position that might be created by any widespread distribution of clothing to the able-bodied and their dependants, apart from the question of the serious additional burden which might therefore be imposed on the ratepayers, the Board will expect the parish council to exercise their statutory powers in the matter with the utmost discretion. The Board also strongly advise that in every case in which clothing is granted a small weekly deduction from the amount of relief paid under the scale should be made.

Govan agreed and a 5 per cent deduction per week was made to those families which had received clothing. Other parishes followed suit.

By early 1922, the Board had established some semblance of a national policy. Parishes could pay no more than the September scale; a full means test was to be imposed; payments for clothing were possible, but only if the weekly allowance was subsequently reduced; and apart from some extreme 'necessitous' case, there was to be no subvention of wages. Nevertheless the Board realised it faced two new problems. Many parishes still resented having to assist the unemployed without Government grants, and their resentment increased when, in May 1922, the Act was extended for another year.[78] The experience of the unemployed, it noted, was also likely to lead to resentment. Although trade had improved and unemployment had fallen to 180 000 (13 per cent), in many parishes there were large numbers who not only had been out of work for a long period, but had also been suspended from unemployment benefit.[80] They, the Board knew, were likely to focus their attention on the one body capable of providing assistance.

One of the first incidents occurred at Bonhill (the Vale of Leven), where the parish had been unanimous in accepting the September scale. In February a group of unemployed, wanting extra assistance, forced their way into a parish meeting and were only prevented from assaulting the councillors by the speedy arrival of the police.[81] But at Port Glasgow more serious trouble occurred. There the local Charity Organisation Society had arranged with the parish to relieve all applicants. This was greatly assisted by Lithgow's agreeing to have some ships broken up on a non-profit making basis. By the end of 1921, 500 were either on the rolls or employed on relief work.[82] But early in 1922, the system began to break down. Many of the shipyard workers objected to being paid less than those on cos – Lithgow's insisted on a maximum wage of 11 pence an hour – and went on strike. At the same time a deputation of those on cos pressed for increased allowances. Although the Society paid the September scale, it would not pay more than 36 shillings. Many labourers, it said, had wages below this.[83] On 17th February, after a week in which the parish offices had been continually besieged and extra police brought in from Greenock, some hasty re-ajustments were made. During the summer further grievances emerged and the Society itself was accused of being too officious. On 4th September, with the Society facing bankruptcy (having spent some £45 000) the patience of the unemployed finally ran out.[84] After three days of rioting and looting, the Town Centre was left in a shambles, the Orange Hall had been sacked and some thirty were in court. The parish agreed to enrol the unemployed at a scale only slightly below that agreed in September 1921.[85] Within a week 600 were being assisted and the town had nearly 20 per cent of its population on Poor Relief.

The disorder also spilled over into nearby Greenock. In February a group of unemployed rampaged through the parish Offices and threatened the Inspector's life.[86] Frustration increased when in April the councillors cut the scale to unemployment benefit level.[87] Some improvements were made in late September, after the Port Glasgow riots, but for many of the unemployed this was obviously not enough. On the 2nd October, headed by the local Communist leader Patrick Geddes, several thousand marched to the council offices and stormed a parish meeting. In some haste, the councillors agreed to reverse their decision, the Chairman being forced to announce the new scales through an upstairs window.[88]

During the spring of 1922 parishes became particularly incensed by another 'gap' in the entitlement to unemployment benefit. Glasgow, whose roll had dropped by more than half (to 8 000) when benefit had been restored in November 1921, now had a dramatic rise in claimants to over 24 000.[89] Other parishes, especially in Clydeside, where disqualifications had also increased, were equally affected. In response, many began to cut their scales to unemployment benefit level. Some were clearly not satisfied even with this. Blantyre, now fully under ratepayer control, agreed to reduce its allowances for those affected by the 'gap' to benefit level and for those disqualified, to only half the September agreement.[90] The local miners' union immediately appealed to the Board. The Board, which had until then had passed no comment on those that had reduced their scale to benefit level, became alarmed and told Blantyre that it had to pay an allowance equal to 'needful sustentation'. A further letter stressed this point and added that, 'any relief granted must be adequate and that they see no reason why persons not entitled to unemployment benefit should be treated differently to those who are'.[91] Blantyre agreed to pay the unemployment benefit scale.

Nevertheless, although the Board was signalling that economy had to be matched with a serious attempt to meet need, it continued to be concerned about the poor state of parish finances. The 'gap' and disqualifications had more than doubled expenditure: Scottish parishes were spending over £30 000 a week on the unemployed. In July a new circular was issued and parishes were told.

> The Board desire to point out that since the scale therein recom-
> mended was drawn up, the cost of living index figure published
> in the Labour Gazette has fallen from 120 to 84 and that in con-
> sequence some parish councils have found it possible to reduce the
> scale payable to the able-bodied unemployed. . . The Board are
> of opinion that in view of the fall in the cost of living, parish
> councils that have not already done so should carefully consider
> whether circumstances do not now justify the payment of relief
> to the able-bodied unemployed on a lower scale than that agreed
> on by the Conference of parish council representatives. While
> parish councils will no doubt see that the relief afforded is
> adequate they should, in considering the question, take into
> account the wages now payable to the lower paid workers in the
> parish, with a view to avoiding the consequences of placing reci-
> pients of relief in a better position than persons who are working.[92]

Not all parishes, the Board found, accepted this and after representations
it agreed to call another conference. This showed that, of the thirty
parishes present, fourteen were paying the full scale, ten the unemployment benefit scale and six, amounts inbetween.[93] With apparently no
agreement amongst the parishes on what 'needful sustentation' meant
and with many tales of demonstrations, the Board was forced to concede
that no reduced scale could be agreed.

The end of 1922, therefore, had seen the establishment of a distinctive
policy on relief. Irrespective of their financial burden, parishes had to
pay enough to prevent a breakdown in public order and they had to
ensure that as far as possible 'needful sustentation' was being met. But
it was still assumed that the Poor Law's crisis was temporary, and that
at some stage the Government would take over the burden. Further,
most had believed those who were unemployed would at some stage
find employment; trade would return to 'normality'. That in itself posed
problems, for throughout 1922 unemployment continued to remain well
above 10 per cent. So instead of meeting a 'temporary emergency',
parishes found themselves faced with a new issue: the physical and
moral condition of the unemployed. The Board itself noted two probable
effects of the continued depression:

> As the months of unemployment drag on, the apparent hopeless-
> ness of the position and the desperate outlook for the future pro-
> duce a condition of nervous strain and considerable strength of
> will is necessary to prevent a sinking into apathy. Some fall under
> the strain and become definitely apathetic and listless. Others are
> inclined to challenge an organisation of society in which such
> conditions are possible. . . Until normal conditions return, how-
> ever, the cumulative effect of prolonged unemployment on morale
> will undoubtedly become progressively more serious.[94]

The new councillors, elected in November and December 1922, it minuted, were bound to reflect this mood.[95] Govan was one of the first to feel this change. The new council immediately pressed the Board for permission to improve children's allowances.[96] The Board refused, but did allow the parish, where there were exceptional circumstances, to increase the maximum payment beyond 40 shillings. In other parishes, the councillors showed they were less concerned about following constitutional paths. At Dalziel (Mother-well), Communist members openly called the Chairman a 'baby starver'.[97] The atmosphere was so bad that the ruling group of ratepayers set up a small sub-committee to carry out the parish's work. It took five months of Communist court action before the council was recon-stituted.[98] But more serious challenges occurred at Bonhill and Old Kil-patrick (Clydebank).

Like Blantyre, Bonhill in May 1922 had reduced its scale to unemploy-ment benefit. This had sharply reduced the numbers being assisted. But unlike many of the coalfield parishes, Bonhill had not seen any revival of trade and with unemployment remaining stubbornly high, the unemployed by the autumn had become distinctly more organised. At the end of October, 1 000 marched on the council's offices and demanded the restoration of the September scale. Although the offices were ringed by police brought in from Glasgow, the councillors were sufficiently alarmed to unanimously agree.[99]

The council's belated move to restore its local prestige was not enough and in December the parish, which had never seen any real political contest before, saw the electorate move sharply to the left. Under the umbrella of the local Trades Council, a loose coalition of Labour and Communist councillors took control. The following month, after a more orderly demonstration, the council agreed to increase the scale's maximum to 47 shillings and 6 pence and to ignore the first 16 shillings of a war disability pension. Parishes, it argued, should neither 'sur-charge the war wounded' nor penalise the large family. But within a week the Board indicated its disapproval. Noting a bank debt of over £19 000, it told Bonhill that other parishes had agreed to take all income into account. The council refused to back down, the Inspector, telling the Board privately, 'the Chairman and other members gave it as their opinion that your letter only contained "observations" and not "instruc-tions"'.[100]

The reply was instant. The Board stated that the question of payment was, in the first instance, always up to the parish, but that if the auditor objected, the Board might, if 'needful sustentation' was exceeded, declare the payments illegal.[101] Nevertheless, as the parish had exhausted its existing loan, the Board agreed to sanction another.

In March, after an inquiry by C. C. Ellis, its Superintendent, the Board's attitude hardened. Bonhill was told there was no statutory authority for it to disregard pensions and that the Board had already received complaints from a number of industrial ratepayers.[102] The parish again refused to back down and its attitude also hardened: one of its Communist councillors declared, 'we are out now against the property owners'. An even stronger letter followed in April, stating that, 'cases will almost certainly arise in which the amount of relief granted will be so extravagant as to leave the Board no alternative but to declare part of the relief to be illegal, and to surcharge the councillors responsible'.[103]

But the parish's financial situation was getting desperate. The council had exceeded its loan and the Bank, taking fright, told the Inspector that unless the Board was prepared to fully support another, no cheques could be cashed.[104] The Board, itself alarmed at the prospect of no payments being made, immediately sent representations to the Bank. Afterwards Bonhill was told the Bank would make one more advance, but it would not make any other without the Board's authority. The following week, with no money to pay its allowances, Bonhill, by the Chairman's casting vote, backed down. The next day credit was restored.

Old Kilpatrick (Clydebank) represented another kind of threat to the Board's policy. Its ratepayer council was badly administered. By the end of 1922 with a quarter of the Old Kilpatrick on Poor Relief – the highest anywhere in Scotland – it neither had the staff nor the office accommodation to adequately implement the September agreement. Early in 1923, to overcome some of these difficulties, the newly elected council (still ratepayer controlled) at first tried to reduce the scale, but after appeals from the unemployed, backed down. Instead it agreed to increase the maximum to 45 shillings.[105] The Board immediately objected. The parish's move, it said, would mean many working labourers earning less than Poor Relief.[106] Nevertheless the payments continued. But when a few months later its bank refused a loan, the parish was forced to seek the Board's advice.[107] The Board immediately approached the bank and secured the loan, but at the same time sent its Superintendent, C. C. Ellis, to make a full report. Ellis found the parish flagrantly breaking the September agreement. Not only was it paying more than the maximum, it was also giving clothing to the the long-term unemployed without deduction. Again the Board suggested the parish return to what had been agreed and again it refused. The parish told the Board that it paid according to the scale and it was up to the Government to prove the payments were excessive.[108] Old Kilpatrick's position was simple; long-term unemployment meant increased needs, especially for the large family.

Unemployment in the parish continued to remain high (at 20 per cent), and at the end of March 1924 the local unemployed committee petitioned the council to increase its scales. After a minor disturbance in the parish's Chambers, it was agreed to hold another special meeting.

Later that week, behind bolted doors, with a demonstration and a pipe-band playing outside, the council rejected a Labour proposal to increase the scale by 30 per cent. Instead, on the Chairman's casting vote, it agreed to 18 per cent.[109] No other parish in Scotland paid as much.

Old Kilpatrick was, however, more fortunate than Bonhill. In 1924 unemployment benefit was increased and despite the new allowances the parish was able to reduce its rate. Although it tried later that year to obtain a Government loan (in order to pay off its accumulated debt), the Board, noting the reduced rate, refused.[110] Instead, with Board approval the council obtained a temporary overdraft. It was only when a supplementary rate failed the next summer that the council was forced into the Board's hands. There could be no new loan, the Board said, until the scale was reduced. Old Kilpatrick, under protest, agreed.[111]

By the mid-1920s the Board had achieved some uniformity in the administration of relief. It had been able to rebuff the more determined ideological attacks on what it considered 'needful sustentation', and had been able to force the more reluctant parishes to pay at least the equivalent of unemployment benefit. Parish bankruptcy had been avoided. The Board's own surveys concluded that its policy had worked reasonably well. After one report on Clydeside, it felt able to comment:

> The medical evidence confirms the opinion formed by lay observers that the public measures taken for the relief of unemployment have prevented any widespread physical distress. In this respect the position has been much more satisfactory than in previous severe trade depressions, when the unskilled and the casual worker, who become immediately affected by a falling off in trade, often suffered acute physical distress and privation because of the lack of co-ordinated efforts to provide relief. In the present depression this class have had available for them, in common with other classes of unemployed, a regular weekly income sufficient to enable an adequate supply of necessaries to be procured.[112]

What had 1921-24 demonstrated? First, caught between its own economic policy and preserving public order, the Government had accepted the necessity of overturning one of the Poor Law's basic and traditional principles – no relief to the able-bodied. Second, in doing so, it opened a new chapter in domestic administration: a highly political and, in some cases, violent conflict between ratepayer and the unemployed. Although the crisis in 1921 was temporary and the numbers on relief fell back sharply from about 50 000, parishes knew that even with a third of this number on relief they could not survive. Indebtedness stood at over £3 000 000. On the other hand, with their right to national insurance severely curtailed, many unemployed had to face the unthinkable: means tested benefit from the Poor Law. Until 1921, the broad mass of the Scottish working class had been brought up to ignore the Poor Law. After it, they could not. (Indeed in Glasgow alone, by 1924, nearly half the working class had received some form of relief.) But there was a third and equally important aspect to what had happened. The Government, having been drawn into breaking the law, had itself created a precedent. It was prepared, if politically expedient, to abandon the Poor Law's established – and legal – doctrines.

The events surrounding unemployment relief were unexpected. The same was not true of the second issue to dominate the inter-war period: poor relief to the dependants of strikers. It began in February 1922, when the Engineers' Union (in an attempt to avert wage cuts) announced industrial action, and ended some four years later with the General Strike. This time, after an initial inquiry, the Board had worked out what it thought was a reasonable policy.

Soon after the Engineers' announcement, Govan, a parish with a considerable number of engineering works, asked the Board for clarification of its legal position: as a destitution authority, could it provide assistance to families of men out on strike? The Board was evidently taken by surprise by Govan's letter because the parish noted that the reply was 'vague and indefinite, if not contradictory in terms'.[113] A further letter soon followed. It stated that the 1921 Act did not cover strike relief, quoted the English Poor Law case of Merthyr Tydfil in 1900, where the dependants of miners had been assisted (the Court had ruled the men were technically in 'desertion') and added: 'Any application for relief on behalf of themselves or their dependants should be dealt with as application for ordinary poor relief under the Act of 1845, and disposed of in accordance with the practice which has obtained in the administration of that Act.'[114] Govan felt that this advice was still too vague, and again pressed the Board on whether or not it could assist families. This time the Board was emphatic. Parishes could not assist strikers as a separate class of applicant, but 'in any particular case in order to prevent hardship through lack of food', they could relieve under the 1845 Act.[115] This meant little because Govan, to avoid any suspicion of illegality, sent all applicants to the Sheriff.[116] Out of 200 applicants only seven were successful.

Further pressure for clarification of parish responsibility came from a Labour M P, F. Rose (Aberdeen North), and Munro, the Scottish Secretary, referred the issue to C. D. Murray, the Lord Advocate and Briggs Constable, the Solicitor-General.[117] They stated, 'there is no difference, so far as the Poor Law is concerned, between men on strike and other men who can, but will not, support themselves'. No reference was made to the 1845 Act. Indeed their opinion indicated that they were more concerned to differentiate between those genuinely locked out, and hence entitled to relief, and those who were on strike. But whatever their opinion, discretion under the Act, according to the Board, remained available.

A number of other parishes were less reluctant than Govan. In Dundee, the parish agreed to treat strikers as if they were locked out and provided some assistance.[118] The following year, during a jute dispute, it again made no differentiation.[119] Some 300 applicants were enrolled, each being paid 15 shillings for their wife and 1 shilling for a child. When, a fortnight later, the Board advised the council that the payments were illegal, they ceased.

A more serious stoppage occurred at Douglas in 1925. There the mine owners told the men they would only be employed if they agreed to wage cuts and other alterations in working practices. The parish considered it to be a lock-out and began enrolling the miners and their families.[120] The Board became alarmed and immediately asked for the payments to be withdrawn. But when it received allegations that children were undernourished, it had second thoughts and permitted the parish to continue the relief on a reduced scale.[121] The inconsistency of the Board's attitude in part reflected a new political development. The Labour Government had added another paragraph to the Law Officer's memorandum. It now specifically stated that discretion was available under the 1845 Act, an action regretted by the Board's Chairman, Ewan MacPherson, who felt 'it gave the whole show away'. Indiscriminate relief, he noted, was a distinct possibility.

With the likelihood of more widespread industrial action, the Government during the summer of 1925 began to review strike relief and Sir John Gilmour, the Scottish Secretary, was asked to reconsider the issue in the light of maintaining a Scottish policy similar to England's. Gilmour told the Board he did not think it was possible to withdraw Labour's additions, although he did insist on adding a paragraph warning parishes not to intervene 'too readily'. This, Baldwin was assured, meant the Board's policy was in line with the Ministry of Health's.

The policy was soon tested, for in November a dispute flared up in the shale oil districts of West Lothian. The parishes, twelve in all, defined it as a lock-out (the employers wanted wage reductions), decided on a scale – 23 shillings for a miner and his wife, and 2 shillings and 6 pence for each child – and enrolled nearly 2 000 families.[122] The Board could not agree and, after some terse correspondence over the strike's status, called a conference. MacPherson told them that no relief could be given under the 1921 Act – work was available to any man – but said:

> They [the Board] had not any wish that any man should suffer any unnecessary hardship whatever. Those in authority over them [the Scottish Secretary] had permitted him to authorise Parish Councils to stretch the law to the extent he had indicated to prevent people suffering. They were satisfied that if the Parish Councils used the 1845 Act properly there would be no undue suffering.[123]

The head of the household (the striker) was to be the applicant and settlement was not to be pressed. The parishes were not pleased: Uphall's Chairman told the Board he felt MacPherson 'had simply brushed aside the difficulties'. The dispute was settled soon after and the policy never became contentious.

At the same time as the Board was agreeing to the use of the 1845 Act, the Court of Session completely overturned its arbitration decisions on the right of dependants to receive relief on their own account.[124] In a 'test' desertion case, the Lord President, Lord Clyde, ruled that relief could only be given if there was 'difficulty in tracing and recalling' the missing head of the family. A *Poor Law Magazine* commentator was very alarmed, because this meant an inspector would have great difficulty in granting 'interim' relief. If he provided assistance before an 'exhaustive' inquiry, the court might rule his action illegal. But if the inspector refused and the applicant died, he might be prosecuted for neglect. It was against the spirit of the 1845 Act.

The beginning of the General Strike led the Cabinet to agree to a Ministry of Health memorandum on relief and a circular was duly issued on 5 May 1926.[125] Three days later, after repeated requests for guidance from parishes, the Board issued a similar circular, which stated that where relief could not 'Lawfully be given to the man [and] where acute destitution and suffering on the part of the man's dependants is immediately threatened, temporary relief in respect of such dependants may have to be afforded.'[126] It stated further that relief could be given under the 1845 Act to a man unemployed if he was physically unable to perform work, and then gave the same scales of relief that were operating in England: 12 shillings for a wife and 4 shillings for each child. The Board stressed that a parish's financial position was not to be endangered.

With the overwhelming majority of parishes controlled by the ratepayers, the Board rarely had trouble from councils seeking to pay allowances over the recommended scale. Labour controlled parishes in Fife, at first, tried to pay extra relief, but soon ran into overdraft difficulties and, after a letter from the Board stressing that it wanted 'uniform action in all industrial districts', backed down from any confrontation.[127] Two parishes, Beath and Culross, which had paid relief to single miners were later surcharged, but this was subsequently withdrawn.[128]

When pressed for the circular's legal authority, the Board frankly admitted there was none. A letter to Bo'ness in August, similar to one sent to Dunfermline in May, stated:

As you are aware. the primary duty of a Parish Council is to relieve destitution where it is found to exist. Moreover, it has been the long-established practice of Parish Councils in cases where actual physical suffering is immediately threatened, not to await the actual emergence of such suffering but to grant relief to prevent it. . . It was having regard to these aspects of the situation that the Board, while recognising that on strict interpretation of the Law it might be held by the Court that there is no power to grant relief to wives and children, as a class, of unemployed able-bodied men directly concerned in a trade dispute, felt justified in issuing to Parish Councils the recommendation.[129]

Virtually all parishes initially agreed to give relief, but as costs increased and the 'lock-out' became a strike in July, many had second thoughts. Scales began to be cut, at first by about 20 per cent, but when ratepayer objections became even more vociferous, particularly in the smaller parishes, all relief was stopped. The refusal of Lord Moncrieff, in the Court of Session at the end of July, to grant interim interdict against Hamilton on the grounds that 'the balance of convenience' lay in the continuance of relief, seemed to have little effect.[130]

At the beginning of July, Labour MPs became alarmed at these developments and at a private meeting pressed Walter Elliot, the Under Secretary for Health, to take stronger action. Their concern was heightened when, at the end of the month, Ayr, Dailly and Carnwath Parishes withdrew all relief.[131] A new circular to those that had withdrawn relief was prepared. Addressed to the Inspector of Poor, it said:

The Board are of opinion that the fact the mines may now be declared open for work on new terms in consequence of the passing legislation [for an increased working day], in no way affects the position of the Parish Council in regard to relief. The Board's circular of 8th May remains operative.

The Board view the Council's attitude with grave concern, as it practically amounts to the Council refusing to perform one of the main duties laid on them by statute, viz., the duty of ensuring that relief is afforded out of the Poor rates to prevent injury through the effects of destitution.

[The Board] also point out that you as Inspector of Poor have a personal responsibility to ensure there is no acute suffering through destitution in cases in which the facts have been brought to your notice. Should any case be brought to your notice, it is your duty in terms of the Poor Law (Scotland) Act 1845, to investigate such cases in co-operation with the Medical Officer and, if you are satisfied that there is such suffering, to take such immediate action as in your discretion seems necessary.[132]

To support this, where there were complaints of distress and malnutrition, the Board sent its General Superintendents to investigate. At Leslie, every house was visited: G. A. MacKay, the Superintendent, reported no ill-health.[133] Avondale received similar treatment and although C. C. Ellis, the Superintendent, reported 'no obvious destitution', he urged the parish to reconsider its decision.[134] Generally such action appears to have had little effect. At Cranston, the parish replied to the Board's letter by saying that only the council had 'a full knowledge of local circumstances' and would continue to deal with each case 'on its merits'.[135] The strike was the miners' own responsiblity. Similar views were expressed by Logie, whose Inspector, Alex Morrison, commented:

> To give relief from the Poor rates to the dependants of strikers whose sole claim is destitution due to the failure of their bread-winner to support them although in a position to do so, is either according to the law of Scotland or it is not. The Parish Council of Logie take the latter view. And now I, who am carrying out the considered instructions of my Council, am threatened by the Board of Health with a criminal prosecution. . . It appears to me to be most unfair that I should be branded by the Board as a hypothetical criminal.[136]

Out of about a hundred mining parishes, at least thirty withdrew relief before the end of the strike.

At the end of July, the Board faced an even more serious problem. Hamilton, although the Court of Session had delayed a final judgment, found its bank would not agree to another overdraft. Its debt had already reached £28 000. The Board tried to reassure the bank, but when this failed, it had to hurriedly secure a Government loan.[137] A few weeks later, fourteen other parishes also said their banks had refused further overdrafts and the Government faced the possibility that all relief would stop. Baldwin immediately informed the banks, confidentially, that the Government would if necessary introduce legislation to 'secure' their advances. But they still refused and the parishes concerned threatened to withdraw all relief unless there was indemnification. The Board, with the consent of Baldwin, was forced to tell them that the Government would fully 'protect their position'. By the end of the strike, forty parishes were receiving Government loans.

Whatever the pressure from the Board and the banks, parishes had also to contend with the local miners. At Dunfermline in June, 3 000 single miners, headed by four pipe bands, marched on the local poorhouse demanding admission.[138] After some 'friendly conversations' and being told any applicant required a medical certificate, they marched away to Kirkcaldy. The threat of the withdrawal of relief at St Ninians (Bannockburn) led to the councillors being told by a deputation 'that the first man who goes outside will be torn limb by limb' unless they continued relief.[139] When West Calder did withdraw relief (in August), a riot broke out and within a week the parish rescinded its decision.[140] At Mauchline, for instance, which as early as June decided to withdraw relief, the Chairman protested that there had been demonstrations in front of his house and that 'a section of the community were treating him badly'. It too rescinded its decision. Faced with ratepayers' complaints and miners' demands, Cumnock and Auchinleck agreed to hold a referendum.[141] Cumnock's ratepayers agreed that relief should continue, while Auchinleck's did not. The procedure was entirely illegal. Other ratepayers were not as contented. In Lanarkshire, the Colville Company notified Dalziel on 12th July that it intended to take High Court action to stop relief.[142] The parish unanimously agreed to defend the action. Lord Constable, the Lord Ordinary, later that month refused the interdict on an understanding that no new assessment would be imposed before November. Nevertheless the extent of local ratepayers' feeling can be seen in the *Hamilton Advertiser*'s Leader on the Government's position:

> The Board cannot make laws; they can only administer laws as they exist, and not as the Board thinks they should exist. Carluke's Chairman has answered that the Government will make it legal. Parish Councils should take notice they are not there to administer illegal relief, in the hope that it may be made legal. They should be brought to the bar of justice whether or not the Government makes illegality legal.[143]

The Parish Councils' Association agreed. By a large majority it approved a motion condemning the Board's action and asking for a withdrawal of the circular.[144] Doubt was even expressed on the legal liability of an inspector who carried out his parish's wish and refused assistance. Tempers amongst this circle continued to rise with the failure of the Colville action to be heard in Court. The *Hamilton Advertiser* noted in late October that many felt the case had been delayed so long that the Government had interfered in the administration of justice.[145]

The declaration by the Court of Session in December, when the strike was over, that dependants' relief was illegal was no surprise.[146] Lord Constable's judgment reflected traditional principles, stating that even if temporary relief had been given, the parish would have had to pursue the miner for the failure to maintain his family. The Scottish Secretary, who had already drafted retrospective legislation, quickly introduced the necessary Bill.[147] At Churchill's insistence (as Chancellor of the Exchequer) only 40 per cent of the relief given, some £703 038, could be reclaimed from the Government. The Bill's passage was, as Gilmour predicted, one of the most difficult the Board had ever faced. The industrial ratepayers, parishes and indeed many Conservative MPs all expressed strong opposition.[148] Only Labour seemed satisfied. Although critical of the Bill's financial clauses, they praised Gilmour for not only 'preventing a breakdown in local government', but also accepting strike relief. It was, said Wheatley, 'a principle of modern civilisation not to punish women and children'.

The development of Poor Law policy has so far indicated that relief was unconditional: that is to receive assistance the unemployed had only to demonstrate the inability to obtain employment. Almost as soon as the 1921 Act had been passed parishes became concerned both at giving monetary benefits without some form of 'test' and the possibility of large numbers of otherwise respectable workers becoming 'demoralised' by public relief.[149] Unless a parish was a landward authority, it did not have the power to offer work in return for relief. (Landward parishes had responsibility for allotments, footpaths and in some cases, minor roads.) However with the Government insisting that the Poor Law continue 'emergency' assistance after May 1922, the clamour for urban parishes to become involved in relief work grew.[150] The 1923 Act, which continued the 1921 measure for another year, allowed this and small schemes began in Edinburgh, Govan and Glasgow.[151]

The following year the Labour Government agreed that the National Insurance scheme should be reorganised and in the summer benefits were increased: 18 shillings for the insured, 5 shillings for an adult dependant and 2 shillings for each child. 'Uncovenanted' benefit was also reformed, and the regulations amended to reduce the number of disqualifications, and more importantly end the use of the 'gap'. Although Adamson, the Scottish Secretary, was forced to continue the 1921 Act for another year, 1924 saw the number on relief decline.[152] Only those who had no insurance record, or those with children were now eligible and by September the numbers assisted had fallen from 37 000 to 22 000.

1924 therefore marked an important turning point in Poor Law policy. Instead of having to assist the 'ordinary' unemployed, parishes now dealt with a much narrower group. The Board commented:

> It should be remembered that the greater proportion of the unemployed do not seek assistance from the poor law. The number of able-bodied unemployed in receipt of relief during the year has been considerably less than 20 per cent. of the number registered as unemployed. Those who do apply probably include, among others, not only a large proportion of casual labourers, but also many of the least satisfactory types in the large industrial centres.[153]

A quarter of those who were on relief, it reported, had been unemployed for over a year. In Glasgow the figure was nearly 70 per cent.

But during 1925 a new problem for parishes emerged (the 1921 Act had again been continued): the stricter imposition of unemployment benefit regulations. By the end of the year, the numbers and costs of relief had returned to pre-1924 levels. Although the Ministry of Labour declared that Scottish parishes were 'too generous', the Board was able to establish that in fact it was applying the regulations more strictly than before.[154] Workers now had to have made eight insurance contributions in the previous two years before they could retain 'uncovenanted' benefit. In Paisley, for instance, one of the towns most affected, the numbers disqualified more than doubled. In Glasgow, where a similar situation had developed, the parish's own analysis not only confirmed Paisley's, but also showed the majority were unskilled and over fifty.

132

Initially the Board complained of the Ministry's policy. Parishes, 'in the absence of specific offers of employment', had no alternative but give relief. But with the Ministry sticking to its policy and the cost of relief increasing (to £30 000 a week in May 1926), the Board's attitude changed.[155]

During the coal dispute the Board withdrew approval of the September scale and stated that only those parishes that paid no more than unemployment benefit would secure a Government loan. It was 'the plain duty' of every parish 'to conserve their financial resources'. Early the following year, this was re-emphasised. Parishes applying for loans were told that 'excessive borrowing was economically unsound' and although none were refused, all came under renewed pressure to cut back even further.[156]

So in 1927, when the miners' strike receded, the Board had a somewhat different perspective and this was reflected in its Annual Report. Ahead of the Industrial Transference Committee (established by the Ministry of Labour as part of its economic recovery programme), it concluded that the Scottish economy could not possibly absorb the 'surplus industrial population' of the coalfields and the Clyde basin.[157] Parishes in these areas, the Board suggested, faced a new responsibility: ensuring that they did not impede the 'natural movement of labour'. It warned that unemployment

affected the possibility of young men and women becoming trained in the habits of industry. The dangers associated with the existence of large numbers of young men and women growing up in the spirit of reliance on a considerable measure of support from public funds are sufficiently obvious and need not here be stressed. Those who show an unreasonable reluctance [to move] should be made clearly to understand that the maintenance out of the poor-rates was never intended to be an alternative to work, and that if work locally is not available efforts must be made to find work elsewhere.

It then insisted, 'unemployment itself is not a qualification for receipt of relief; there must also be genuine inability to find work.' The Report suggested that parishes should offer to pay the expenses of those willing to migrate. Those who were unwilling to move should be sent to the poorhouse. By an active policy of disqualification, the Poor Law, it hoped, would 'push' labour away from 'stagnant pools' of industry.

Thus during 1928, after a special investigation by one of the Superintendents, C. C. Ellis, and an Assistant Secretary, George Henderson, Cambuslang was specifically told that families of the long-term unemployed should not receive outdoor relief unless the man himself accepted relief in the poorhouse.[159] In their view, 'the automatic and unconditional payment of outdoor relief must inevitably result in the perpetuation of the problem'. The parish, although under ratepayer control, was appalled. It replied, 'It has never been the practice of this Council to send a householder to the Poorhouse and run the risk of breaking up a home. To do so in an able-bodied case would mean keeping the breadwinner in an Institution where he would be unable to look for or obtain employment, and would entail extra cost on the rates.' Other parishes on Clydeside were equally appalled. Bonhill dismissed the Report out of hand, the ratepayer councillors said they 'could not subscribe' to its contents.[160] Bothwell, after being told loans 'might have a deterrent effect on preventing unnecessary applications' (permissable after the 1927 Act) at first agreed, but then refused to consider any specific case.[161] Only Blantyre, where the Board itself had added:

> It is common experience that a great many of the unemployed are able to obtain short spells of work. . . Complete failure to do so over long periods affords *prima facie* grounds for suspicion that reasonable efforts to find employment have not been made. From this point of view the Board suggests the classification of the roll into 1) those genuinely unfortunate and 2) those who are 'work shy'.

did withdraw relief.[162] But when the local miners' union told them that breaking up families was inhumane and would lead to 'trouble', the councillors backed down. Each case was to be treated 'on its merits'.

By the autumn of 1928 the Board's attempt to use the Poor Law as an active instrument in the relocation of labour was a failure. But there still remained the policy of offering work both inside and outside the poorhouse for those deemed lacking in the 'work ethic'. The early attempts to promote relief work as a way of testing the unemployed had not turned out to be a success. By the sheer pressure of the more 'respectable' short-term unemployed, Glasgow had been forced to utilise its scheme at Woodilee Asylum for them and not the long-term unemployed. As a result Glasgow, like other large parishes, sent more and more to the poorhouse.[163]

This change in the use of poorhouses did not go unnoticed. Glasgow's Governor, George Gillie, as early as 1924 felt compelled to comment:

> The year [1923] has seen a large increase in the admission of young able-bodied men most of whom admit that they have done no work for two and three years, and, as a result of the 'Dole' system, they are not likely ever to settle down to work outside. A General Poorhouse is not a suitable place for such as these and the problem they involve will not be solved until something in the nature of a Labour Colony is provided for their reception and detention.[164]

Similar views were expressed by Governors in Edinburgh, Dundee, Govan and Omoa (mid-Lanark). After a strike of inmates in 1927, Govan decided to act and a special work retraining scheme was launched at their Gartlock Asylum.[165] Glasgow soon followed with a similar one at

Lenzie. Edinburgh used its Distress Committee labour colony at Muiriston, Mid-Calder. This time the parishes all set wages below trade union agreed rates. It was important, Glasgow's Inspector said, for the workers to realise that any form of Poor Relief was 'less eligible' than regular work.

By the end of 1928 this tough policy of offering indoor relief to large numbers of unemployed and forcing them, if they wanted their families to receive any benefit, to accept relief work, began to worry some of the Labour councillors.[166] In Glasgow, after hearing reports about Barnhill, the councillors inspected it and found their worst fears substantiated. Between forty and fifty men, mostly those disqualified from unemployment benefit, were being sent there each week. Poorhouse clothing, drugget, was mandatory. But the councillors also found considerable problems over segregation. Barnhill's lack of accomodation, they said, meant the young had to mix with drunkards, petty criminals and other 'dissolutes'. Sodomy was said to have taken place. At the same time, encouraged by the National Unemployed Workers' Movement, the relief workers went on strike.

When Labour returned to power the following year, the Labour councillors approached Adamson and Johnston, the new Scottish Ministers, and within a month of taking office Johnston called a conference of the parish, the Labour group and the Trades Council. The use of a poorhouse for the unemployed, Glasgow was told, had to stop. Relief work, Johnston said, should be reformed to allow for two categories of workers. The first and most numerous class, those who could not find any employment and were otherwise 'respectable', should be offered work with a 'fair wage and conditions' clause. Any employment, Johnston went on, should simply be to maintain a work record. For the others – the beggar, the petty criminal, the bookie and the hardened drinker – the 'test', as Johnston put it, 'ought to be not what the man was actually able to turn out but evidence of his willingness to work'. A special scheme of work for self-improvement ought to be devised.

After Johnston had arranged a favourable Government grant for the Lenzie retraining scheme, Glasgow agreed to adopt Labour's policy.[167] The parish also agreed to use the poorhouse only for those who had been unemployed longer than five years. Within two years, Glasgow had 48 in its Poorhouse (compared with 128 in 1929), 1 250 at Lenzie and 343 on a special scheme at Palacerigg, the old Distress Committee colony. The poorhouse test was dead. So too was the use of relief work to test the claims of the ordinary unemployed. As the Department explained in its 1929 Annual Report:

> To force the head of the household into the poorhouse, involving his temporary separation from his family savours of hardship. Again a man who has experienced a long period of unemployment may, although he had made reasonable efforts to find work, have

been unfortunate in his search for work and he resents being classed with, and compelled to live in close association with, men of bad character.[168]

Character reformation, the Department said, could only be aimed at a very small minority: those who were both unemployed and had clearly defined handicaps. For the unemployed, detailed inquiry into character was no longer a condition of relief, all that counted was unemployment.

The withdrawal of the September scale in 1926 had meant parishes no longer supplemented unemployment benefit. This, together with further improvements in national insurance and the change in regulations which allowed those previously disqualified to receive 'uncovenanted' benefit, meant that the numbers on Poor Relief declined.[169] In Glasgow, one of the areas most affected by the Ministry of Labour's 'not genuinely seeking work' test, the number dropped steadily from nearly half of those out of work (16 000) in 1927, to less than 10 per cent (4 000) in 1930.

By then parish councils had been abolished. The 1929 Local Government Act transferred their powers to the local authority, either burghs over 20 000 in population or county councils. Afterwards the Department of Health (which had taken over the functions of the Board in 1929) commented:

Certain results automatically follow the spreading of the burden of poor law expenditure over a wider area. Among these are the removal of the glaring inequalities in the poor rates of parishes comprised in a county or large burgh, and the dimunition of the difficulties of a number of small industrial parishes which had to carry a heavy burden of expenditure due to unemployment. . . On average, the allowances paid by the new authorities appear to be slightly more generous than those previously paid by parish councils.[170]

This was particularly the case on Clydeside where some unemployed saw their allowance increase by over 15 per cent.[171]

This increase was welcome news for the Department. During 1930 it had come under pressure from Labour MPs to demonstrate that, despite the financial stringency of the previous decade, the children of the long-term unemployed had not suffered.[172] A new survey, based on the school and child welfare medical records of over 100 000 children was instituted, and its results again emphasised the conclusions of earlier work. The major factor affecting the growth and development of children, it said, was the size of family income. Nevertheless no widespread concern was noted and the Department's Secretary, John Jeffrey felt able to write that if there had been deprivation 'it was difficult to point to a failure in the social services'. The Report's value, he told Adamson, lay 'in showing no action was called for other than in indicating new lines of social amelioration'. His statement was soon tested, for with the demise of the second Labour Government in August 1931, cuts in benefit were announced.

Within a few weeks of the National Government being formed, national insurance benefits were reduced by around 10 per cent. At the same time, the Government scrapped the existing scheme of assistance for those who had received 'uncovenanted' benefit. New Transitional Payment regulations were introduced which, although they embodied the first nationally defined needs level, also introduced a household means test. It was to be operated, until a national administrative scheme could be devised, by the local public assistance committee.[173] At the same time, in order to conserve public expenditure, councils also came under pressure to reduce their own Poor Law scales to Transitional Payment level, which virtually all of them did.[174]

The issue for the unemployed, approaching 40 per cent in many towns, had changed. With mass unemployment and a worldwide depression few, even in Government, believed that there could be any immediate return to 'normality'. Instead what had become important was the benefit rate and for the Labour Party, the committees of the unemployed and others, there was an instant target: the local council. If the council could not by law increase Transitional Payment (it was fully funded by Government), then they should supplement it through the Poor Law. In Glasgow, the council received virtually every month a deputation from local trade unions and ex-servicemen's organisations pleading for some modification of the scale. In Renfrewshire, even the Paisley Presbytery joined in the action and wrote to express its concern at 'those suffering hardship under the means test'. It urged the council to 'operate it with sympathy and generosity'.[175] Elsewhere more direct action was taken. Fife found that the Labour controlled District Committee at Lochgelly refused to implement the cuts, and the council was forced to establish a separate sub-committee to administer the scheme.[176] But even where Labour councillors were able to persuade others to adopt a more ameliorative policy, the Department was soon in action. Dunbartonshire was told that its proposal to ignore the value of war disability pensions was 'contrary to the principle of the Poor Law'.[177] All household income had to be taken into account.

By the middle of 1932, with little sign of the Government's changing its attitude, the issues became clearer. Labour and the deputations of the unemployed concentrated their attacks on three areas of policy: the inadequacy of the scales, the failure to ignore the full value of war disability pensions, and the household means test. In Greenock alone, 40 per cent of recipients suffered some means tested reduction.[178] Glasgow, at 45 per cent, was even worse. Although it was strenuously denied by public assistance committees, many believed the test broke up family homes. Why this happened was explained to Glasgow by its Director of Assistance, Matthew Reynard:

> The opponents of the [means] test have stated that it has resulted in the "break up of the home" due to the fact that, when parents become idle, working members of the family refused to remain in the family as their earnings are taken into account in fixing the amount to be paid as transitional benefit to the parents and that, when the adult members of the family became idle, the parents refused to allow them to remain in the family and to maintain them out of the earnings of the household. Consequently, it is alleged that such adult members of the family left home in order to secure the full allowance payable as transitional payment.[179]

Throughout 1932 and 1933 an alteration in the political control of Scotland became apparent. The ratepayers' hold on local councils began to dissolve. In Glasgow, under mounting pressure of unemployment and wage reductions, the traditional affiliation of the skilled Protestant working class to 'moderate' Conservatism broke. At first they voted for a new Party, Protestant Action, ostensibly over Catholic interests on the Education Committee, but then as the depression worsened, in greater numbers for Labour candidates. In other areas, although the fracturing was less religiously orientated, with Labour promising to restore all cuts the same process occurred and the Party moved from controlling less than 5 per cent of the population in 1931 to over 40 per cent by 1935.[180]

This alteration in political control was underlined during the Communist-inspired NUWM marches of 1932 and 1933. Their first march, on the Scottish Office early in 1932, attracted only minor attention.[181] The next one in June 1933 was different. A much longer march from different areas of Scotland was organised, and when it reached Edinburgh, thousands of local unemployed, many of them skilled, joined the procession. An Assistant Secretary at the Scottish Office, J. L. Jack, was quick to complain about the disruption it caused and noted in particular that while many in the clubs and offices felt uneasy, the local police seemed reluctant to make any arrests. He told his Permanent Secretary that 'it was by no means an edifying sight and the scene at Princes Street after 10 p.m. was a very disagreeable reminder of what had taken place during the General Strike'. Another Assistant Secretary, J. N. Duke, went further and commented that although 'opinion' had been on the side of the marchers, if they 'had broken loose, the police could not have prevented a serious riot'. He hoped the new national scheme for the unemployed (the Unemployment Assistance Bill) would help prevent another disturbance.

A more direct challenge to Government policy came at the end of 1933, when Labour swept to power for the first time in both Glasgow and Greenock. Yet despite overwhelming support, Glasgow's Labour administration moved cautiously. It delayed implementing the Party's election promises until it had sought the Department of Health's views. After a meeting with Noel Skelton, the Parliamentary Under-Secretary, Glasgow seemed satisfied that there would be no intervention but asked for written confirmation.[182] On two specific questions – the right of the council to increase the scale of allowances beyond Transitional Payment and on the Secretary of State's attitude – the Department's Secretary, J. E. Highton, replied:

I have to observe scales of relief are not recognised by the Poor Law Acts. The statutory duty of the authority is to afford needful sustentation appropriate to individual applicants for Poor Relief having regard to the whole circumstances of the particular case. A scale of relief may be useful as an administrative expedient in helping to avoid inequalities of treatment among poor persons whose circumstances are approximately similar, but, whether high or low, a scale cannot as a general measure of needful sustentation be legally substituted for the individual determination required by statute.

The decision as to the amount of relief to be given to any applicant who has been held to be eligible for relief is a matter for the local authority alone. Neither the Secretary of State nor the Department can relieve the local authority of the responsibility for that decision which they take subject, on the one hand, to an appeal on the ground of inadequacy of relief, and, on the other, to a risk of challenge by the auditor that the expenditure is excessive with the result that the local authority may be surcharged for the excess by the Secretary of State.

Later Skelton underlined the point by declaring the issue a 'purely domestic one'. Glasgow, nevertheless, still moved with caution. There was still the possibility of ratepayer action. It originally proposed to restore part of the head of household's cut.[183] Only at the last moment, after taunts from the splinter ILP councillors, did the ruling Labour group change its mind. An increase in the child's allowance to 3 shillings was also accepted.[184] It meant that a family with three children would receive 33 shillings and three pence a week – more than they would have received under the old September agreement. Within a week the number of unemployed on relief had doubled to 42 000 and some 20 per cent of the city were being assisted.

Greenock was less hesitant. After an extraordinary campaign, when even the local press came out in Labour's favour, the new council felt little need to be cautious. Children's benefit went up immediately to 3 shillings and 6 pence.[185] The maximum was abolished and the means test modified for family earnings and pensions. Again the Department refused to be drawn on the legality of Greenock's move. Skelton, in particular, would not say whether he felt national insurance was adequate for 'needful sustentation'.[186] The council's auditor, J. B. Wallace, had different ideas. He did object and the Scottish Secretary, Sir Godfrey Collins (the local M P), was forced to establish a Court of Inquiry under J. R. Dickson, the Sheriff of Argyll.[187] It sat in August 1934.[188] The issues before the court soon became clear. Wallace maintained that Greenock's payments were illegal for three reasons. First, although willing to admit poverty in the town was 'rampant', he felt the council had departed from the Poor Law's basic and traditional function – 'the relief of destitution'. In adjusting its scales Greenock had introduced a new issue, a concern for the people's health. Second, he felt the means test was there to enforce family obligations and only when its members had fully exhausted their own income was there a role for the State. Greenock, he said, wanted to ignore it. Thirdly, in his 'unbiased and unprejudiced view', the more children one had the 'cheaper' it was, and he thought a more appropriate scale would have been 3 shillings for the first child, 2 shillings and 6 pence for the second and 2 shillings for the third. That would have meant for a family of three, 30 shillings and 9 pence.

Ranged against him, the Labour Councillors, headed by Provost Bell, argued that times had altered. Long-term unemployment had sapped the energy and the savings of the ordinary, decent working man. In Greenock alone, the Provost revealed, 7 000 had drawn out all their savings. The means test, he said, was 'unjust and barbaric'. It meant even the earnings from a child's part-time work were deducted. To avoid this, Treasurer Barr added, many sent their daughters away to become domestic servants. Breaking up homes, he said, was evidence of society's 'moral degeneration'. Another councillor, A. Porter, was even more emphatic on what the means test had done. He told the Inquiry that where there were working daughters, under the old scale, a husband, wife and daughter would receive 30 shillings and 3 pence. If the daughter earned £1, the parents received 15 shillings and 9 pence and if she earned 30 shillings, it would be 5 shillings and 9 pence, and if 35 shillings and 9 pence, none. 'It was not possible', he added, 'for such a girl to prepare herself as a citizen of the community and to provide for the "bottom drawer"'. The chairman of the Public Assistance Committee, Mrs McLeod, was equally opposed to the old scale. She told the Inquiry that many mothers had 'starved themselves for their children'; she had known some that lived on milk, bread and margarine. Other councillors gave similar evidence. One said that benefit should allow for the costs of recreation, because without it, the long-term unemployed would become 'progressively demoralised'. Another (a previous ratepayer councillor) argued that the longer one remained out of work, the greater the need for increased allowances. To round off its evidence, the council introduced Edinburgh's past Medical Officer of Health, Dr W. Robertson. He claimed that the old scale, under British Medical Association guidlines, was 30 per cent below what was necessary for reasonable physical efficiency.

After seven days of inquiry, Labour's defence seemed impressive. The 'atmosphere' the local press felt, had been with them. Indeed in its final Leader it could comment, 'all the Labour Councillors were as full of facts and figures as a high civil servant' and went on to add, 'they have devoted years to civic administration and have seldom been caught unawares'. What had been in the dock, it thought, was not Labour's expansive policy, but the Auditor's acceptance of traditional philosophy.

Collins, the Scottish Secretary, early in 1935 announced that the payments were not illegal.[189] That he had accepted Labour's campaign was seen in the Department of Health's Annual Report. Explaining why the cost of Poor Relief had increased, it commented:

> Not only has the volume of unemployment been unprecedented, but the savings and other resources of those who have experienced long periods of unemployment have been eaten into and in many cases exhausted. Relatives have been less able, or, realising their own precarious position, have been less willing to assist those who are in need.[190]

and on the adequacy of relief, added, 'Many scales are. . . defective in that they make no provision for adjustment to meet differences in such matters as rents and the ages of children.'

This change of view in fact reflected another development. Unknown to Greenock, and indeed to anyone outside the Government, the Department in the spring of 1934, under Cabinet instructions, had begun yet another survey of the physical condition of the long-term unemployed.[191] Using more sophisticated methods, the medical officers again showed the effects of low income. The unemployed had fewer household goods, fewer personal possessions, lived in poorer quality homes and ate an inferior diet. Moreover for any given length of unemployment, the larger the family the greater the distress. The results sufficiently worried its authors for them to comment 'that it could possibly be a prelude to a more serious organic breakdown if conditions prevailed over a long period'. A senior medical officer was more than worried. He told his Assistant Secretary that he had, 'read with some unease the report of the effects of unemployment on health and he had encountered enough danger signals to render necessary a continuation of more direct Departmental supervision.'[192] He thought the situation would only be eased with the restoration of the cuts.

Collins, now armed by a public Court of Inquiry and his own Department's survey understood that there had been a shift in public attitude. Throughout late 1935 and the first half of 1936 he pressed on the Cabinet Committee dealing with the new Unemployment Assistance Board regulations the need for special consideration to be given to the long-term unemployed.[193] He estimated what with the Poor Law supplementing Transitional Payments in Glasgow, Greenock, Clydebank and many other towns, if the U A B proposals were implemented, 50 per cent of the unemployed would suffer substantial cuts in benefit. Not only would this renege on the 1935 National Government election promise, but it would also lead to a lowering of health standards. The industrial part of Scotland, he told his colleagues, was 'one large distressed area', and he believed that 'public opinion had come to the conclusion that generous treatment of the unemployed was a right cause'.[194] His sustained campaign had its effect, and the Cabinet agreed to a package that would reduce the numbers affected to only a third. In half of these the cut was to be less than 2 shillings.

Why had Collins taken up Labour's campaign? First of all he had realised that, in a period of economic depression, any working-class belief in 'sound money' had evaporated. Its economic application had neither produced sufficient material reward nor sustained public order. If the National Government was to retain an electoral hold on the working-class vote, particularly amongst the skilled, then the recasting of unemployment relief had become an urgent priority. Moving the unemployed who had exhausted their insurance entitlement to a national means-tested scheme was, in itself, not sufficient. An ameliorative scheme had to be established which neither impinged on character reformation nor upheld the values of rugged individualism – one, in fact which acknowledged the struggles of the unemployed 1921-34. If that meant Scottish circumstances should dictate British policy, then so be it.

NOTES
1. Sir George MacCrae on Poor Law Reform (5.12.12), in *Scotsman*, p.12.
2. See, for instance, The Social Significance of Medical Inspection (1913), in *The County and Municipal Record 21*, pp.121-124, and, Health and the State (1914), in *ibid. 24*, pp.17-22.
3. Question from Scott, M. (Liberal, Glasgow Bridgeton) (24.7.17), in *Hansard 92 (Fifth Series)*, pp.2202-3. Munro was the Liberal M P for Wick Burghs.
4. Deputation to the Secretary for Scotland (24.9.17), in *British Medical Journal(2) 1917*, p.464. Actually the issue had been raised by the Society's President, Dr A. Robb (Midlothian), at its A G M the previous year, but it had taken the Society twelve months to prepare a deputation. Robb was particularly concerned about 'compensating' for losses on the battle-field. Their A G M had taken place just two months after the opening of the Somme offensive. See, Robb, A. (1916), After the War, in *The County and Municipal Record 27*, pp.322-6.
5. Report from the Annual Conference of the Scottish Association of Insurance Committees (27.10.17), in *Scotsman*, p.8 and

(29.10.17), in *ibid.*, p.10. Interestingly the Conference was just as keen for Scotland to have its own separate Ministry and not be included in an all-UK one.

6. Statement by the Royal College of Physicians of Edinburgh (6.12.17), in *British Medical Journal(1) 1918*, pp.33-4; but see opposition of the Medical Guild, (a group which included the President of the Royal College of Physicians) to 'State servitude', Report of A G M (29.10.17), in *Scotsman*, p.7. The College too was keen for Scotland to have its own Ministry.

7. Report of an Interview of Lanarkshire County and District Council with Secretary for Scotland (22.2.18), in *British Medical Journal(1) 1918*, p.271; Report of a Conference of the Convention of Royal Burghs, the Association of County Councils, the Association of District Councils and Glasgow Corporation (7.3.18), in *Scotsman*, p.4; Report of the A G M of the Scottish District Committees (26.6.18), in *ibid.*, p.6.

8. Questions from Hogge, J. M. (Edinburgh, East) (30.5.18) and Miller, D. (Lanarkshire North-East) (13.6.18), in *Hansard 106 (Fifth Series)*, pp.957 and 2367.

9. See, Meeting of Ayrshire, Dumfriesshire and Kircudbrightshire Poor Law Officers Association (30.3.18), in *Poor Law Magazine 1918*, pp.176-7; Smith. T. C., Some After-War Problems in Relation to Pauperism, in *ibid.*, pp.212-21; A G M of the Association of Parish Councils (12.6.18), in *ibid.*, pp.328-30; note comments by Hogge to a Local Authority Deputation to Parliament (17.7.18), in *Scotsman*, p.4 and by Munro to Deputation of Scottish Miners, in *ibid.*

10. Question from Dalziel, Sir H. (Coalition Liberal, Kirkcaldy) (26.2.19), in *Hansard 113 (Fifth Series)*, pp.1751-2.

11. Second Reading of Bill (1.4.19), in *ibid.* 114, pp.1135-60; this pledge had been given by his English counterpart the previous December, see Report on Ministry of Health Bill (3.12.18), in *Scotsman*, p.8.

12. *Scottish Board of Health Act, 1919. Ch. 20 (George V 9 & 10).*

13. See, Presidential Address by Munro at the Board's first meeting, 18.7.19, in *Poor Law Magazine 1919*, p.279. Note that of the Board's members only Macpherson was a Conservative.

14. Speech to the A G M of the Association of Parish Councils, in *ibid.*, pp.332-3.

15. *Annual Report of the Board of Health, 1920. Cmd. 1319 (P.P. 1921 Vol. XIII)* p.241.

16. The parishes were Wemyss, Beath, Ballingry, Auchterderran, Culrose, Newbattle, Carmichael, Blantyre, Falkirk and Larbert. Labour also held a third of the seats on Glasgow, Govan, Rutherglen, Cambuslang and Bothwell.

17. *op. cit.*, pp.337-40 and 366-69.

18. MacKenzie, *Report on Physical Welfare, op cit.* The child welfare scheme provided free medicines and food to pregnant and nursing women.

19. Rattray Parish Council v Coupar Angus Parish Council (30.11.03), in *Poor Law Magazine 1904*, pp.14-21. Sheriff Jamieson was said to hold Conservative opinions. He later became Lord Ardwall, Senator to the College of Justice.

20. Fordyce Parish Council v Bellie Parish Council, (18.11.03), in *ibid.*, pp.46-7. Board arbitrations could occur only where both

parties agreed on the facts of the case. There was no further appeal. The growth in arbitrations reflected the fact that they involved little cost; the Board's services were offered free.
21. G.M., Relief to the Able-bodied and their Dependants, in *ibid.*, pp.418-21.
22. Inverness Parish Council v Forfar Parish Council (8.4.04), in *ibid.*, pp.115-7.
23. Coupar Angus Parish Council v Tibbermore Parish Council (15.8.04), in *ibid.*, pp.193-5.
24. Inverurie Parish Council v Forgue Parish Council (18.11.04), in *ibid.* 1905, pp.27-8.
25. Houston Parish Council v Dumbarton Parish Council (10.10.11), in *ibid.* 1912, pp.129-31.
26. Glasgow Parish Council v Rutherglen Parish Council (7.8.18), in *ibid.* 1918, pp.153-7.
27. *Annual Report of the Local Government Board, 1919. Cmd. 824 (P.P. 1920 Vol. XXI)* p.vii.
28. Auchinleck Parish Council Minutes, *ADA CO.3.22.5.*
29. Ballingry Parish Council Minutes, 18.4.21, *FRCR 6.8.3.*
30. Shops looted in Cowdenbeath (9.4.21), in *Dunfermline Free Press,* p.2; Batons out to Dispose of Disorderly Mob at Bannockburn (7.5.21), in *Falkirk Mail,* p.1; Baton Charge on 90 men looting Shops (30.4.21), in *Hamilton Advertiser,* p.4.
31. Chapter VI, Prevention and Relief of Distress, *Annual Report of the Board of Supervision, 1921. Cmd. 1697 (P.P. 1922 Vol. VIII).*
32. Newbattle Parish Council Minutes, (passim, 22.4. to 1.6.21), *Midlothian District Council Records.*
33. See, Reports and Memorandum by the Board of Health into Industrial Unemployment and Distress, 1921, *SRO HH 31.36;* Distress in Dunfermline (14.5.21), in *Dunfermline Free Press,* p.5; Feeding the Needy (30.4.21) and Relieving Distress in Falkirk (25.6.21), in *Falkirk Mail,* pp.2 and 1. Once an unemployed person had exhausted their national insurance benefit, they would not be entitled to a second period until November.
34. Wemyss Parish Council Minutes, 21.7.21, *FRCR 6.56.14.*
35. For instance, Galston Parish Council Minutes, 7.9.21, *ADA CO.3.38.7.*
36. Blantyre Parish Council Minutes, 3.8.21, *SRA CO.1.22.10.*
37. Govan Parish Council Minutes, 25.8. and 14.9.21, *SRA D-HEW.5.1;* Glasgow Parish Council Minutes, 24.8.21, *op. cit.;* Helping the Unemployed; Should the Parish Step in? (5.8.21), in *Govan Press,* p.4.
38. *SRO SC 36.7.30.*
39. Letters of 8.8. and 9.8.21, Bothwell Parish Council Minutes, 8.8.21, *SRA CO.1.23.19.*
40. Dundee Workers' Plight (15.8.21), in *Dundee Advertiser,* p.7.
41. Cabinet Meeting No. 71, *PRO CAB 23.27;* for Churchill's account of the meeting see, Churchill's visit to Dundee (24.9.21), in *Scotsman,* p.9.
42. To relieve Unemployment Churchill announces new Proposal (23.8.21), and, Relief for Dundee's Unemployed (25.8.21), in *Dundee Advertiser,* pp.1 and 5.
43. Letter of 22.8.21, Govan Parish Council Minutes, *op. cit.*
44. Old Monkland Parish Council v J. McCormick (27.8.21), in *Hamilton Advertiser,* p.3.

45. Ballingry Parish Council Minutes, 16.8.21, in *op. cit.*
46. Fife Miners' Deputation to Board of Health (3.9.21), in *Scotsman*, p.7.
47. Memorandum for the Information of Parish Councils to whom Application for Relief is made by Able-Bodied Men in Acute Distress through Unemployment (2.9.21), in *Annual Report, 1921, op. cit.*, Appendix XLVI, pp.359-60. Morison was Coalition Liberal MP for Inverness-shire.
48. Dundee Parish Council Minutes, 6.9 and 9.9.21, *TRA TC.PCM.26*; see Reports, *passim* (7.9. to 10.9.21), in *Scotsman* and *Dundee Advertiser*; see also, Report (17.9.21), in *Forward*, p.8.
49. Cabinet Meetings Nos. 74 and 75, *PRO op. cit.*
50. Edinburgh Parish Council Minutes, 9.9.21, *op. cit.*; Cabinet Papers Nos. 3294, 3295, 3451 and 3478 gave information on the disturbances and Communist strength in each town, *PRO CAB 24.127-129* and Cabinet Committee on Unemployment Papers Nos. 212, 225, 242 and 248 gave information on economic conditions and the Poor Law, *PRO CAB 27.119*; see also Reports and *passim* (10.9. to 23.9.21), in *Scotsman*.
51. Uphall Parish Council Minutes, 22.9.21, *op. cit. 1.1.5.*
52. Kirkliston Parish Council Minutes, 15.9.21, *Edinburgh District Archives*.
53. Bothwell Parish Council Minutes, 15.9.21, *op. cit.*
54. Ardrossan Parish Council Minutes, 20.9.21, *ADA CO.3.21.15.*
55. Cabinet Meeting Nos. 71 and 80 (17.10.21), *PRO op. cit.*; see also Relief of Distress Committee Report (11.10.21), Paper 3391, and Cabinet Unemployed Committee Report (13.10.21), Paper 3403, *PRO CAB 24.128-129*; for the Board's continued concern over parish finances, see Letter of MacPherson to Scottish Office (28.9.21), Paper 233, Cabinet Committee on Unemployment, *ibid. 27.119.*
56. Second Reading, Poor Law Emergency Provisions (Scotland) Bill (27.10.21), in *Hansard 147 (Fifth Series)*, pp.1181-1203; Special Parish Councils' Association Meeting (10.11.21), in *Poor Law Magazine 1921*, pp.348-52; Circular on Loans to Poor Law Authorities (1.12.21), in *ibid., 1922*, pp.25-6. The loans were made available through the Vote for the Relief of Unemployment and were administered through the 'Goschen' Committee. They were for those whose banks refused a commercial loan.
57. See for instance, Can the Able-bodied Claim Relief (20.8.21), in *Forward*, p.7.
58. Speech by Duncan Graham (Hamilton) during Second Reading of Poor Law Bill, in *op. cit.*, p.1199.
59. *SRO HH 40.121.*
60. Scale of Relief for Destitute Able-Bodied Unemployed Persons, in *Annual Report, 1921, op. cit.*, Appendix XLVII, p.360.
61. For parish reaction to this scale see Edinburgh Parish Council Minutes, 26.9.21 (reduced), *op. cit.*; Glasgow Parish Council Minutes, 30.9.21 (increased), *op. cit.* Small town parishes were allowed scales below this level (the Board argued they had lower living costs), see for instance, Irvine Parish Council Minutes, 1.11.21, *ADA CO.3.40.40*; Stevenson Parish Council Minutes, 10.10.21, *op. cit. 59.11.* At that time 'general' labourers in Glasgow received from 35 shillings to 42 shillings a week, and skilled

workers in the engineering trades, about 60 shillings. An unemployed labourer with three children, if paid to the September scale, would therefore receive about 85 per cent of their wages, and a skilled worker about 55 per cent. Glasgow's inspector of poor reckoned an employed labourer with three children would spend about 25 shillings a week on food, 2 shillings on fuel, and 5 shillings on rent. This was assumed to be adequate.

62. Falkirk Parish Council Minutes, 27.9 and 25.10.21, *Central Regional Archives, FA1.8.1*; Demands of Unemployed (5.11.21), in *Falkirk Mail*, p.3.
63. Reports (12.11. and 19.11.21), in *Falkirk Herald*, pp.7 and 6.
64. Workless Men Demonstrate (19.11.21), in *Falkirk Mail*, p.5.
65. Falkirk Parish Council Minutes, 29.11.21 and 17.1.22, *op. cit.*
66. Reports (3.12.21), in *Falkirk Herald*, pp.5 and 6.
67. Audacity Wins (14.1.22), in *Forward*, p.3; *SRO HH 40.122.*
68. Board's Letter, 6.2.22, in Parish Council Minutes, 20.2.22, *op. cit.*
69. Minutes, 9.3.22, *op. cit.*; Excessive Relief Payments (11.3.22), in *Falkirk Herald*, p.6.
70. Blantyre Parish Council Minutes, 6.10.2 and 3.11.21, *op. cit.*
71. Letter of 18.10.21, in Inspector's Letter Book, *SRA. CO.1.2.31.2.*
72. Letter of 27.10.21, *ibid.*
73. Letter of 1.11.21, *ibid.*
74. Report of comment at parish meeting (5.11.21), in *Hamilton Advertiser*, p.4; Minutes, 3.11.21, *op. cit.*
75. Minutes, 28.11.21, *ibid.*; Letter of 20.12.21, *op. cit.*; see also, Cabinet Paper No. 3497, Memorandum by Pratt, J. W., Under Secretary for Health (19.11.21), *PRO CAB 24.129.* The Board feared further retrospective legislation.
76. Minutes, 5.1.22, *op. cit.*
77. Necessitious Children and Memorandum on Circular 51, *SRO ED 7.7.7, 7.7.8, 7.7.10 and 7.7.11.*
78. Board's Letter of 28.12.21, Govan Parish Council Minutes, 26.10, 16.11 and 29.12.21, *op. cit.*
79. See for instance, Secretary for Scotland and Greenock's Claims (1.4.22), in *Glasgow Herald*, p.5.
80. See, for instance Letter of Board (21.12.21) on disqualifications through 'not seeking work', in Rutherglen Parish Council Minutes 10.1.22, *SRA CO.1.53.7.* The regulations imposing 'seeking work' and other tests came into force after the November 1921 Insurance Act. The severity of their imposition varied, but Ministry of Labour officials in the Clydeside area seemed unusually harsh in their interpretations.
81. Bonhill Parish Council Minutes, 17.2.22, *SRA CO.4.12.6.*
82. Port Glasgow Voluntary Relief (1.3.22), in *Greenock Telegraph*, p.5.
83. Reports, *passim* (6.2. to 9.3.22), in *ibid.*
84. Reports, *passim* (5.9. to 11.9.22), in *ibid.*; Reports, *passim* (5.9. to 12.9.22), in *Glasgow Herald*.
85. New Scale of Relief at Port Glasgow (15.9.22), in *ibid.*, p.10.
86. Unemployed on the Rampage; Parish Council Offices Raided (10.2.22), in *Greenock Telegraph*, p.4.
87. Unemployment Relief; Greenock's Heavy Burden (5.4.22), in *Glasgow Herald*, p.5.
88. Parish Council Held-up; Remarkable Scenes at Greenock

(3.10.22), in *ibid.*, p.10.

89. Adjustment Committee Meeting of Edinburgh, Glasgow and Govan, 21.4.22, in Edinburgh Parish Council Minutes, *op. cit.*; Notes of Deputation Received by Secretary for Scotland (21.2.24), *SRO HH 31.36.2*; Ministry of Labour (26.10.26), Relationship between Disallowance of Unemployment Benefit and Receipt of Poor Relief, *SRO DD 10.192*.

90. Blantyre Parish Council Minutes, 4.5 and 8.6.22, *op. cit.* At the height of the 'gap' in June, despite the cutbacks, the Board recorded 71 000 Scottish unemployed on Poor Relief. The weekly cost was £47 000. The Board's one-day count for January 15th had shown 29 000 (with 72 000 dependants). The weekly cost was then £13 000.

91. Letters of 7.6. and 14.6.22, in Minutes, 6.7.22, *ibid.*

92. Relief of the Able-Bodied (19.7.22), in Edinburgh Parish Council Minutes, 25.9.22, *op. cit.*

93. Relief to Destitute Able-Bodied Unemployed Persons (20.10.22), in Minutes, 6.11.22, *ibid.*; Blantyre Parish Council Minutes, 5.10.22, *op. cit.*; Report, in *Poor Law Magazine 1922*, p.346. The Board's one-day count for the 15th September showed 45 000 unemployed (with 98 000 dependants) on Poor Relief. Even with the reduced scales, the number of 'ordinary' and unemployed Scottish poor stood at 5.3 per cent of the population, compared with 1.5 per cent in 1920. If all had paid the September scale, then this figure would have been over 7 per cent. See, *Annual Report of the Board of Health, 1928. Cmd.3304 (P.P. 1928-9 Vol.VIII)* Appendix XV, pp.358-9.

94. Chapter VI, Survey of Unemployment and its Effects, in *Annual Report of the Board of Health, 1923. Cmd. 2156 (P.P. 1924 Vol. X)* pp.200-1.

95. Minute of Muriel Ritson, Board Member, 1.12.22, *SRO ED 7.7.7.*

96. Govan Parish Council Minutes, 7.12., 22.12.22 and 19.1.23, *op. cit.*

97. Dalziel Parish Council Minutes, 15.12.22, *SRA CO.1 37.6*; Report (16.12.22), in *Glasgow Herald*, p.5.

98. Bill Chamber to Interdict Dalziel Parish (1.2.23) and Reports (13.2. and 7.5.23), in *Glasgow Herald*, pp.7, 3 and 5.

99. Bonhill Parish Council Minutes, 20.10.22, *op. cit.*; Report (28.10.22), in *Lennox Herald*, p.3.

100. Minutes, 19.1. and 26.1.23, *op. cit.*; Inspector's Letter (1.2.23), in Letter Book, *CO.4.12.21.41*; Report (27.1.23), in *Lennox Herald*, p.2.; see also Cabinet Committee on Unemployment, Paper Nos. 503 (29.12.22) and 515 (23.1.23), *PRO CAB 27.193.* Lord Novar had been unable to secure a direct Government grant for parishes. But the Cabinet agreed, confidentially, that if parish administration did break down, loan repayments could either be extended or deferred.

101. Minutes, 23.2.23, *op. cit.*

102. Minutes, 2.3. and 23.3.23, *op. cit.*; Report (3.3.23), in *Lennox Herald*, p.3.

103. Letter of 6.4.23, in Minutes, 20.4.23, *op. cit.*; see also comment of deputation of Labour M Ps to Lord Novar, Scottish Secretary, 18.1.24, on his hard attitude towards 'excessive' relief, *SRO ED 7.7.6.*

104. Minutes, 14.5., 18.5. and 25.5.23, *op. cit.* A surcharge of £255 for the disablty pensions and £176 for the increased maximum was withdrawn by Adamson the following year.
105. Report (30.3.23), in *Clydebank Press*, p.3.
106. Report (1.6.23), in *ibid.*, p.3.
107. Report (3.8.23), in *ibid.*, p.5.
108. Report (25.1.24), in *ibid.*, p.5.
109. Report (4.4.24), in *ibid.*, p.3.
110. Report (31.10.24), in *ibid.*, p.5.
111. Reports (31.7. and 7.8.25), in *ibid.*, pp.5 and 3; Letter of Board on, the Administration of Able-Bodied Relief (15.3.26), Old Kilpatrick Parish Council Minutes, *CO.4.20.34.*
112. *Annual Report, 1923, op. cit.*, p.193; see also, Report by the Scottish Board of Health on Unemployment in Glasgow and the Clyde Area, 14.9.23, *SRO DD 10.363*; and, Scottish Board of Health Report by Drs Dittmar and Cruikshank on the Physical Condition of Children in the Clyde Valley, 30.1.24, *SRO ED 7.7.7.*
113. Govan Parish Council Minutes, 17.3.22, *op. cit.*
114. Board's Letter of 22.3.22, Minutes, 28.3.22, *ibid.*
115. Board's Letter of 5.4.21, Minutes, 10.4.22, *ibid.*; Report (28.4.28), in *Govan Press*, p.1.
116. *SRO SC 36.7.31.*
117. Minute (12.4.22), Industrial Unrest...Parish Councils and Strikers, *SRO HH 56.15.* Both Murray and Constable were Conservatives.
118. Dundee Parish Council Minutes, 25.4.22, *TRA TC.PCM.27.*
119. Minutes, 23.1. and 23.3.23, *ibid. 28.*
120. Douglas Parish Council Minutes, 9.2.25, *SRA CO.1 39.6.*; Reports, *passim* (20.6. to 28.11.25), in *Hamilton Advertiser.*
121. Minutes, *passim* 14.5 to 23.9.25, *op. cit.*
122. Uphall Parish Council Minutes, 18.11., 20.11. and 27.11.25, in *op. cit. 1.1.6.*
123. Report (2.12.25), in *Edinburgh Evening News*, p.8.; see also, Board's Letter (29.11.25), Uphall Parish Council Minutes, 30.11. and Report of Meeting, Minutes, 4.12.25, *op. cit.*
124. Rutherglen Parish Council v Glasgow Parish Council (30.11.24), in *Poor Law Magazine 1925*, pp.3-30.
125. Cabinet Meeting No. 24, *PRO CAB 23.52.*
126. Edinburgh Parish Council Minutes, 17.5.26, *op. cit.*; see also, Poor Relief during the Coal Dispute, in *Annual Report of the Board of Health, 1926. Cmd. 2881 (P.P. 1927 Vol. X.)* pp.332-4. By June some 40,000 families were on relief.
127. Report of Deputation to the Board on 22.5.26, Beath Parish Council Minutes, 25.5., 26.5. and 27.5.26, *op. cit. 6.10.8*; Board's Letter (17.5.26), Culross Parish Council Minutes, *ibid. 6.19.7.*
128. Board's Letter (13.10.27), Culross Parish Council Minutes 18.10.27, *ibid.*; Board's Letter (13.10.27), Beath Parish Council Minutes, 25.10.27, *op. cit..*
129. Report (31.8.26), in *Edinburgh Evening News*, p.7; Letter of Board (19.5.26) in Report (29.5.26), in *Dunfermline Free Press*, p.2.
130. *Poor Law Magazine 1926*, pp.225-8.
131. See Supply Debate (17.6.26), in *Hansard 196 (Fifth Series)* pp.2487-2551; question from Brown, J. (S. Ayrshire) (22.7.26),

in *ibid. 198* pp.1425-6; and Supply Debate (28.7.26), in *ibid.* pp.2134-2236.

132. Board's Letter (8.9.26), Cadder Parish Council, 13.9.26, *SRA CO.1.24.18.*

133. Board's Letter (13.10.26), Leslie Parish Council Minutes, 1.11.26, *FRCR 6.41.7.*

134. Avondale Parish Council Minutes, 5.10.26, *SRA CO.1.20.6.*

135. Cranston Parish Council Minutes, 25.8.26, *Midlothian District Council Records.*

136. Inspector's Letter (23.8.26), Logie Parish Council Minutes, 11.10.26, *Central Regional Archives XA.2.2.3.*

137. Hamilton Parish Council and the 1926 Emergency Loan, *SRO DD 10.242;* Loans from the Committee on Poor Law Authorities, *ibid. 243;* Memorandum by Gilmour, Sir J., on Poor Relief to Miners' Dependants (8.11.26), Cabinet Paper No. 374, *PRO CAB 24.181.*

138. 3 000 Miners Invade Dunfermline (26.6.26), in *Dunfermline Free Press,* p.2.

139. Miners Demand Relief at Bannockburn (19.8.26), in *Stirling Journal,* p.4; St Ninians Parish Council Minutes, 11.8. and 17.8.26, *Central Regional Archives XA.2.1.11.*

140. West Calder Parish Council Minutes, 10.8. and 31.8.26, *West Lothian District Archives 2.1.5.*

141. Cumnock Parish Council Minutes, 12.8. and 2.9.26, *ADA CO.3.52.5;* Auchinleck Parish Council Minutes, 9.9. and 23.9.26, *op. cit. 22.6.*

142. Dalziel Parish Council Minutes, 13.7.26, *SRA CO.1.37.6;* Court of Session, Lord Ordinary, Colville and Sons and others v Dalziel Parish Council (31.7.26), in *Scotsman,* p.7.

143. Poor Law Relief (24.7.26), in *Hamilton Advertiser,* p.6.

144. Parish Councils' Association Conference (2.10.26), in *Scotsman,* p.9.

145. Court of Session Action (16.10.26), in *Hamilton Advertiser,* p.2.

146. David Colville and Sons and Others v Dalziel Parish Council (15.12.26), in *Poor Law Magazine 1927,* pp.1-22.

147. Cabinet Meetings Nos. 57 (10.11.26), 62 (8.12.26) and 66 (17.12.26), *PRO CAB 23.53;* Memorandum by Secretary of State for Scotland on Poor Relief to Miners' Dependants (1.2.27), Cabinet Paper No. 34, and, Memorandum by Chancellor of the Exchequer (9.2.27), Paper No. 44, *PRO CAB 24.184.*

148. Second Reading (22.2.27), in *Hansard, 202 (Fifth Series)* pp.1609-89; see also, Leader (21.2.27), in *Glasgow Herald,* p.10; Conference of Coal, Steel and Iron Masters, in *Poor Law Magazine 1927,* pp.33-6.

149. Evidence of Jeffrey, J., (Secretary, Department of Health) (22.1.31) and Reynard, M. A., (Inspector of Poor, Glasgow) (30.3.31), to *Royal Commission on Unemployment Insurance (Evidence).* (London, 1933).

150. Edinburgh Parish Council Minutes, 10.5.22, *op. cit.*

151. Board of Health Circular on New Emergency Provisions Act (18.5.23), in *Poor Law Magazine 1923,* pp.145-7.

152. Cabinet Paper No. 65, Memorandum by Secretary for Scotland (6.2.24), *PRO CAB 24.164;* see also, *SRO HH 40.128, 130* and *Annual Report of the Board of Health, 1924. Cmd. 2416 (P.P. 1924-5 Vol. XII)* pp.206-8. During 1924, Scottish unemployment

averaged 156 000 (12 per cent), a slight decrease on 1923.
153. *Annual Report of the Board of Health, 1925. Cmd. 2674 (P.P. 1926 Vol. XI)* p.275.
154. Resolutions, Relief, etc., 1925-8, *SRO DD 10.182, 192*; see also Resolutions on Unemployment, 1925, *SRO HH 31.36.2.*
155. See *Annual Report, 1926, op. cit.,* pp.325-31. At the height of the strike 400,000 (8 per cent of the population) were on various forms of relief.
156. Board Notes (22.2.27), Resolutions, Relief, etc. . . , 1927, *SRO DD 10.193.* Some forty parishes had been given loans, totalling £4 000 000, for up to fifteen years. The parishes most indebted were on Clydeside.
157. *Annual Report of the Board of Health, 1927. Cmd. 3112 (P.P. 1928 Vol. X)* pp.328-32; see also Inter-Departmental Committee on Unemployment, 1928, *SRO DD 10.184.* During 1927, Scottish unemployment fell to its lowest inter-war level, 130 000 (10 per cent).
158. Report of General Superintendent of Poor and Mr Henderson (20.4.28), and Reply, Cambuslang Parish Council Minutes, 21.6.28, *SRA CO.1.25.24.*
159. Bonhill Parish Council Minutes, 11.6.28, *SRA CO.2.12.8.*
160. Bothwell Parish Council Minutes, 13.9.28, *SRA CO.1.23.23.*
161. Board's Letter (21.6.28), Blantyre Inspector of Poor's Letter Book, *op.cit.*
162. Blantyre Parish Council Minutes, and passim (3.5 to 1.11.28), *SRA CO.1.22.12.*
163. In May 1922 there were 116 unemployed in Scottish poorhouses and in 1926, 502. Return of Destitute Able-bodied in Poorhouses 1922-30, *SRO HH 40.123-148*; see also *Annual Report, 1924, op. cit.,* p.209.
164. Governor's Annual Report for 1923, Glasgow Parish Council Minutes, 23.1.24, *op. cit.*
165. Strike at Merryflats Poorhouse (3.6.27), in *Govan Press,* p.3.
166. Lennox Castle Relief Works, *SRO DD 10.237*; Glasgow Parish Council Minutes, 28.12.28 and 5.2.29, *op. cit.*; Glasgow Trades Council Minutes, 2.8. to 10.12.29, passim, *Glasgow Mitchell Library.*
167. Glasgow Parish Council Minutes, 3.9.29, *op. cit.*
168. *Annual Report of the Department of Health, 1929. Cmd. 3529 (P.P. 1929-30 Vol. XIV)* pp.168-9.
169. See for instance, Memorandum by the Corporation of Glasgow to the Royal Commission on Unemployment Insurance , Glasgow Corporation Minutes, 23.2.21, *SRA C1.3.*
170. *Annual Report of the Department of Health, 1930. Cmd. 3860 (P.P. 1930-1 Vol. XIV)* pp.157 and 162.
171. Evidence of Anderson, R. (Chief Public Assistance Officer, Lanarkshire) (20.3.31), to *Unemployment Insurance Commission, op. cit.*
172. Inquiry into the Physical condition of Children in Scotland whose Parents have been in receipt of Unemployment or Poor Relief for a prolonged Period, 1930-1, *SRO HH 64.51.*
173. See, Letter from the Department of Health on the Order in Councl Imposing Duty on Local Authority (7.10.31), in Glasgow Corporation Minutes, 9.10.31, *op. cit.*
174. See, Memorandum by Director of Public Assistance on the

Order and Scales of Benefit, and, Memoramdum on Disablity Pensions, in Minutes, 2.11. and 16.11.31, *ibid.*; for comparision of scales, see, Edinburgh Corporation Minutes, 21.11.31, *EPLER YJS.4245A2*. For a typical scale see Appendix 6.
175. Renfrewshire County Council Minutes, 10.10.32, *SRA CO.2.3.1.136*.
176. Fife County Council Minutes, 6.11. and 18.11.31, *FRCR 3.11.1*.
177. Department's Letter (4.1.32), Dunbartonshire County Council Minutes, 8.1.32, *SRA CO.4.3.1.133*.
178. Greenock Town Council Minutes, 26.11 and 10.12.31, *Greenock Public Library*.
179. Report by the Director of Public Assistance in Connection with the Request by the Deputation of Women Members of the ILP that the Corporation petition the Government to abolish the Means Test, Glasgow Corporation Special Report (4.8.32), *SRA D-CC.3.39.1. No.1394*. In July 1932 the reasons given for reduced benefit were as follows: 1. Interest on Capital, 302; 2. Earnings of family living in household, 10 220; 3. Disability pensions, 2 567; 4. Superannuation allowances, annuities, etc., 1 418; 5. Short time employment, 277; 6. Subsidiary occupations, 286; 7. Profit derived from boarders, 2 436; 8. Scale reductions while living with relatives, 6 375; Total, 23 881. In Glasgow all an unemployed claimant's capital above £100, and 75 per cent of part-time and subsidiary occupations were taken into account. The profit from boarders was assumed to be one-sixth of the rent and this too was deducted. For those who lived with relatives, it was assumed they lived rent free and their benefit was reduced accordingly. Disabled pensioners could keep a small percentage of their pension (depending on disability) up to a maximum of 15 shillings a week. All family earnings, apart from work expenses, were taken into account. Relatives of sick and disabled claimants (the 'ordinary poor') were treated differently, see Chapter 8.
180. Municipal Election Reports, October to December 1931-5, *passim*, *Scotsman*, and *Glasgow Herald*.
181. NUWM, 1929-36, *SRO DD 10.245, 246.1, 246.2*; The Control of Unemployment Marches 1933, *ibid. 365*.
182. Letter of Department (22.12.33), Glasgow Corporation Minutes, 15.1.34, *op. cit.*; Relief Scales; 1s. 6d. More (16.1.34), in *Glasgow Herald*, p.3.
183. Minutes, 22.1. and 1.2.34, in *op. cit.*; Report (2.2.34), in *Glasgow Herald*, p.11
184. Minutes, 9.2.34, *op. cit.*; Reports, *passim* (6.2. to 12.2.34), in *Glasgow Herald*.
185. Greenock Town Council Minutes, 1.12. 15.12.33, *op. cit.*; Greenock Relief Increases passed by Corporation. Town Clerk's Opinion that they are Illegal (16.12.33), in *Glasgow Herald*, p.7.
186. Letter of Department, 28.12.33, Minutes, 2.1.34, *op. cit.*; Report (28.12.34), in *Greenock Telegraph*, p.2.
187. Greenock Relief Payments. Bombshell to Labour Members. Court of Inquiry Surprise (13.6.34), in *Glasgow Herald*, p.14; see also Collins's reply to question from R. Buchanan (Labour, Gorbals), in *Hansard 288 (Fifth Series)* p.487. Collins said the Auditor had not provided details of family circumstances and

so could not comment on the payments' legality.
188. Reports of Proceedings, *passim* (3.8. to 11.8.34, in *ibid.* and *Greenock Telegraph*. Dr T. Ferguson, an Assistant Medical Officer at the Department of Health was one of the Sheriff's assessors. He later became Professor of Public Health at Glasgow.
189. Greenock Town Council Minutes, 15.1.35, *op. cit.*; see also, Labour Councillors Vindicated (14.1.35), in *Greenock Telegraph*, p.2; Relief Awards not Illegal (14.1.35), in *Glasgow Herald*, p.11.
190. *Annual Report of the Department of Health, 1935. Cmd. 5123 (P.P. 1935-6 Vol. XI)* pp.144-5.
191. Enquiry into the Physical Condition of Children in Scotland whose Parents have received Unemployment Benefit or Poor Relief, 1934-7, *SRO HH 64.151.*; see also Cabinet Meeting No. 7 (28.2.34), *PRO CAB 23.78*. The first survey was completed by February 1935. Its authors were P.L. McKinley and Dr G. W. Simpson.
192. Minute of Dr T. Ferguson to G. H. Henderson, 29.3.35, in *SRO HH 64.161*.
193. Committee on the Regulations of the UAB, 1934-6, *PRO CAB 27.575*.
194. Especially Statements at Meetings on 11.5., 27.5. and 19.6.36, and, Memorandum by Secretary of State for Scotland (23.6.36), Paper No. 179, *ibid.*

7
PROVIDING HOSPITALS 1914-45

On the day war was declared many of the larger poorhouses were transferred to the military. A year later, the Government froze all new local projects, and further development of Poor Law medical care came to an abrupt halt. After the war, when the poorhouses were eventually returned, the Minority Report's medical-care recommendations had been considerably enhanced by the Maclean Report. It emphasised yet again the basic problem: stigma. In Scotland the result was self-evident. Even in Glasgow, the pre-war showcase of integrated care, the working classes still preferred to join the waiting lists of a voluntary hospital. The voluntary hospitals, with their extensive and extending facilities offered the kind of treatment and services they desired. The problems of maintaining regular financial contributions, the perennial flag days and the innumerable special appeals did little to diminish their overwhelming sense of awe and respect.

Nevertheless, for the voluntary hospital the failure of the Poor Law to develop a complementary service meant even greater pressure on their already stretched resources. By 1914 this problem had alarmed the Board's sister Department, the Health Insurance Commission. Faced with local demands for improved care, the Commission agreed to an inquiry. Its Report, Scotland's first comprehensive review of hospital services, revealed an alarming and worrying picture. The conclusion was stark enough:

> In Scotland with its concentration of specialist skill and large general and specialist hospitals in urban centres situated asymmetrically to the less thickly populated areas dependent upon them, there is normally a lack of accessability to and of adequate accomodation for institutional treatment for other than a simple kind [in the latter areas]. The lack of accomodation in voluntary hospitals is mainly surgical, but it extends to convalescent treatment, epilepsy, neurasthenia, paralysis, chronic affection of the heart of respiratory organs, and incurable diseases generally. Many of the smaller hospitals are ill-equipped with modern appliances and this makes difficult not only treatment but also the early diagnosis of disease. In hospitals controlled by the local authorities, there is a need for more accomodation for TB and infectious diseases.

There is no convincing evidence that the flow of income to voluntary hospitals is diminishing, but it does not grow in sufficient volume even with the flow of funds raised by special appeal, to meet the ever increasing pressure upon accommodation in hospitals situated in the more thickly populated areas. One is struck by the fact that the large general and special hospitals work on the whole independently of one another, and by the casual relation between them and the rural hospitals. There may be difficulty in achieving some joint arrangement where medical and nursing services are run on a voluntary and private basis and under separate management, but the need is clear.[1]

Scotland's hospital provision did not just suffer from the Poor Law, for the Report highlighted other basic inadequacies: an uneven distribution of beds, a lack of comprehensive specialist care, doubt over future financing, no policy to guide development and no system to co-ordinate efforts. So with voluntary hospitals that rarely talked to each other, and pauper ones that had seen better days, the new Board of Health faced a formidable problem. If there was no national policy, inadequate funding and insufficient accomodation, how could its statutory responsiblity – promoting the people's health, their 'personal fitness', as MacKenzie had argued – be achieved?[2]

In contrast to the trouble over unemployment relief, the 1920s witnessed little overt political agitation to rationalise and improve hospital services. Few Labour councillors openly campaigned for a State system. Even James Maxton, the ILP MP for Bridgeton, who was notorious for his outspokeness on social matters, found it hard to advocate radical change. In his evidence to the Hospital Services (Scotland) Committee in 1925, he recognised that although working men often felt annoyed and irritated by the voluntary hospital waiting-list, they also saw them as centres where 'the finest equipment and the most skilful physicians could be obtained' and 'they did not want anything inferior under a public service'.[3] Labour's desire for a State-organised system, he added, could only be brought about by 'the least disturbance possible to the existing agencies'. That meant giving voluntary hospitals three options: nationalisation, receiving some form of grant, or remaining independent. If they chose the last, then the State, through the local authority, should 'fill up the gaps'.

There was little doubt what the voluntary hospitals preferred. Their views were eloquently expressed by an eminent Glasgow surgeon, Sir George Beatson.[4] He fully recognised that times had changed and that hospitals had to reform their financial structure. After all, they were no longer solely providing treatment for the sick poor, but to a wide and growing section of the community who could easily afford a contribution for their care. The way forward was obvious: self help through Hospital Savings Associations. This voluntary system would not only keep out the 'class interference' of compulsory National Insurance, but also protect the public's wider interest, for only if there was medical control could professional dedication be engendered. In the early 1920s, Beatson's views embodied the central problems facing the voluntary hospital, namely: how to obtain a secure income, how to extend treatment to all those in need and how to maintain their professional independence. Change was necessary, but not if it meant State control.

The remainder of this chapter will therefore be devoted to how these issues were resolved, how in fact Scotland's institutional environment, statutory and voluntary, helped finally shape a much more radical solution – one that few during the 'reconstruction' debates would have thought politically feasible. The first part will look at Government policy towards the voluntary movement in the 1920s; the second, what happened within the Poor Law during the same period; the third, at the issues surrounding the 1929 Local Government Reform Act; and the fourth, at the changes within national policy as the Government tried to implement what the reform intended.

After the war the difficulties the voluntary movement faced did not go unnoticed. At the beginning of 1920 the Board, as part of its general review of health administration, established a Consultative Council to report on hospital services.[5] Over the next two years it specially surveyed the Edinburgh area, and concluded that there were 'serious shortages' in accomodation. The voluntary hospitals, it said, with their overstretched finances could not cope with the growing demand for care. The report recommended government assistance and the establishment of a Scottish Commission to co-ordinate the movement's work. At the same time, the Government-sponsored Voluntary Hospital Council (chaired by Lord Onslow) had wound up its post-war disbursement of grants (in aid of service work) and some of its Scottish members also began to argue for a Commission to maintain their interests.[6] So at the end of 1922 the Board found itself undertaking its first serious review of hospital provision. In March Lord Novar, the Scottish Secretary, was informed of its conclusions. Unless voluntary hospitals obtained greater funds to secure additional beds, the Board said, the whole movement faced collapse. A 'formidable body', it added, was in favour of rate-aided hospitals and 'it would become increasingly difficult to prevent this if accomodation was not provided'.[7] Nevertheless the Board would not commit itself on how the extra funds could be generated or how they would be disbursed. All it could suggest, for increased 'efficiency', was greater voluntary co-operation.

The Board's principal difficulty was the unwillingness of the voluntary hospitals to be in any scheme that hinted at 'State management'. But a year later, after much internal deliberation, its views hardened; unless there was some 'machinery' to co-ordinate the voluntary and

Dr R.S. Aitchison and the Medical Staff at Edinburgh Craigleith Poorhouse, c. 1895.

Some Edinburgh Lodging House Men, c. 1908.

Some Glasgow Paupers apprehended for deserting their children, *c.* 1910.

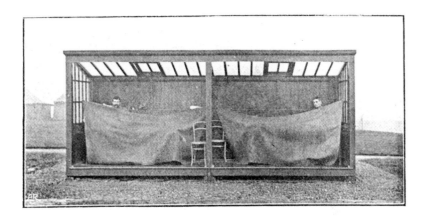

Open Air Shelter for Tuberculosis Patients, Stobhill Hospital, Glasgow, 1905.

Children's Ward, Craiglockhart Poorhouse, Edinburgh 1917.

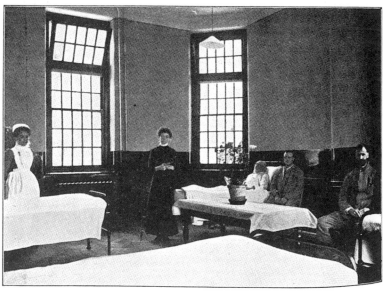

The Male Ward, Eastern District Hospital, Glasgow Parish, 1904.

DEMONSTRATION BY UNEMPLOYED: JOHN M'LEAN ARRESTED

FOR GREENOCK UNEMPLOYED

PORT-GLASGOW SHOP WINDOWS SMASHED AND LOOTED

Edinburgh Parish Council, 1930.

An Unemployed Dundee Family on Poor Relief, 1922.

DISTRESS IN EDINBURGH: DEMANDS BY UNEMPLOYED.

HUNGER MARCHERS ON THE TREK

A STONY COUCH IN PRINCES STREET

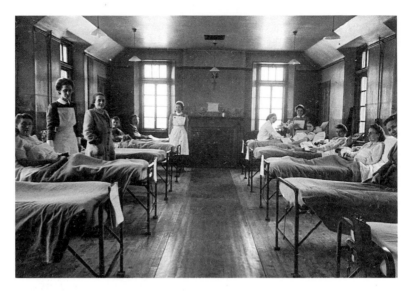

Western District Hospital, Edinburgh, 1943.

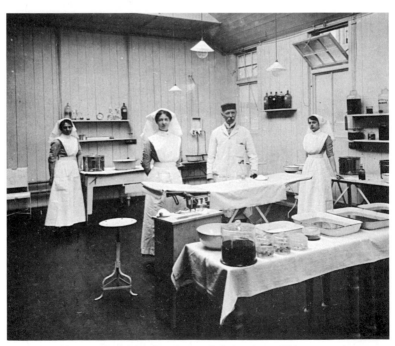

Operating Theatre, Craigleith Poorhouse, Edinburgh, c. 1920.

statutory sectors, the co-operation its Consultative Council had suggested would not occur.[8] There needed to be 'concerted action' and in a Memorandum to Adamson, Labour's Scottish Secretary, it urged a Departmental Inquiry. Adamson agreed and a Committee was established under the chairmanship of Lord Mackenzie 'to enquire into and report upon the extent and nature of the inadequacies of the present hospital and ancillary services in Scotland and to make recommendations for the development and the maintenance of those services to the needs of the community'.

Although the Committee reviewed all aspects of hospital care –Adamson had specifically requested that it did – the emphasis of the review lay with the voluntary movement.[9] In part this no more than reflected the Committee's composition; three quarters came from the voluntary sector. But equally it was a reflection of what it thought was the movement's popular support; any State interference, the Committee suggested, which 'impaired' the movement's 'voluntary character' would be rejected out of hand. So despite reiterating the Maclean recommendations on separating medical care from the Poor Law, and accepting the development of local authority 'general' hospitals, the Report (published in February 1926) argued that the direction of future development should be through the voluntary movement. It concluded: 'Our recommendations are an attempt to formulate a hospital policy for Scotland which will preserve and maintain the voluntary hospital and secure by co-operation all round and not least between the voluntary hospital and the local authority a continuously adequate hospital service.'[10]

The perceived lack of 3 600 hospital beds could be met by extending voluntary provision through a 'once and for all' Government grant (50 per cent of the capital cost).[11] At the same time, to secure the movement's finances, the Report also urged that the National Health Insurance system should make an annual contribution. Many insured workers whose approved society could make a contribution were in fact receiving free treatment. These grants, it was felt, would overcome any deficiency in philanthropy, and maintain the movement's supremacy in the face of a reformed local authority. Finally, to administer the grants and to assist in voluntary and statutory co-ordination, the Report recommended a Scottish Hospital Commission.

The Board was delighted. It noted:

> The solution, according to the Committee does not lie in administrative effort to improve poor law hospitals, for even if the effort succeeded, it would carry the poor law hospitals in a direction that might be inimical to the future development of the hospital service on sound lines. The poor law authorities would move into the position of general hospital authorities, providing a service of the same kind and to the same social class as the voluntary hospital, with a third authority, the local health authority,

providing a service to all classes of the community. This new alignment might make a co-operative policy even more difficult than at present.[12]

and added:

The shortage of general hospital accomodation in Scotland is still a serious gap in the community's organisation against disease and ill-health, and the need for a national hospital policy that will equip Scotland with a reasonably adequate service is no less urgent than it was when the Mackenzie Committee was appointed.

So at the end of 1926 the Board wrote to the Scottish Secretary, Sir John Gilmour, and said, 'we felt that if the Voluntary Hospital problem was not solved then local authorities would feel obliged to build them and that would lead consequently to a deterioration of charity to voluntary hospitals and eventually to a complete State-aided system'.[13] The Board also reiterated the legal position which prohibited local authorities from building general hospitals, and argued that it was a way to save the ratepayer, already hard pressed with funding unemployment relief, a future burden. Unlike the English Ministry of Health, it believed that aid to this sector could be an alternative to reforming Poor Law hospitals: the Scottish voluntary movement, the Board said, was not only held in high public esteem, but was much larger. Gilmour agreed and wrote to his opposite number in the Ministry, Neville Chamberlain, 'I am satisfied that a measure of Government assistance is necessary if my responsiblity for the health of the Scottish people is to be discharged'.

But Chamberlain had other views. Poor Law reform could release beds for acute illnesses and perhaps enable voluntary and public sector co-operation. In the long run, he told Gilmour, it would be cheaper. With the Treasury about to receive the bill for reimbursing parish strike relief, Gilmour reluctantly wrote back to the Board saying the issue could not be pressed – the time was 'not ripe'. The Board's retort that some action was necessary went unheeded.

In early 1927, when again pressed by the Board (which itself had been pressed by the voluntary hospitals) Gilmour re-affirmed his position. The Board was told that, 'the Government was not in a position to make a statement or to bind a future government and while there must be some loss in the development of beds this clearly must be faced'. In less than a year after the publication of the Report, Scottish hospital development was in some disarray. A little later Gilmour was forced to inform a Hospital Association deputation that it was 'now essential' poorhouse medical treatment was brought up to 'modern standards'.[14] Sooner or later he said, they would develop into general hospitals. What had been poorhouse policy?

Although the Board of Health Act did nothing to separate medical care from the Poor Law, the Local Government Board, in its final Report, commented:

> Within its limits, the Poor Law Medical Service is an efficient service; but the new conception of the State's duty in relation to the health of the people as expressed in Acts of Parliament passed in recent years and administered by us and by other Government Departments, has gradually diminished the scope of the Poor Law Service. And further developments that may be expected will not improbably lead to the entire dissociation of the treatment of disease from destitution.[15]

Whatever its view, the new Board still had to administer the Poor Law and by the end of 1922 it found the number of sick in poorhouses had returned to pre-war levels. So early in the following year when its Consultative Council suggested Poor Law hospitals ought to be part of an integrated national service, the Board again sent its medical inspectorate (principally Dr Dewar) to review the standard of care and, if necessary, urge improvement.

The inspectors' reports soon confirmed what previous surveys had indicated; the standard of provision remained well below the voluntary hospital, especially in the smaller and older poorhouse. For instance at Inveresk, (sanctioned accommodation 128) the inspectors reported that the staff included a governor, a nurse, a labour master, two attendants and a visiting medical officer.[16] But with a building of only six wards (two for the sick, male and female) they discovered it was virtually impossible to introduce new medical practices. The Board agreed and commented generally, 'To some of the older Poorhouses, hospital extensions have been made, but. . . while efforts have been made to brighten the sick wards, the structural difficulty remains and prevents any possiblity of keeping pace with advancing medical knowledge and practice'.[17] And on the nature of the care provided, it added:

> It is clear that the medical work of many of the smaller Poorhouses falls far short of the standard reached in respect of precisely similar cases, not only in city infirmaries, but also in the hospital wards attached to the city Poorhouses. It is realised that an elderly patient with a chronic malady may not require medical attention or examination or what might be called 'a visit' more often than once a month or possibly at even longer intervals; but it too frequently happens that these very prolonged cases of illness remain for many months without any re-examination or any attentative revision of their circumstances.

Even a larger and more modern poorhouse like Omoa (Mid-Lanark), with accommodation for over 250, had difficulties. Here not only was there the usual conflict between governor and trained nurses over hospital administration but also the three parishes concerned, Bothwell, Shotts and Cambusnethan, frequently clashed over policy. In one incident Shotts suggested removing the unemployed; it felt that they prohibited hospital development.[18] But the others, wanting to keep some 'test' for their larger outdoor roll, remained uninterested. Despite the Board's insistence on better segregated wards, they attracted few patients.

City poorhouses also had problems. Dundee, a nurse-training school, was one authority the inspectors found consistently refusing to employ extra medical staff; the ratepayer Council told Dewar it was too costly.[19] Only in 1924, when the General Medical Council withdrew its training school recognition (there was not enough surgical work), did the Parish agree to act. An Ear, Nose and Throat Department was quickly established. New visiting surgeons and gynaecologists were also appointed.

Edinburgh's Craiglockhart suffered a similar fate. Additional visiting consultants, resident doctors and radiographers all had to be appointed. But as in Dundee, such moves made little impression and hospital admissions remained constant. Its facilities were still below the more prestigious Royal and other infirmaries. Edinburgh's difficulties did not go without comment, as its Medical Officer reported:

1. There are no wards available for the separation of the foul or offensive cases. These cases have, at present, to be mixed with the ordinary medical and surgical patients. 2. The absence of day-room accomodation for convalescents is a great drawback e.g. (a) of the wards has to be kept higher for patients who are up (b) of convalescents in day-room is more hygenic than by giving meals to them in wards (c) the wards would be less noisy for seriously ill cases and the practice of convalescents wandering indiscriminately through the corridors could be stopped. There are no arm chairs or couches. Replacement of remaining straw mattresses by hair mattresses would be an improvement. Mental observation cases have to be kept in the ordinary wards until they are certified. They disturb all the patients in the ward and are occasionally a source of danger to themselves and to the nurses. 3. operating theatre is suitable and well equipped, the only defect being that it is lit by a centrally placed incandescent gas lamp. Electric lights placed on each side of the operating theatre would be more aseptic and less dangerous when Ether was used as an anaesthetic. 4. The sanitary arrangements of the Poorhouse generally are not good. Manure heaps are in close proximity to the Poorhouse. Flies breed out in great numbers in the summer and are a menace to the health of all the inmates. The slunging of foul linen in the ordinary baths in wards by nurses is to be deprecated.[20]

His conclusion, like that of the Parish's more progressive councillors seemed obvious: no one really wanted to be cured in an institution that mixed all sorts together, could not perform advanced surgery, forced patients to wear coarse drugget, had poor sanitary arrangements, and used inmate labour to serve food and keep the wards clean.

Only Glasgow appeared willing to re-assess its provision. During early 1921, in an attempt to fill some of its vacant beds, approval was sought for admitting paying patients. This the Board refused. It said the proposal was of 'doubtful legality' and added:

> Primarily the Board would require to be satisfied that there is ample accomodation for the ordinary poor entitled to treatment in these hospitals; but as to this they have some dubiety. Further, it is doubtful whether it would be administratively feasible to attempt to treat in one Institution numbers of Poor Law cases and paying patients as complimentary and disciplinary difficulties could quite conceivably arise.[21]

If a claimant applied for treatment and there was not a bed, they could sue the Parish for a failure to provide adequate care. The Board, supported by Munro, the Scottish Secretary, suggested Glasgow improve its medical status. In that way it might attract sufficient numbers of claimants who otherwise looked to the voluntary hospital. After considerable discussion, Glasgow agreed to allow doctors complete control over indoor admissions. This move, together with the appointment of more consultant and resident staff and an extension of medical facilities, did actually increase the number of sick seeking admission.[22] Stigma could be overcome, but at a price.

Thus apart from Glasgow, the early 1920s saw little real effort to rid poorhouses of 19th century philosophy and practice. Indeed, the major influence on development was not the parishes or the Board, but the General Medical Council who, by answering wider changes in medical practice, wanted its nurses trained in the more advanced aspects of care. The Board's own position seemed contradictory: on the one hand it argued poorhouses should have better medical services, but on the other accepted their use to control the unemployed.[23]

The Board in 1927 began to recognise the contradiction and acknowledged that there was widespread 'disquiet' over poorhouse medical services. It stated: 'the divergence between the best and the least good is indefensibly great; and in respect of a number of the poorhouses of middle size, the principles of equality of standard with the voluntary hospitals should, without delay, be carried into practical effect.'[24] The only way forward, the Board suggested, was for the full implementation of the Poor Law Commission's recommendation: poverty should cease to be the 'essential factor' in determining an applicant's case; all that mattered was medical need. Parish development of hospital care had failed; it was simply not feasible under the existing philosophy, or system of local government, or indeed, with the nature of central control.

The reform of local government had been a smouldering issue since the Poor Law Commission. The Maclean Report revealed over 1,300 units of public administration, and provided ammunition for those who believed 'progressive' services could only come through amalgamation and simplification. But Scottish opinion had never been entirely happy with the way the Maclean Report had resulted in the Board of Health, and to offset the criticism that English circumstances had led to Scottish reform, Munro established a Consultative Council (in 1920) to review local health administration. It too reported in favour of 'sweeping' reform.[25] The parish, it said, should be abolished and its functions transferred to the county and those burghs with a population over 50 000. These new authorities should control public health. This in fact was the unofficial view of the Board and the Scottish Office; their hospital policy already encouraged burghs under 50 000 to combine.[26] So despite a vigorous parish defence of 'ad hoc' welfare services, the Conservative Government accepted that some action was necessary. Addressing a medical audience in 1925, Gilmour stressed the need for the local authority to become much more involved in the co-ordination and planning of administrative tasks.[27] His view, like Chamberlain's (the Minister of Health), was that each area should have sufficient rateable power to sustain development. Resources could then be pooled, with larger, more efficient hopsitals replacing many of those that were too small and isolated. If this were to occur, a much broader perspective on local government might actually overcome parochial (and hence Poor Law) backwardness. The necessity for some action became even greater when the Board's final Report acknowledged its years had not been a success – 'more could undoubtably have been achieved'. Mass unemployment combined with financial restriction had undermined its statutory responsibility, that of promoting health.[28]

But Government had another problem, to reconcile the public's demand for better welfare with their own Conservative ideology of slow but continuous change. To abolish the parish, as Walter Elliot noted, 'would disturb one of the foundation stones of Scottish society', one he accepted had stood it in good stead for a considerable period.[29] Moreover, both he and Gilmour acknowledged that too drastic a reform might lead to an expectation of greater statutory involvement, at the expense of those forces so applauded by Conservatives; self-help, mutually generated aid and private property.[30] In consequence Gilmour decided to tread a cautious path. His Local Government Bill proposed to abolish parish councils and transfer their functions to the county and the burgh. But unlike the English Bill, it made no reference to the provision of hospital services. Further, to offset some likely criticism about the destruction of local tradition, he decided to over-rule his Scottish Office advisers. They had wanted the minumum size of public health and assistance authorities to be 50 000; he choose 20 000.[31] It meant three authorities rather than one in Fife, Ayrshire and Dunbarton and six instead of two in Lanarkshire.

Opening the Commons debate, Gilmour summed up the rationale for reform by saying, 'the [existing] administrative areas are too small to discharge their duties efficiently or to justify a separate organisation for the great major services with which we have to deal in these times.'[32] Labour remained hostile, attacking both his destruction of local government democracy and the failure to abolish the Poor Law. Outside Parliament, local authority reception was equally cool and a petition, organised from Glasgow, was sent seeking the mandatory development of public hospitals.[33] Matters soon became heated for the voluntary lobby was aghast. A counter petition was quickly lodged.[34] Public hospitals, they said, meant a new welfare ideology which threatened not only their financial solvency but also their independence. The clause was only acceptable if it included an obligation to seek local voluntary agreement. Gilmour sympathised and told the local authorities that while he was not 'unfriendly' to their suggestion, his Bill was essentially aimed at political and not social reform. Concerned not to generate new demands for Government grants, all he was prepared to offer was the possiblity of 'experimental' action. With the voluntary hospitals perturbed even at this, Gilmour refused any further concessions. Thus a new clause, twenty-seven, was inserted. It allowed the reorganisation of local medical services and for the building of general hospitals, all under Public Health control. But this could only happen if the Department was satisfied the need was not being met by voluntary hospitals. Moreover local authorities, in drawing up a new scheme, had to secure the area's voluntary hospital co-operation.

Explaining this departure in policy, Gilmour told the Commons:

one of the greatest difficulties which anybody in dealing with this problem has to keep in mind is the relative balance between the position of the Voluntary Hospitals and the Voluntary Services and the services which may be created by the Local Authority. . . They [the opposition] would make a very great mistake indeed if they endeavoured, certainly under present conditions, to impose definitely upon a Local Authority a task of which they have no conception and as to which they are not in a position to judge whether the Local Authority can reasonably and fairly undertake.[35]

For Gilmour his Bill represented an advance; there was now a way to 'break-up' the Poor Law.

Labour were not satisfied. Because the Act would allow 'reasonable charges' for hospital treatment, a new 'means test' would be born, one alien to Scottish traditions. Instead of diminishing Poor Law doctrines, Labour said, the Government were merely transplanting it to another, previously unsullied local service, the Public Health Authority. Moreover, the Act was not mandatory, so there was no certainty that a coherent, rational and nationwide service would develop. As Maxton argued, the abolition of parish councils did not mean the abolition of poverty, and assessing poverty still came before meeting medical needs.

Almost immediately the Act was passed, the Department began to ask local authorities to review their medical services.[36] Special attention was to be paid to hospital accomodation. By 1932 the Department itself had conducted another national survey and made detailed recommendations on its improvement. Although voluntary hospitals were reassured about their 'pivotal' role, the Department stressed that the 1929 Act had at last brought a coherent structure to the previously unrelated Public Health, Poor Law and Educational Welfare services.[37] Its Chief Medical Officer left medical audiences in no doubt that past failures could now give way to co-operation, with the Local Authority initiating change.

The Department soon realised that it faced three particular problems. First, the acute shortages of accomodation – in Fife, Lanarkshire, Ayrshire and Renfrewshire the existing accommodation was only 50 per cent of perceived needs – meant it would be legally difficult for many authorities to convert their poorhouses into general hospitals.[38] If Poor Law claimants were left in the queue for treatment, their position would be worsened and the Authority might be open to prosecution. Second, there were many authorities who by themselves could not finance any new capital development. Even if they abandoned traditional poorhouse philosophy, they would still have to combine with others in selecting a site and deciding their own contributions. Thirdly, the Department would have to generate and sustain the willingness of voluntary hospitals to agree to rate-aided general hospitals in their area, hospitals which might draw away patients and contributions. Each of these problems can be looked at in turn through the experiences of Glasgow, the six Lanarkshire authorities and Greenock.

Glasgow illustrates the first problem, converting Poor Law institutions into general hospitals. Under the new administrative scheme, all hospital care came under the control of the local medical officer of health. However until the local authority implemented Section 27, the patients of existing Poor Law institutions were still classified as Poor Relief recipients. Their names, settlement, family income and liable relatives all had to be entered into the poor roll, the same as any other claimant. Thus, although the two district and one general hospital of the old Glasgow Parish were transferred to the administrative control of the Public Health Department, its patients came from the Public Assistance Department.

By early 1931 Glasgow had drafted a scheme but it soon became apparent that implementation was not going to be easy. The voluntary hospitals had huge waiting lists and the Poor Law was itself receiving growing numbers of legally entitled applicants seeking an alternative source of care. As the Corporation stated:

The hospitals must take charge of those who are considered

beyond the scope of the voluntary hospital, and consequently admit large numbers who are not in actual need of continuous skilled nursing and who require only intermittent medical attention. The greater part of [our work therefore] is concerned with pregnancy, insanity, respiratory diseases – both acute and chronic – apoplexy, malignant disease, senility, cardiac disease, and diseases of the skin and subcutaneous tissues. With the exception of pregancy, the age incidence of patients is well over the middle period of life, as one would expect. In 1933 [with over 26,000 admissions] the average duration of stay was 44.55 days, but in certain groups the period of stay was very much longer; for example, non-pulmonory tuberculosis averaged 135 days, syphilis of the central nervous system 160 days, and post-encephalitis lethargica 500 days. As regards particular groups of affections, a ward is set apart at Stobhill and at the Southern General for patients with advanced tuberculosis, some 436 cases, of whom about 40 per cent died in hospital. Cases of senility occupy a relatively large amount of accomodation, some 523 cases, their average duration of residence being 71 days. Diseases of the central nervous system, 1,805 cases, have a high frequency and include neurosyphilis and general paralysis of the insane admitted for malaria therapy. The majority are of cerebral haemorrhage, etc., with a fatality of about 50 per cent. Diseases of the circulatory system accounted for 1,352 cases, chiefly valvular disease of the heart, which had a case mortality of 35.6 per cent.[39]

Thus the hospitals had accumulated two distinct types of patient: large numbers of chronically sick, for which there was no alternative provision, and in response to its own campaign, many more expectant mothers. Nearly half of the available beds had to be reserved for these two groups alone. As the Corporation further explained: 'while home conditions, indifferent housing, poverty and ignorance must be determining factors in regard to hospital treatment, the provision of institutions is a costly way of treating conditions which do not of themselves require hospital treatment'. In consequence, there could be little scope for developing surgical care, no matter what the need.

Its draft scheme therefore depended on extra accommodation and a reorganised G P service. Only then could a more rational administrative system develop which, while extending surgical facilities, would permit more specialised assistance for elderly, the chronically sick and the child. Glasgow's right-wing ruling party stalled on the cost and it was not until Labour entered office at the end of 1933 that development began. Within two months the old Renfrew Poorhouse at Crookston had been converted into an old people's home. Over the next few years new detached homes for the elderly were built, five hundred extra beds at the Southern General created, inmate labour abolished and Barnhill provided with extra medical staff.[40] By 1941 all the administrative arrangements had been completed and Section 27 was duly implemented.

In Lanarkshire the Department was faced with another problem, inducing local authority co-operation. The Act had produced six authorities – one county council and six burghs – and each controlled their own provision for infectious diseases, TB, child welfare and Poor Relief. In all there were thirty-three public institutions.[41] As each authority had both a Public Assistance and a Health Committee, it meant that the county, which also had twenty voluntary hospitals, was served by well over forty bodies – all separately pledged to provide institutional care.

The Department's survey of medical provision, published in 1932, was not complimentary.[42] It commented that only Motherwell had a poorhouse with any potential for development, as an outbuilding for the nearby Burgh Hospital. The others were either too poorly sited, small, or inadequately constructed. Airdrie's was one of the most appalling its medical officers had ever seen, housing its sick poor in an attic. The public health hospitals were not much better: Carluke and Shotts had no operating or X-ray facility, and Stonehouse had ninety-six TB patients in a building licenced for just fifty-four.

At a series of local conferences the previous year the Department's Chief Medical Officer of Health had already decided action was necessary. He told the County and Burgh Councils that because 'hospitals now needed elaborate equipment and specialisation', local authorities on their own could not provide the necessary services.[43] Co-operation was essential and the Department, he added, would not allow any of the existing authorities to develop by themselves. He urged a new general hospital. The county agreed but the burghs, distrustful of the county's motives, remained doubtful. Motherwell was the most unwilling of the five and decided to promote its own provision, a new block for the sick poor at its poorhouse, not as part of the 1929 Act, but under the Poor Law.

By the beginning of 1935 Motherwell's plans had reached an advanced stage and despite the burgh having changed control to Labour, they approached the Department for approval. This it refused. The burgh was told that the Department's 'conviction remained unshaken', Motherwell 'should not prejudice the District's ordinary development of hospital services'. If the poorhouse was overcrowded, then it should transfer some of the less infirm to either Hamilton or Omoa, both of which had vacant accomodation. The Department wanted the sick 'out of the poorhouse'. The burgh was not happy and again approached the Department to review its case. After a further conference, the Department summed up its position and what it saw as the county's problem:

The existing hospital system, or group of systems, viewed in the light of modern conditions and requirements, shows needless duplication and overlapping, multiplication of small, relatively costly institutions, wide discrepancy of standards and generally, the anomalies that might be expected to arise in a service founded by a large number of independent bodies acting for the most part in isolation from each other.

. . . Hospital provision for the sick poor. . . should, the Department are convinced, satisfy two main conditions: to secure maximum efficiency it should be so planned and staffed as to make available all the resources of modern medicince: and to secure economy and avoid duplication it should be capable of development to serve the needs, not of the patients of one authority only, but all patients in the area for whom such a hospital may be required.[44]

The case against poorhouse development, the Department privately minuted, 'was unanswerable' – even if there were 'political trouble'.[45]

Motherwell remained adamant. All it wanted was to move the sick into 'more commodious' buildings. The Department, it said, was being 'unreasonable'. But the council also raised two other objections to the county's scheme. First, there was no evidence that people in the town had turned against the voluntary movement, and although the council accepted subscriptions had fallen, it thought this was temporary. Second, it was illusory to believe medical treatment was of any benefit to the aged and infirm, the bulk of those in the poorhouse. At best they had a condition 'which could only be alleviated and not cured'. It was a problem of public assistance, not health.

Departmental frustration grew. Here was a burgh that dissented from its accepted view of health care. Not only did the Department feel that many chronically ill could respond to curative care, it also felt they required greater care than most poorhouses offered. A Special Areas grant was held out as 'bait', and although the other burghs agreed to participate in a 400-bed County Hospital, Motherwell still refused. At the end of 1936, the Department was forced to minute that the burgh 'did not appreciate the best interests of its population'.[46] By 1939, with costs rising above £1 000 000, the others also began to have serious doubts and when war broke out the scheme was abandoned.

Greenock's problem represented the last of the Department's difficulties – securing the co-operation of voluntary hospitals. Although Greenock's slums were on a smaller scale to Glasgow's, it had perhaps the worst record of public health in Scotland. The damp climate combined with a northerly exposure for most of its housing meant that TB, pneumonia and bronchitis were endemic. To combat this the town had a Royal Infirmary with 200 beds, a Public Health Hospital with 120 beds and, for sick paupers, a poorhouse with accomodation for another hundred patients. The town's institutional deficiencies had been recognised, and in 1930 after much deliberation, the Infirmary added a new auxiliary hospital at a cost of £60 000.[47] Half of its forty beds were for paying patients. owever the Hospital did not boast a high medical reputation. Until the late 1930s, when a number of specialists were appointed, most of the work was done by local GPs. With the onslaught of the depression, many, including the Department, doubted the move into paybeds would yield an economic return. Nevertheless its Management Committee, with an usually large number of workmen's representatives, enjoyed considerable support. Its Saturday Fund alone attracted over £6 000 a year, mainly from the local working class.

The poorhouse too, was not noted for its medical care. Not only was it mixed, but it was also one of the few still to have licensed wards for the mentally insane. The hospital accomodation for men was described in detail by one Departmental inspection:

Ward 1, 20 beds. At one end are two ward annexes. The one contains a single water-closet in one apartment and a sink in the other. There is no slunge, and bedpans have to be cleaned in the open sink and stored in the same apartment. In the other annexe are a bath and two wash-basins. Most of the patients are able to get up, and some use the common bathroom. A number (probably about twenty per cent) are incontinent or dirty in their habits, and it is obviously a herculean task to keep the water-closet in a decent condition. The ward has one open fire and a protected central radiator. The beds are about six feet apart, between centres; Ward 2, has fourteen beds. The sanitary offices consist of one water-closet and a sink but no slunge, and on the other side an old tin bath; Ward 3. This is a six bed ward with an open fire but no central heating. The sanitary arrangements are similar to Wards 1 and 2, viz. one water-closet, surrounds of which are very damp: a sink and an old fashioned bath. This ward contains out-patients only, most of whom are able to look after themselves and go to the common bathroom; Ward 4, is identical. Patients are mostly up but in both wards there are a number of dirty patients who give a good deal of trouble, and the somewhat defective sanitary arrangements accentuate the difficulties in looking after them. In addition there is a single-bed unit with a separate water-closet and old fashioned bath which is used for the treatment of bad cases, e.g. cancer. The unit is not very satisfactory, as free ventilation is difficult. On the opposite side of the corridor a similar room is used for special treatment, including ultra-violet light. The general bathroom for males is on the ground floor opposite the theatre. This dismal old single-storey room has a central radiator and eight old porcelain baths, many of which are cracked. The floor is tiled. There is one water-closet at the end of the room. As an overflow three rooms have been taken over in the main 'poorhouse' block. On the north side is an 'infirm' ward of eight beds. This room has no sanitary conveniences apart from the 'house'. The ward is intended for aged infirm males. With regard to the fabric, we are aware that dry rot has been prevalent and that it is impossible to get at the fungus in the joints of the stonework. We believe that dry rot is still present in the dining rooms and we expect that the plaster work on the walls and ceilings will have to be entirely removed to deal with it.[48]

Other inspections revealed the widespread use of inmate labour, defective operating equipment (the resident refused to perform all but the most simple of tasks) and the continued fear of internally spread epidemics. With a northerly exposure, little sunlight and gross overcrowding – expectant mothers were frequently placed in sick wards – few disagreed with its label as the country's worst poorhouse.

The Department's first attempt to rationalise the area's hospital accommodation immediately incurred the council's opposition. But unlike the Lanarkshire burghs, who principally feared the loss of autonomy, Greenock also had ideological objections. The ruling right-wing Moderate Party was adamant that the townsfolk should look towards the Infirmary for treatment, and provide it with funds. The poorhouse, the Department was told, was simply a home for the aged, the infirm and the 'wanton' mother. Anyway, with the depression gathering pace, the group's immediate concern remained reducing the rates. Discussion was not resumed until 1934 when the new Labour administration, faced with even greater overcrowding, sought the Department's advice. The Department, after hearing privately from the local Medical Officer of Health that what was really required was a new general hospital, suggested that this was what they should consider. A Special Areas grant of 50 per cent of the capital cost was again held out as bait.

By early 1936, the Council had drawn up plans for a 140-bed hospital. Although twenty beds for general provision had been included, it had been specifically designed for the non-pauper chronically ill. Greenock told the Department it would 'fill a gap in the local social services'. The Department greeted the proposal with satisfaction and commented, 'the scheme now put forward may be regarded as a reasonable attempt on the part of the Local Authority to make such hopsital provision as is immediately necessary in the interests of the general health'.[49] However the Infirmary managers, sensing the possibility of a rival, began to raise objections. The Department tried to reassure them, stating that the scheme was no more than what 'was reasonably required for orderly flexiblity of administration' and underlined this by saying, 'it certainly affords no grounds for apprehension that what may be described as "poaching on the preserves" of the Infirmary is contemplated'.[50] They were not reassured, replying that the Infirmary had virtually no waiting

list and that the extra twenty beds were 'quite without present necessity'. Pleas that the Infirmary did not provide a service for many acute
areas, like orthopaedics, failed to change their mind.

The Department soon encountered a more serious problem. In
November 1937 the council swung back to Moderate control. With their
eyes still firmly on the rates, the Infirmary's managers were invited to
make further comment. In fact the Moderates had come under intense
Infirmary pressure, and by March the Department became seriously
alarmed. A few weeks later the managers formally announced their
opposition, stating they themselves intended further expansion. Faced
with such open hostility, the Department was forced to reconsider its
policy. Previously it had tried to be even-handed, stressing that its
primary aim was not to encroach on voluntary interests, but to end the
mixed poorhouse. Where new local authority hospitals were to be built,
its policy had been to ensure they would no more than complement
existing voluntary institutions. Now in Greenock a voluntary hospital
was not prepared to accept the rationale behind Section 27; tradition,
independence and financial solvency all told against co-operation. The
Department recognised the issue's wider implications. It minuted:

> There may be grounds for the fear of the voluntary hospital that
> the advent of the local authorities in the general hospital field is
> the beginning of the end for them, but even if there be this danger,
> it must be faced as inescapable and the best possible arrangements
> made to maintain their claims on public generousity and gratitude
> for services provided.[51]

In Greenock, the voluntary movement had singularly failed to provide
for local needs.

A month later the Council withdrew the scheme, and development
came to a temporary halt. Although the Department expressed regret,
it was in fact holding back: the November elections, it thought, might
see a swing to Labour. To maintain the pressure, the Chief Medical
Officer of Health, along with the Department's Architect, conducted
another inquiry. Like others before him, Dr Mackintosh was appalled
by the poorhouse, believing that even the chronically sick could not
acquire proper medical attention. Labour did regain control, and to
assist them further the Scottish Secretary, John Colville, reiterated the
Government's belief in the development of local authority hospitals.
An audience of voluntary managers was told that while their hospitals
were 'the national expression of the spirit of liberty', it would be a 'bad
mistake' if they refused local authority co-operation.[52] But at Greenock
one of the Labour councillors, under heavy pressure from workman's
representatives, switched sides, and with only a one-seat majority the
scheme failed.

With the sheer density of Poor Law medical needs, with the unwillingness of local authorities to combine, and with voluntary hospitals refus-

ing to agree to general hospitals, Gilmour's 'experimental' Section 27 had floundered. By 1939 only Aberdeen, Bute and Edinburgh had adopted the section and of these only Edinburgh's conversion of Craigleith into the Western was deemed a success. Permissive powers and the traditional tool of Scottish government, administrative action had, led neither to the abandonment of the Poor Law nor to the meeting of medical need.

The early difficulties to initiate greater statutory and voluntary co-operation had led the Department to commisison another Report by its Consultative Council.[53] But like the Mackenzie Committee, although re-iterating the Maclean recommendations, it too was dominated by the voluntary movement. It still held the belief that voluntary hospitals should occupy the central role in any reorganisation of services. But unlike Mackenzie, the Council recognised that the voluntary movement would have to alter its own finances. he legal restrictions on charging patients, it said, should be removed – many Scottish hospitals had charters which specifically prohibited 'paying' patients. Any discussion on the recommendations, however, was soon overtaken by events. Another Committee, this time on local government expenditure, reported that in order to achieve economy, there ought to be greater co-ordination of services.[54] A more exhaustive inquiry into health care was urged. Collins, the Scottish Secretary, concerned that the 'expected' improvement in health had not occurred, agreed and in June 1933 he announced the establishment of a Scottish Health Services Committee.[55] Its aim was to review the existing services and make recommendations on any policy thought necessary for the 'promotion of efficiency and economy'.

The Committee soon found many of its witnesses were advocating greater statutory involvement. The BMA were emphatic on this need, stating quite openly that 'the community in its corporate capacity must assume a part of the burden if the minimum reqirements are to be met'[56] Faced with this and evidence on inadequate health provision, the Commmittee in its conclusions stressed:

> The existing health services are not fully adapted to modern conditions and outlook, and it is inherent in their more or less haphazard and sectional growth that they do not constitute a national health policy. The first essential is to integrate the separate services into a national health policy. The general aim of this policy should be to promote the fitness of the people.[57]

It indicated that the voluntary hospitals, given their precarious financial position, should play a less pivotol role. Instead the Report that recommended the local authority assume a definite obligation to provide for all types of hospital care, and that the Department increase its control, whether it was statutory or voluntary provision. It was suggested that this might be acceptable if the voluntary movement secured a reasonable guarantee over their future status. What exactly these controls and guarantees would be, however, was not fully discussed. Despite this, the Report did serve one useful purpose: increased statutory involvement was legitimate.

Medical reaction was almost uniformly positive. The BMA applauded its recommendation and called for immediate legislation.[58] A group of Edinburgh surgeons also welcomed it. One, although unsure about the prospect of greater departmental direction, commented, 'but I recognise that it is inevitable and I suppose, viewed in its widest sense, beneficial'.[59] In 1938, armed with this Report and faced with the complete failure of Section 27, the Department approached the prospect of war with some anxiety: how could Scotland's hospitals cope with the expected bombing raids, gas warfare and troop casualties? How in fact were new hospitals to be built? On the one hand, it recognised local authorities were too numerous and in most cases too small for quick and effective action. On the other, voluntary hospitals admitted that there was little they could do. Indeed if anything, given their financial problems, many in the movement felt that the Government ought to help them.[60]

With no faith in 'municipal arrangements', and voluntary hospitals facing bankruptcy, all the Government could do was to authorise the Department to build and maintain the necessary emergency hospitals.[61] Six were eventually built, all from scratch, with four sited at or near shortage areas. Many other hospitals and asylums were extended by grants. This policy of State-managed hospitals was in contrast to England, where the Ministry of Health allowed local authorities full control.

Once the hospitals had been built, it was not long before consideration was given to the eventual post-war system of administration. In early 1941 Labour's Joe Westwood, the Under Secretary of State, suggested the possiblity of a free medical service, with all hospitals under some regional control.[62] The Department, severely pressed by war-time demands and low staff morale (it had just lost its Chief MOH), felt it was not the right time for an enquiry. The Scottish Secretary, Ernest Brown, a National Liberal, agreed. But within three months, and unknown to the political secretariat, a Departmental 'office' committee was established to consider the whole post-war system.[63] G. H. Henderson, an Assistant Secretary and the Committee's Chairman, noted in his opening memorandum:

> Unless destruction of hospitals through enemy attack is on a scale which we have not yet contemplated, we shall find ourselves after the war with sufficient beds to meet all the estimated needs for hospital treatment in Scotland. The new hospital units that have been built for EMS purposes will, with proper care to maintenance, serve for some twenty years. They are sited in areas where the need for hospital beds is greatest. The problems [now] are to find the best methods of integrating the hospital service and of financ-

ing it. We must firmly establish the principle – without heed to the squealing of those whose corns are trod on – that the voluntary hospitals must co-operate with the local authorities and the local authorities with each other. That is essential if economy and efficiency are both to be secured not only of expenditure but of medical and surgical personnel. The general principle broadly outlined. . . involves a regional organisation and is in line with policy which was being slowly, though with great difficulty, developed before the war. The increasingly precarious position of most voluntary hospitals will help to make the transition easier.[64]

After some considerable discussion of the issues, the Committee agreed that the long-term solution to the country's poor health record was a free health service. But it recognised that tradition, local democracy and possible post-war revulsion from State control would probably preclude discussion of such a service. Instead the Committee suggested that future policy should be based on four principles: an extended insurance system; a continuance of grants for voluntary hospitals; a statutory responsiblity on local authorities to develop facilities where need had not been met; and regional boards to co-ordinate development. But equally importantly, it argued that any re-organised system should have a new philosophy: treatment without 'fear of poverty'. The Committee's Report was welcomed by the new Scottish Secretary, Labour's Tom Johnston.[65] But he was less cautious about the Government maintaining control over the emergency system. These new hospitals, he suggested, although sited in areas of greatest medical need had not exhausted all the Department's 'objectives'. Their development could not only ease future 'pressure points', but also ensure that Scotland retained its position as a medical 'pioneer'. He envisaged establishing something similar to the Scottish Special Housing Association. To assist this, he agreed to another Hospital Committee and the Principal of Glasgow University, Sir H. J. W. Hetherington, a distinguished medical scientist, was appointed its Chairman.

Unfortunately for Johnston, Hetherington refused to consider the possiblity of any State involvement. His Committee stuck rigidly to a voluntary and local authority division in the provision of care. Five regional boards, composed of equal representatives from the two sectors, would manage the post-war system. Johnston, on hearing the Committee's likely proposals, immediately wrote to Hetherington and told him that in his view any abandonment of the Emergency Service 'would be regarded as disastrous'.[66] Hetherington refused to accept the proposition, arguing that a 'Public Corporation' would cut across the whole basis of his Committee's calculations.[67] But so appalled was Johnston that he ordered the Committee's Report be given only minor consideration. Instead he proposed to his newly created Secretary of State's Council on Post-War Problems that the State should continue to manage the Emergency Hospital Programme. Despite the other members, past Secretaries of State, being either Conservative or Liberal, they agreed.[68]

Thus by the middle of the war, Scottish hospital policy was looking to the government to undertake three things: grants for voluntary hospitals; the control of all development; and the building and maintaining of State hospitals. The political debate over voluntarism, public sector stigma and local accountability had been resolved. It was a complete reversal of Scottish tradition. The pursuit of the people's health – their 'personal fitness' – over-ruled other considerations.

NOTES

1. *Report on the Hospital and Nursing Services in Scotland. Cmd. 699 (PP 1920 Vol. XXII)* pp.26-7. The survey was completed in 1917.

2. See, MacKenzie, W. L. (1921), The Production of Fitness, in *Journal of the Royal Sanitary Institute XLII*, pp.11-17. (Presidential Address to the Society's Annual Congress); (1924), The Problem of Fitness, in *Glasgow Medical Journal 101*, pp.192-7; (1925), The Problem of Psycho-Physical Fitness, in *Journal of the Royal Sanitary Institute XLVI*, pp.72-86. (Lecture addressed to the Society's Annual Congress.)

3. *British Medical Journal 1925(1)*, p.280.

4. Quoted in, A Maintenance System for Scottish Hospitals, in *ibid. 1923(1)*, p.532.

5. See, *Poor Law Magazine 1920*, p.104; see also, The Interim Report of the Scottish Consultative Council on Medical and Allied Services, *A Scheme of Medical Service for Scotland. Cmd. 1039 (P.P. Vol. XXX 1921)*.

6. Voluntary Hospital Commission: Proposed Scottish Consulative Commission, *SRO HH 65.49*.

7. Submission of Board on Health Services in Scotland, 8.3.23, in *SRO HH 65.49*. In 1923 the annual income of Scottish hospitals was £1.1 million. 21 per cent came from investments, 5 per cent from fees, 47 per cent from legacies and 18 per cent. from subscriptions. By 1937 these figures were £2 million, 20, 25, 24 and 21. In England in 1937, the percentage figures were, 12, 45, 11 and 24.

8. Submission of Board to the President 4.4.24, in Voluntary Hospital Commission: Grants, *SRO HH 65.50*; see also, *Annual Report, 1923, op. cit.*, p.15; and *Annual Report, 1924, op. cit.*, p.16.

9. *British Medical Journal 1924(1)*, p.1151. It had five doctors, three infirmary managers, two insurance committee members, two public health officials, a BMA representative and one from the Labour Housing Association, J. Waugh; evidence reported in *ibid. 1925(1)*, pp.136-317 and *passim*. Mackenzie, a retired Court of Session judge, had been a Unionist Parliamentary candidate.

10. *The Report on the Hospital Services of Scotland, 1926. (Edinburgh, 1926)* A Minority Report was signed by Waugh stating the voluntary movement had failed and that 'the State should recognise its duty'. For the favourable press comment, see Leader (8.2.26), *Scotsman*, p.7.

11. 600 of this total were in fact allocated for local authority maternity and child welfare work. It also recommended an unspecified increase in local authority beds for TB, measles, whooping-cough and pneumonia.
12. Chapter VIII, The Hospitals, in *Annual Report, 1926, op. cit.,* pp.154-8.
13. Departmental Committee on Hospital Services, *SRO HH 65.51.*
14. Comment at meeting with the Scottish Regional Committee of the British Hospitals Association, 9.12.27, *ibid.*; see also, Chapter VII, Co-operation in the Scottish Hospital Service, in *Annual Report, 1927, op. cit.,* pp.145-7. All the Government would concede was a relaxation of its curb on local authority maternity schemes.
15. *Annual Report of the Local Government Board, 1919. Cmd. 824 (P.P. 1920 Vol. XXI)* pp.vii-viii.
16. Inveresk Combination Poorhouse Minutes, 15.11.18 to 31.4.24 and *passim., SRO C.O. 97.1*; see also, *Annual Report, 1923, op. cit.,* pp.160-1.
17. See discussion on poorhouses, *Annual Report, 1924, op. cit.,* pp.187-90.
18. Omoa Combination Poorhouse Minutes, 17.5.23, *SRA CO1.23.51.*
19. Medical Services; Dundee East Poorhouse, *SRO HH 60.65*; Dundee Parish Council Minutes, 18.10.23 and 19.2.25, *TRA TC.PCM.28, 30.*
20. Medical Officer's Annual Report, 1923-4, Edinburgh Parish Council Minutes, 3.3.24, *op. cit..*
21. Board's Letter, in Glasgow Parish Council Minutes, 24.3.21; see also Reynard, M. A. Inspector of Poor, Memorandum on the Classification of Indoor Sane Poor, Minutes, 21.2.22, *op. cit.* and *Annual Report, 1921, op cit.,* p.188.
22. Evidence of Reynard M. A., Inspector of Poor, to Hospital Services Committee (7.2.25), in *British Medical Journal 1925(1),* p.281 and to (30.6.25) *The Royal Commission on National Health Insurance, 1925 Part IV,* pp.982-8. (London, 1925).
23 *Annual Report, 1924, op. cit.*pp.187-90 and 204-9.
24 The Poor Law Medical Service, in *Annual Report, 1927, op. cit.,* pp.337-352; see also Keay, J. W., (1928) The Future of Poor Law Hospitals, in *Edinburgh Medical Journal 35,* pp.69-75.
25. The Report of the Scottish Consultative Councils, *A Reformed Local Authority for Health and Public Administration.* (Edinburgh, 1923).
26. Evidence of the Board and the Scottish Office (21.10.26 and 23.11.26) to *The Royal Commission on Local Government, 1928* Part 8, pp.1543 and 1592. (London, 1928).
27. Address by Sir J. Gilmour (1925-6), in *Journal of the Royal Sanitary Institute XLVI,* pp.65-71.
28. *Annual Report of the Board of Health, 1928. Cmd. 3304 (P.P. 1928-9 Vol. VIII)* pp.13-14.
29. Address to Glasgow Businessmen, in *Poor Law Magazine 1927,* p.172; see also, *British Medical Journal 1927(1),* p.639.
30. Speech by Gilmour at the Opening of Glasgow Victoria Infirmary's Auxiliary Block, in *ibid.,* p.489.
31. Local Government Act 1929, *SRO DD 5.693-721; Proposals for Reform in Local Government in Scotland. Cmd. 3135 (P.P. 1928*

Vol. XIX).
32. Second Reading (3.12.28), *Hansard 223 (Fifth Series)* p.859.
33. General Hospital Policy, *SRO HH 65.52-3; DD 5.700;* Mac-
    Gregor, Chapter 9, in *op. cit.* MacGregor claims he was instru-
    mental in pressing for action, but the Departmental files
    indicate Dr J. P. Kinloch, the Chief Medical Officer of Health
    and his senior officials were already in favour of permissive
    development.
34. *British Medical Journal 1929(1),* pp.171, 413-4 and 472-3.
35. Committee (7.2.29), *Hansard 224 (Fifth Series)* p.2081.
36. Kinloch, J. P. (1929), The Meaning of an Adequate Health Ser-
    vice, in *Transactions of the Royal Sanitary Association of Scotland,*
    pp.1-24.
37. Kinloch, J. P. (1930) Conference Addresses, in *British Medical
    Journal 1930(1),* pp.562-3 and, *ibid. 1930(2),* p.35; (1931) The
    Science of Life, in *Transactions of the Royal Sanitary Association
    of Scotland,* pp.2-18; see also Chapter 7, Hospital Services, in
    *Annual Report of the Department of Health, 1931-2. Cmd. 4080
    (P.P. 1932 Vol. X)* and *ibid, 1932-3. Cmd. 4338 (P.P. 1933 Vol. XII).*
38. For a breakdown of deficiencies see, The Department of Health,
    The Scottish Hospital Survey. (Edinburgh, 1946).
39. Glasgow City Corporation (1933) Evidence to the Scottish Hos-
    pitals Services Committee, in *SRA D-HE 1.1.3,* pp.50-67; see
    also, Glasgow City, *SRO HH 9.24.*
40. Glasgow City Corporation Minutes, 8.1.34, 20.3.35, 24.3.36,
    22.5.36, 23.10.36, 20.11.36 and 3.5.37, *op. cit.;* see also, Mac-
    Gregor, A. S. M. (1937), Administration of the Sick Poor, in
    Public Health 50, pp.213-6 and (1938), The Future Development
    of the Hospital System, in *British Medical Journal 1938(2), Supple-
    ment,* pp.199-202.
41. Surveys and correspondence, Lanark County, Motherwell and
    Hamilton, Airdrie, Coatbridge, *SRO HH 9.54, 35, 3, 5.*
42. See also, supporting Leader (17.2.32), *Glasgow Herald,* p.13.
43. Statement by Kinlock, Dr J. P. to Deputation of County Council,
    10.7.31, *op. cit.;* see also, Health Services in Lanarkshire: Prop-
    osed Co-ordination, in *British Medical Journal 1931(1),* pp.369-
    70.
44. Letter of Vallance, J. M. (Assistant Secretary), 9.8.35, *SRO HH
    9.35.*
45. Minute of Vallance to Highton (Permanent Secretary), 2.9.35,
    ibid.
46. Letter of Taylor, Dr. P. (Head of Hospital Section) to Special
    Areas Commissioner, 14.12.36, *SRO HH 9.54.3.*
47. *British Medical Journal 1930(1),* p.84; Special Areas Commis-
    sioner's Reports, *DD 10.169.;* Surveys and Correspondence,
    Greenock, *SRO HH 9.25.*
48. Mackintosh, Dr. J. M. (Chief Medical Officer of Health), Report
    on Smithston Institution, 5.11.38, *ibid.*
49. Minute of Vallance, 2.3.36, *ibid.*
50. Letter of Taylor, 6.10.37, *ibid.*
51. Minute of Taylor, 21.4.38 and approved by the Chief Medical
    Officer of Health, 4.5.38, *ibid.*
52. Speech given to Glasgow Victoria Infirmary, in *British Medical
    Journal 1938(2),* p.1223.
53. Department of Health, Consultative Council on Medical and

Allied Services *Report on Hospital Services*.(Edinburgh, 1933). It was published in May. For comment on Scotland falling behind England in hospital income, especially legacies, see *British Medical Journal 1929(2)*, p.1018.

54. Chapter 7, Public Health, in *Report of the Committee on Local Expenditure (Scotland)*. *Cmd. 4201 (P.P. 1932-3 Vol. XIV)*; see also, Committee on National Expenditure, especially Minute of Department on need for Public Health Inquiry, 23.1.33, *SRO HH 1.486, 496-507*. It had been established under the National Government's economy programne.

55. Memorandum by the Secretary of State on the Report of the Committee on Local Expenditure (Scotland), *PRO CAB 24.242; British Medical Journal 1933(1)*, p.1022.

56. Evidence of BMA (7.7.34), in *ibid. 1934(2), Supplement*, pp.1-18.

57. *Report of the Committee on the Scottish Health Services. Cmd. 5204 (P.P. 1935-6 Vol. XI)*. J. Westwood M.P. (Labour) and seven others signed a Minority Report suggesting the long-term need was for a free health service. Only one member, A. Grierson, was against further State involvement.

58. Leader, in *British Medical Journal 1936(2)*, pp.27-8.

59. Discussion (4.11.36), The Report of the Committee on Scottish Health Services, in *Transactions of the Obstetrical and Medico-Churigical Society of Edinburgh (1936-7) CXVI*, pp.1-24.

60. Comment by McFarlane, Sir J. (Chairman of Glasgow Royal Infirmary); see also comment of Little, J. R. (Chairman of Edinburgh Royal Infirmary), in *British Medical Journal 1939(1)*, p.132.

61. Dunn, C. L., *The Emergency Medical Services*. (London, 1952).

62. Minute of 9.1.41, in Post War Hospital Policy, *SRO HH 65.93*.

63. Minute of 15.4.41, in Office Committee on Post-War Hospital Policy, *ibid. 65.70-2*. It included G. H. Henderson (the Assistant Secretary and chairman), the Chief MOH, Mrs M. Ritson (health insurance) and Dr P. Taylor (hospitals). Ritson shared Westwood's concern over means tests and the ability of insurance to cover all medical needs, Minutes of 14.1 and 5.3.41; see also, Leader, Scotland Deserves Better Social Legislation, in *British Medical Journal 1941(1)*, pp.631-2.

64. Preliminary Notes by Henderson, 5.3.41, *SRO HH 65.70*.

65. Minute of 24.9.41, *ibid. 65.93*.

66. Minute of 7.6.43, in Post-War Hospital Problems, *ibid. 65.94*.

67. Minute of 16.6.43, in Hetherington Committee, Meetings, *ibid. 65.63*; evidence to Committee, *ibid. 65.62, 64-7*; *Report of the Committee on Post-war Hospital Problems in Scotland. Cmd. 6472 (P.P. 1942-3 Vol. IV)*.

68. Meeting of 21.5.43, in Scottish Council on Post-War Problems, *ibid. 50.166*.

8

THE COURTS, PARISHES
AND THE MEANS TEST, 1908-39

The failure of the Poor Law Commission to reach a consensus had severely affected the prospect of immediate legislation. However, the Commission's deliberations had helped focus on the third of the Poor Law's problems: could a legally based system be compatable with an expansive view of social need? The Majority Report had argued that it could, but had tinged its recommendations with the need for character reformation. The Minority had argued that it could not, but had recommended that administrators have unlimited powers of intervention. Neither appeared acceptable to a more popularly based electorate. One implied the inferior status of a citizen, the other negated ballot-box control of Government. The resolution of the debate, from 1908 to 1939, centred largely on the meaning of poverty and the method of its relief. In doing so, it helped form a key element of the new Welfare State: administrative regulation detached from any moral stance. To understand this debate, it is first important to relate how the existing system determined eligibility.

The predominant aim of the 1845 Act had been to provide a legal definition to poverty, one which could protect a pauper's rights. This resulted in an administrative system where officials were supposed to work not only for their parish, but for the good of the poor. Thus if an inspector felt the parish was not providing adequate maintenance, he not only could, but had a duty to supplement relief. Indeed if a case was really urgent, an inspector could on his own authority grant immediate (interim) relief. As a Board official explained to the Poor Law Commission: 'The responsiblity resting on an inspector is somewhat serious, especially in cases where he refuses relief, for not only is he liable to dismissal by the Board for neglect of duty, but if the life or health of a poor person is endangered by such neglect, he is liable to prosecution on a criminal charge.'[1] Only when the parish had met and considered the case was there the possiblity of this being discharged.

The Poor Law's principle task, of course, was to meet material needs. But needs could vary considerably between claimants. It was therefore essential for parishes, inspectors and the Board to know what conditions would ensure a pauper's claim being met. In practice it meant a very special relationship had to be created between the legal system and the inspectors. What kind of relationship was explained by the *Poor Law*

Magazine:

> Judicial interpretations of a very generally worded statute [the Poor Law Acts] should, above all, be simple and easily understood, even if it is somewhat arbitary and occasionally imperfectly reconcilable according to pure reason. This, of course, is simply because Inspectors of Poor have before them, weekly and daily, problems arising in different circumstances, which it is desirable that they should be able to solve by a kind of footrule judgement. The Poor Law should be such that cases fall readily and clearly into well defined categories, and do not hover, like uneasy spirits between heaven and earth.[2]

As the Magazine suggested, it was not the function of the Supreme Court (the House of Lords) or the lower courts to meet weekly, or even annually, to review the Poor Law. They were there to adjudicate when either a pauper, the Board or another parish (in disputes over settlement) rejected a parish's decision. If a case did arise, the court's function was simple: to provide an authoritative interpretation of Statute Law that would leave eligibility in no doubt.

Thus within the limits set by the Statutes, the Poor Law was ultimately a contestable system. That meant two things. First, any alteration in practice, whether by an inspector, his council or indeed the Board, had always to consider the possibility of the court's construing their action illegal. Second, the court would always be the last port of call for any pauper who wanted to challenge the prevailing notion of what constituted a parish's obligation to meet need. In practice there were two legal processes and two legal concepts which greatly influenced how much a pauper received: they were the appeal to the sheriff, the appeal to the Board, the concept of 'needful sustentation' and the means test. Before considering how policy changed it is necessary to consider what each entailed.

The Sheriff's appeal was designed to be a swift and inexpensive method of reviewing an inspector's decision to refuse relief. The system was described to the Poor Law Commission by Sheriff MacKenzie of Glasgow:

> Where an applicant has been refused relief he is entitled to demand a 'line of refusal', specifying why relief has been refused. He can then apply to the sheriff, who, after hearing this statement, may either confirm the refusal or may appoint the inspector to lodge with the Sheriff-Clerk within a specified time a detailed statement of his reasons, and the inspector is ordered meantime to give interim relief. If the inspector does lodge a statement the sheriff appoints one of the agents for the poor to answer it for the pauper, and thereafter the case goes on as an ordinary action.[3]

For the claimant the system's critical element was its speed. In Glasgow, as in Edinburgh, a claimant refused relief could be back at the inspector's office within an hour. But the Sheriff could only determine that relief ought to be given. He could not indicate how much or in what form. This aspect was the Board's responsiblity.

The appeal to the Board, because it concerned the adequacy or the amount of relief, was more complicated. Under the Old Poor Law a claimant's only appeal had been direct to the Court of Session, which unless there was a willing agent to shoulder the financial cost, meant few could pursue their legal rights. With the central authority acting as an intermediary between the parish and the court, the claimant was, in theory at least, in a better position. After due consideration of the case, which might include a visit from a General Superintendent of poor, the Board would issue its 'determination'. If it felt the claimant was entitled to a specified amount and the parish refused, it could issue a Minute entitling the claimant to the benefit of the poor's roll in the Court of Session. A further appeal could be lodged with the House of Lords. In the 1900s the Board received about a hundred such appeals a year. What then constituted entitlement?

First and foremost in determining entitlement was the concept of 'needful sustentation'. Thus was used by the courts to determine the amount of relief that was appropriate in each case. Ewan Macpherson, the Board's legal member, was quite open as to what it meant: 'Such an amount necessarily varies in accordance with the standard of living in the locality. We aim at giving the pauper an allowance sufficient to maintain himself, without putting him in a position better than that of those in his own class who support themselves'.[4] To the Board, the maintenance of life, and hence 'needful sustentation' was therefore a comparative term, linked not to some absolute concept of physical fitness, but to the moral and economic propriety of allowing the non-productive, publicly dependent person State support. How much this was at the turn of the century can be seen from one of Barclay's half-yearly reports:

> I observe a tendency to give larger weekly aliment to Outdoor Poor. There are now few cases to be found at 1s. or 1s. 6d. a week, and those still on the Rolls at these allowances are mostly old cases in which the Boards have not cared to interfere with previous practice. The stereotyped allowance of 2s. 6d. for a single person is rapidly being replaced by 3s., and the allowance for children is frequently 1s. 6d. a week for each child, while formally it was invariably 1s. This is a step in the right direction, if tempered with careful discrimination. No absolute rule can of course be laid down, but each case must be judged on its own merits, but where there are children the allowance should be ample to secure the building up of a sound and healthy constitution.[5]

Related to the concept of 'needful sustentation' was the means test. No claimant could escape from its application to both their own and their family's income. All of a claimant's own income was deductable, including any benefit from a friendly society.[6] Nevertheless, the court had issued a ruling, that gave the claimant some protection and made Scotland's relief quite different from England's. In 1885, it had stated that, 'the relation of debtor and creditor never exists between the [claimant] and the parish which relieves them. The money is expended and presumably properly expended, and no claim arises thereout'.[7] Putting it more simply, because Scottish Law granted individuals a greater recognition of their right to relief as 'free' persons the parish could not claim any monies expended from the claimant's future estate. Poor relief was not a loan.

In contrast to a claimant's future estates, the estates of their relatives were at risk. Following the Hoseason v Hoseason case in 1870, husbands had to support their wives (though not necessarily the reverse), fathers, mothers and grandparents their children and grandchildren, and children their parents and grandparents.[8] Those who benefitted from a father's estate within the family (e.g. an eldest son), also shared in this duty. Parishes were also keen to emphasise the moral obligation of brothers and sisters. This was strongly supported by the Board, who in their 1878 circular stated that 'persons having collateral relatives in comfortable circumstances ought not to receive outdoor relief'.[9] They should be offered the poorhouse.

Whatever the Board or parishes decided, there were two important court decisions that mitigated the wholesale application of the concept. First, the courts had decided that a parish's attempt to enforce familial obligation by an offer of the poorhouse had to be tempered. In 1867 it ruled that the 'test' was not to be a 'test of ability to endure privation'.[10] The parish had to demonstrate the family could actually provide support. And in 1877 it also ruled that children ought to have a 'superfluity of means after providing for the maintenance of themselves and their families'.[11] Although in the 19th century 'superfluity' was not very generously construed – relatives were allowed between 10 and 30 per cent of earnings before aggregation – parishes had been forced to acknowledge the limits of 'moral' administration.[12]

'Needful sustentation' and the means test were therefore important concepts which delineated how much and in what form relief ought to be given. The court was there not only to adjudicate on excessive amounts but also on the paucity of relief. In essence it was a system designed both to protect the poor from the vagaries of ratepayer control and ensure some consistency in the method and amount of relief. Yet its very nature entailed its chief shortcoming. The Sheriff's appeal may have been swift and inexpensive, but the need for well defined rules meant that a system which was inherently conservative in its view of change. Established rules were there to be followed. To do otherwise, thought the proposers of the 1845 Act, would have left everyone unsure of their rights. It would have been the very antithesis of a sound, efficient and controlled welfare system. How then did policy change?

With an established philosophy stressing discriminatory treatment, all parishes operated their relief committees on the principle of 'each case on its merits'. In the smaller parishes which met every few months, councillors would make this decision collectively, and if necessary, after a vote. In larger ones, like Bothwell, separate committees composed of a number of councillors would operate on a more frequent basis.[13] In city parishes with thousands of applicants each year, a more elaborate structure was obviously necessary. The 1905 Report explained Glasgow's system:

> The parish is divided into 12 relief districts. While the Relief Committee nominally consists of the whole Council (of 31 members), in actual practice the administration of relief is remitted to the individual members; and two committees (each consisting of a single councillor) sit daily on five days of the week. A councillor's turn for duty on the Relief Committee comes round once every three weeks. . . any applicant, councillor, or the inspector of poor may appeal against a single member's decision to a Relief Appeal Committee, consisting of 11 members, who meet once a month.[14]

A further appeal by any party could be made to the full council. Each of the other city parishes, Edinburgh, Govan, Dundee and Aberdeen had different committee systems, but the same principle held: a pauper's case was individually assessed and individually determined.

After 1900 this method of individualised treatment began to break down. The evidence to the Poor Law Commission seems to have suggested three particular reasons. First, with the increasing number of claimants, especially in the larger parishes, less time became available for each councillor to consider cases.[15] Second, the early 1900s witnessed a general concern over the Poor Law's adequacy to meet needs. These two factors were combined with a third which, for contemporaries, seemed much more worrying: it was difficult to persuade councillors to stand for re-election.[16] At Leith, for instance, a third of those elected in 1901 stood down in 1904 and a similar proportion did the same in 1907.[17] Many councillors, the general superintendents reported, had little knowledge of the Poor Law, or of entitlement, or even of paupers.

The 1905 Committee had noted these problems and suggested not only a closer scrutiny of relief work by the whole council but also the introduction of fixed scales.[18] This, it argued, would enable the parish to set the boundaries of individual decision-making. All the parishes concerned refused to consider the issue; they believed they that could continue with traditional practice and maintain the viability of their relief policy. This was soon tested in Glasgow, where the 1908-9 trade depression caused a 30 per cent increase in applications. The ability of the Relief Appeal Committee to monitor and standardise policy came under particular stress. In 1909 when a Labour councillor, James Stewart, suggested the possiblity of introducing 'set' allowances, the other councillors willingly agreed to establish a Committee to review its potential.[19] But Stewart's proposal was also helped by another set of events.

When the Board in 1902 suggested an allowance of 3 shillings per week for widows, they were breaking with tradition.[20] No recommendation on benefit levels had ever been made. The Board's concern was primarily to encourage parishes to give an allowance that would prevent a widow from having to work. By 'devoting herself' to the proper care of her children the growth of the next generation of paupers could be stemmed – or so it believed. But in the process the Board was also raising the general subject of adequacy: were allowances sufficient to meet needs? This was underlined two years later when at an international Poor Law conference held in Edinburgh, a number of contributers spoke openly of a parish failure to address the issue 'scientifically'; little work, they said, had been done to measure a pauper's standard of living.[21] This issue was taken up by the Dundee Social Union and as a result of its investigations its Secretary informed the Poor Law Commission:

> It is not unusual for an old woman to receive 2s. 6d. a week from the Parish, 6s. a month from Charity, and 2s. 6d. a month from the Female Society, thus making a total allowance of 4s. 6d. a week. The Parish is aware that 2s. 6d. or 3s. a week is not sufficient to maintain an old person, but they expect this allowance to be supplemented from some other source. Friends and neighbours are often very good to these old persons, but in many cases there is great privation.[22]

and she added:

> The following estimate [of expenditure] is based on the budgets of two old infirm women.

	s.	d.
Rent	1	6
Coals and gas	1	3
Bread	0	6
Meat Fish	0	4
Butter	0	3½
Sugar	0	2½
Tea	0	3
Ham or Eggs	0	2
Milk	0	2
Potatoes	0	1
	4	9

The two women, the Secretary noted, had nothing for clothing, houshold amenities, entertainment or insurance. Similar evidence came from Edinburgh, where its cos Secretary, reported that many paupers were expected to 'hang on' in the hope of receiving 'extras' from their church or mission.[23] The final seal of inadequacy came from the Parsons inquiry. Dr Parsons reckoned that a family of five required an income of at least 21s. a week: 13s. 6d. for food, 3s. 6d. for rent, 2s. for fuel, 1s. for clothing, 6d. for soap and another 6d. for insurance. This would be sufficient, he said, for an ordinary working class diet: milk and porridge for breakfast, soup, stew, vegetables and pudding for lunch and a piece of bread with cocoa or tea for supper.[24] But a third of the pauper children he surveyed were grossly underfed: their allowances had not been supplemented. Many others, despite good domestic management, were ill-nourished. Glasgow, reckoned a generous parish, assumed that a total of 15s. a week for a family of five was adequate. Even if this family were to obtain another 6s. from relatives, part-time work or charity, the parish would simply deduct it and they would be no better off. Allowances were less than two-thirds of what Parsons thought adequate. Stewart's proposal, therefore, came at a time not just of considerable debate over adequacy, but when parishes had at last some definite information on what need was.

During the Review Committee's discussions, the issue soon became clear. Stewart knew he was suggesting a radically different method to meet need and he left no one in any doubt what he thought the level of allowances should be: 'adequate to enable a person to live in such conditions as will promote their physical and mental health'.[25] Benefit levels, he suggested, ought to be sufficient in themselves and he recommended an increase of about 50 per cent; 23s. a week for a family of five. Another councillor suggested a different scale, increasing allowances by about 20 per cent and after considering a study of working class budgets completed by one of the other councillors, the Committee duly recommended this scale. The Inspector, James Motion, was aghast. He vigorously attacked any notion of change, arguing that:

> At present, a Councillor, by what he learns from the Inspector and applicant, can use his own judgement as to the truth of the particulars given to him, and fix or refuse that ailment accordingly; whereas, if he is tied down by a fixed scale, while perhaps convinced that he is being deceived, the hopelessness of proving the deception is such, that there is nothing left for him but to grant relief according to scale.[26]

In other words, a councillor would lose power. He had other objections also. First, the new scales might allow deserted wives unconditional outdoor relief. This and the higher payments, he said, would probably mean many of the 'industrious poor' giving up 'the struggle' and applying for relief. The fight against 'pauperism' would be nullified. Second, he stressed that the present practice meant all of a relative's income was taken into account; those the parish felt should make some contribution and did not, found the claimant being offered the poorhouse. Under what was being proposed this could not occur. Those who gave something would be in the same position as those who avoided support. It struck at the heart of established policy, discriminatory treatment based on family obligation.

The councillors remained unimpressed. They wanted change and in September 1910 the new scales were introduced, the first anywhere in Scotland. Within three weeks, however, some of Motion's fears had been substantiated. The rigid application of the scales did lead to many 'respectable' poor, whose families had provided some support, being struck off the roll and others whose families now refused, being added. The scheme was temporarily abandoned. What the councillors had neglected was the need to formalise the means test; setting a level of 'necessitious sustentation' was not sufficient. Although Motion continued to argue against any scale he presented a modified one with a set of 'disregards' for family earnings.[27] It increased allowances by nearly 30 per cent and allowed relatives to retain a third of their income before aggregation; a family of five would now receive 19s. 6d. With the councillors agreeing that some form of discretion was still important, the new scales were introduced with the proviso that they should be regarded as a mimimum.

The issues which Glasgow had debated for over a year had thrashed out an important redirection of policy. A new consideration had been given to the way the Poor Law treated poverty. The previous fusion of legal and moral concepts had been replaced by administrative regulation, which ensured that a claimant was treated according to the formal categorisation of his circumstances. Hidden within this new scheme lay another important shift, one which lessened the power of officials and councillors to deal individually with any case. By knowing in advance the minimum they could obtain and the dedutions they would suffer, a claimant now had a greater degree of protection from any sudden shift in a relief committee's attitude.

With war-time inflation many other parishes found it difficult to maintain traditional policy and scales became widely adopted.[28] But, by then, the issue of 'set' allowances had been affected by two other important factors. Beginning with the Lindsay study in 1913, Professor Noel Paton's team working for the Medical Research Council slowly gained a more precise notion of an average working-class budget and what constituted a proper diet.[29] As a result of their work, one Govan official (in 1916) was prepared to put a definite sum on minimum benefit.[30] Using the investigations, he reckoned that each man required an income of 7d. a day for basic physiological needs. With the needs of a woman being set at 80 per cent of this, and a child depending on age between 20 per cent and 70 per cent, this meant each week for a family of five, 14s. for food, 4s. for rent and 2s. for fuel – 20s. in total. As this did not include other household items like soap and clothing, it meant

his mimimum level was considerably higher than Glasgow's allowances. In fact, his mimimum more resembled Stewart's.

The second important factor, as seen in Chapter Six, was Labour's
substantial increase in parish representation. It was in the left-wing
dominated parishes of West Fife – Auchterderran, Ballingry, Beath and
Wemyss – that the issue of 'set' allowances was again tested. With the
arrival of the new councillors, the Labour Party felt it was time to launch
a more co-ordinated attack on the Poor Law and in early 1920 the Party
called a parish conference. During the discussions the West Fife representatives all confirmed that they thought their existing allowances
were inadequate. Although Beath and Ballingry had 'set' scales – introduced before Labour took control – they were only marginally higher
than Glasgow's. At the end of the meeting the councillors were unanimous: the war had seen an improvement in working class living
standards and that, in turn, meant a more generous interpretation of
'subsistence' was necessary. Post war Scotland, they said, demanded
'maintenance' at a 'higher degree of comfort'. A new scale of allowances,
some 40 per cent above Glasgow's (in real terms) was recommended.[31]
With minor modifications Auchterderran, Ballingry and Wemyss
adopted the suggested scale. Beath also adopted the scale, but went
further.[32] It almost abolished the means test: family earnings below £3
were to be ignored.

The difficulties that this created for established policy soon became
apparent. Within four months, Beath found the nearby parish of Dollar
raising objections. It had discovered that one of Beath's claimants residing in their area was receiving 86s. a week. This was well in excess of
its own scale and, what made it much worse to them, she was a mother
with eight illegitimate children. The Board was equally shocked and
told Beath it had committed a 'serious act of maladministration'.[33] This
was an encouragement to 'extravagance and profligacy' and the Board
urged the parish to send the woman to Dunfermline Poorhouse and
board out her children. Beath remained unimpressed. The Chairman
said the Board was really objecting to the fact that the woman had eight
illegitimate children: there was little evidence that her house was untidy
or the children ill-treated. Another councillor stated that it would actually cost more to board the children and would probably harden the
mother into being 'immoral'. After the Board told a deputation that its
view had not altered, the parish agreed to bring the family to Beath for
more direct 'supervision'.

The Board remained unhappy. At the end of 1920 with the decline in
the cost of living, it wrote to the four parishes warning them that their
auditors might regard the allowances as excessive. Beath, like the others,
was told:

> The powers and duties of a parish council in regard to poor relief
> are limited to the provision of 'needful sustentation'. While

generally the question as to what is 'needful sustentation' in any
particular case is left to the discretion of the parish council, the
Board are charged with the duty of seeing that excessive expenditure is not incurred, it becomes liable to surcharge. The Board
have given careful consideration to the scale adopted by your
parish council, and while recognising the present need for substantial increases over pre-war rates, they are of the opinion that
the scale is excessive.[34]

The councillors, already contemplating further 'disregards' for friendly
society payments, refused to consider the issue. The other parishes also
refused, Ballingry informing the Board that 'they had not gone as far
as they might'.

The Board hastily replied to Beath's proposal. It would require legislation which it would not support and again urged reconsideration of
the scale. Beath agreed only to a stricter means test. The other parishes
also refused to reduce their scale, and Auchterderran re-affirmed Beath's
stance on relief to single parents. Women whose husbands were in
prison were to receive outdoor relief. By the spring of 1921 the parishes
were in open conflict with the Board and the prevailing Poor Law
philosophy.

The Board's attitude hardened and in April two General Superintendents were dispatched to conduct a special inquiry. Afterwards Beath
was told that reductions were 'essential'. With other parishes reducing
their allowances as wages fell, West Fife, it said, had a scale of relief
some 30 per cent higher than anywhere else. The parish was specifically
asked to introduce sliding allowances for additional children. The Board
stated: 'The system under the scale adopted by your parish Council of
granting a fixed allowance of 10s. per week for each dependent child is
obviously unjustifiable. It should be borne in mind that a family of five
children may be adequately fed for a lower sum per head than is the
case with say, a family of two'.[35] It then urged a more rigorous application
of the means test:

Apart from the legal obligation on working members of a family
to support their parents, there is a moral obligation on such members to contribute towards the support of their younger brothers
and sisters and the parish council ought to keep this strictly in
view. Looking therefore to these obligations, a son or daughter
is not to be regarded merely as a lodger and his or her contribution
to the household expenditure must not be limited to the amount
that would be paid for his or her board and lodging.

Beath again refused to consider the issue. The councillors disputed all
the Board's assertions. Wage levels, in particular, were irrelevent; what
mattered was meeting need. It was only when Ballingry received notice
of a surcharge of £181 that the parishes began to alter their stance.[36]
While some councillors had declared themselves ready to go to prison

over the fixed scale of relief, that crisis was soon eclipsed by the scope of the unemployment problem. Worried about the debt that might create, and the general illegality of the payments before the 1921 Act, they all reduced their allowances. By early 1922 their scales were only 10 per cent higher in real terms than the pre-war Glasgow scale.

Whatever the failure of their action, the West Fife parishes had confirmed one thing; there was now a new breed of councillor who was openly hostile not only to the prevailing notion of 'needful sustentation' but also to the means test. Throughout Scotland, other parishes under ratepayer control similarly began to recognise these issues. Glasgow, when it re-examined its scales, agreed to 'disregard' a higher proportion of family income and also increase allowances.[37] By 1922 virtually all industrial parishes had followed suit. Basic allowances had been pushed up 10 per cent in real terms, and in the application of the means test up to two-thirds of a family's income was being disregarded instead of one-third.[38] All agreed that the increased standard of 'comfort' meant families now wanted to spend more on their own needs. In consequence they had less to contribute to support of less fortunate relatives.

Thus parishes and the Board had acknowledged that, through 'set' allowances it was possible to develop administrative regulations to mitigate traditional Poor Law philosophy. However West Fife had demonstrated their limits. In a period of economic retrenchment, many parishes, although willing to accept the 'evidence' that basic needs had increased, still preferred to define poverty in established legal and moral terms. Apart from some extra assistance to the elderly, little else occurred in the 1920s to increase the Poor Law's minimum.[39]

One of the central themes of the Poor Law Commission in 1909 had been the need to improve both Poor Law administration and the condition of the poor. Even the Majority Report questioned the suitability of judicial control over the elaboration of need. Adherence to procedural rights, inherent in a legally-based system, would not necessarily promote more substantive rights.[40] With the prospect of reform diminishing as the Liberals pushed through the new social insurance legislation, the immediate problem was whether or not the existing legal system could make some positive reponse and become adaptable to meeting need. This was soon tested, for by January 1909 Cuthill v Inverkeillor parish Council had reached the Court of Session.

Mary Cuthill was an aged widow with a resident but mentally and physically weak, son who earned about 14 shillings a week in casual labour.[41] She had three other married children, who had given varying amounts of support. In 1906, she was residing in Carmyllie; with her son's earnings very irregular, Poor Relief was applied for and given. The parish of settlement, Inverkeillor, accepted the claim and duly paid Carmyllie the appropriate amount of relief. A year later Inverkeillor changed its mind; it believed that her children's legal and moral duty to support her had been neglected and to enforce this, the parish offered Arbroath Poorhouse.

The reaction was immediate: Carmyllie and the Board expressed horror that a 'home for two respectable people' would be broken up. An appeal was lodged with the Board, who stated that the offer was inadequate and that relief should continue as Carmyllie had decided. A Minute was duly issued. Two years of litigation then ensued. First of all, Inverkeillor tested the legality of the Minute in the Court of Session, arguing that the Board had no power to determine the form of relief, only its amount if given outdoors. The ploy failed; Lord Guthrie held that where the 1845 Act had stated the Board could pass Minutes affecting the 'amount of relief', it was, in his view, equivalent to covering any 'relief' offered.

Some months later the case was heard again; this time Inverkeillor was disputing the Board's and Carmyllie's decision to grant outdoor relief. Mrs Cuthill's legal agents argued that the poorhouse offer was tantamount to testing her ability to 'endure privation'. She would never accept the offer, preferring to live on her son's earnings and whatever meagre amounts her other children could provide. Moreover, they argued, the 'adequacy' of relief ought to be judged by its 'suitableness', not its amount. In essence, they were suggesting that times had altered and that moral and legal responsibilities had to be tempered by changes in relative standards of living. Much broader considerations of 'needful sustentation' could be subsumed under a new concept of 'suitablity'. Offering the poorhouse to a claimant who was neither sick nor a casual labourer represented the worst aspects of discriminatory relief. The court agreed and one of the judges stated that 'the offer of the poorhouse would amount to a harsh administration of the Poor Law, and be contrary to the public interest'. The Court of Session, a few months after the publication of the Poor Law Report, had effectively revoked the legitimacy of the poorhouse 'test'. In future parishes would have to pursue a family's legal and moral obligations in some other manner.

Soon after the Cuthill case the Board itself underlined this change of mood. In one arbitration case it held that a man, Sam Todd, earning £1 a week (as a stone-dyker) could not be compelled to wholly maintain his widowed daughter and two children. With a parish contribution set at 4s., it meant that the Board also considered Glasgow's one-third earnings 'disregard' to be acceptable.[42] Three years later this disregard was confirmed. A man with five children, two of whom were working, and a family income of 28s. could receive poorhouse treatment for TB. Pleas from the parish of settlement, Hamilton, that 28s. was more than many rate-paying workers earned, did not impress the Board.[43]

But it was at the end of the war that a more fundamental review of family obligations occurred, again through a Board arbitration. In 1918,

Mr Brown's wife became mentally ill and was removed to an asylum by Sorn, the parish of residence.[44] He had four children, two of whom earned £1.13.9d a week. His own wages came to £2.7.6d. Although an able-bodied man's family could legally receive asylum treatment, it was means tested and Mauchline, the parish of settlement, objected to Mrs Brown receiving Poor Relief. It felt that with an income of over £200 per annum the family ought to afford the full cost of care, £40. To support its arguments, Mauchline quoted 19th-century decisions which had stated that a smaller sum was sufficient to prevent a person claiming assistance. The Board backed Sorn. It argued that with war-time inflation eroding the real value of earnings, and the father maintaining a daughter who acted as a housekeeper, only a proportion of the costs should be paid. The Board acknowledged that material circumtances had altered and families required a much greater part of their income for their own needs.

Within two years of the Mauchline judgment, however, any further elaboration of entitlement came to an abrupt halt. As the judge in Glasgow v Rutherglen was to state, many inspectors had become unsettled; there were now too many inconsistencies for them to accept with comfort. One of the first cases restricting any elaboration was Macpherson v Kilmore.[45] Duncan Macpherson, a widower, was left to look after four young children. His work as a quarrier became interupted by poor health and he found caring for the youngest increasingly difficult. The local parish, Kilmore, at first accepted the child, but when it reached the age of one, despite Mr Macpherson's reduced income, refused further support. On appeal, the Sheriff agreed and commented:

> Mr Macpherson contends that, although his bodily condition is not such as to render himself as a proper subject of relief, the child's age and his disablity to maintain and look after it are such as to make it necessary in the child's interest that the parish Council should relieve him of a burden which, through no fault of his own, his shoulders are not broad enough to bear. . . The law presumes. . . that every able-bodied father is capable of maintaining his family, however different the fact may be. He had hitherto maintained himself and his three elder children, if not without difficulty, at any rate without invoking parochial aid. No doubt he is not as strong as some other men, nor even so strong as the average man. He appears to suffer from some gastric trouble and some functional irregularity of his heart, which at intervals cause him to suspend his activities for some days or even weeks. And, no doubt, his wages are small. But while, as I have said, his case is one which calls for sympathy, I must perforce judge it according to the law.   .

The Court of Session also agreed; although the child obviously required assistance, Mr Macpherson was able to work. No Poor Relief could be given. Three years later the Court of Session was again in action.

George Darrie was an unemployed labourer who had lost an arm in a farming accident some years previously. During and immediately after the war he had been able to obtain regular work (as a travelling salesman, a coal-dealer and a nightwatchman), but as trade declined he began to suffer long bouts of unemployment. He had a family to support and so when he exhausted his national insurance he applied to his local parish, Melrose for relief. Melrose promptly enrolled him, but under the 1845 Act. It considered a one-armed man to be both destitute and disabled. The parish of settlement, Gordon, was quick to object, saying that he was able-bodied and should therefore be placed on the unemployed (1921) register, at a lower rate of benefit. At the Court of Session, Lord Alness agreed. In his view:

> Age, rheumatism, indigestion, intemperence, ill-health may affect the earning capacity of any man, but they do not necessarily, any more than the loss of a limb, affect his "able-bodiedness" in the statutory sense. The test is not, Has a man lost an arm or a leg? It is rather, Can he earn a living?[46]

Two other judges agreed, but Lord Hunter, the fourth, did not, To him it was important to recognise that the depressed state of trade effectively prevented Mr Darrie from competing equally in the labour market and obtaining regular employment. So long as this condition remained, he would never be able to fully maintain his family.

A few months later, the Glasgow v Rutherglen judgment barred an inspector from providing interim relief to a deserted wife whose husband's address was known. This cycle of judgments was completed with Lord Constable's decision in the 1926 Dalziel v Colville case preventing relief to strikers' dependants. With these decisions the court had narrowed both a parish's power of discretion and the Board's own ability to elaborate new categories for assistance. By the early 1930s it was forced to employ some very odd precedents to permit what it saw as appropriate relief.

The 1920s had therefore witnessed a period of retrenchment in the way the court interpreted the Poor Law. The Board's determinations, the Poor Law inquiries, the growth of new forms of welfare, and the 1921 Act had all created uncertainty. What did 'needful sustentation' actually mean? How should a family's obligation be maintained? When was a 'disabled' person really disabled? Even inspectors of poor, who in 1920 had agreed the only condition for Poor Relief ought to be 'necessity', had found it hard to reconcile themselves with its wholehearted application. Glasgow v Rutherglen had been a test case generated largely by the inspectors' concern over the legality of their own actions. The majority of them although agreeing to disburse strikers' relief in 1926, remained unsure about its propriety. Clawing back the frontiers of legality reflected their wider concern with the need to maintain administrative order.

Inspectors and claimants, of course, were not necessarily of the same opinion and by the beginning of the 1930s, the Department was finding more of the latter pursuing appeals both through them and the Sheriff.[47] Claimants were beginnning to resent the financial restrictions that many parishes had placed on improving benefit. In the early 1930s there were two significant cases inititiated by claimants which significantly altered practice and helped to reshape policy. The first occurred in early 1932.

William Stephens, an unemployed disabled war veteran, applied to Edinburgh for assistance under the 1845 Act.[48] The council quickly granted relief. His county of settlement, Caithness, objected, arguing that as Mr Stephens had worked in a poppy factory he was able-bodied. Relief could only be given at a lower level under the 1921 Act. The Sheriff-Substitute agreed. Relying on the Darrie decision, he said that although disabled there was 'a not inconsiderable class of jobs at which he could earn a living'. On appeal, Sheriff Brown of the Lothians disagreed. Questioning how far the Darrie decision could be applied, he declared:

> ... so far as the applicant's physical condition is concerned... it is clear that [he] is suffering from osteo-arthritis with definite rheumatic change also in the lumbar spine, and... that this disease is not likely to be arrested but rather to advance. The question then narrows to this: Can a man suffering from this definite ailment earn his own livelihood in any reasonable sense of that expression? The medical referee makes it clear... that, while the applicant is not unfit for work of any kind, he is unfit for anything other than 'light occupation of a sedentary nature'. We learn... that he was invalided out of the Army in June 1918, and that he has done no work except raffia work for the Earl Haig Poppy Factory. It is notorious that this work is designed for disabled soldiers.

Mr Stephens was therefore not able-bodied within the meaning of the Poor Law and entitled to relief under the 1845 Act.

A year later, creating something of a sensation, the same Sheriff virtually destroyed the moral obligation of collateral relatives to support each other.[49] Archibald Clark, a young man disabled by physical infirmity from working, lived with his widowed mother, uncle and brother in the mining vilage of Newtongrange. He applied for relief from his local public assistance officer, stating his that mother had a pension of 10s. a week and his brother and uncle, both working, contributed 53s. for board and lodgings. The officer refused relief and Mr Clark applied for a Sheriff's order. The Sheriff-Substitute also refused, stating:

> ... it is no doubt true that neither the appellant's brother nor his uncle is legally liable to support him. That liability is upon his mother alone. But the mother controls the finances of the house-

hold. She receives the income and makes the necessary disburse-
ments. On a consideration of the whole evidence I think it has
been established that after providing food for [the uncle] and food
and clothing for her [other] son. . . she has sufficient money left
for the maintenance of herself and the appellant.

On appeal, Sheriff Brown disagreed. The mother was the only person
legally liable and her income was 10s. a week pension. The collateral
relatives' contribution was a separate account, fully used by the mother
to supply board and lodgings.

The court had thus shown it could move in both directions. In a period
of expanding social welfare, when new philosophies were being discussed, it had recognised that the legal basis of poverty ought to be
redefined. That was followed by a period of retrenchment in the 1920s.
The early 1930s had seen that process reversed, and the court continuing
the previous trend.

On balance it cannot be said the court failed to acknowledge the
sentiments of the 1909 Report, but it had found that there existed a
considerable number of Poor Law administrators who resented the
overturning of established principles. For a Department that had seen
its own plans for improving the health of the nation truncated, by both
economic depression and ratepayer intransigence, the Poor Law in its
present form had ceased to be an efficient method of meeting need. It
was not the case that the court could not be progressive or active in
promoting a new definition of poverty, it was simply too unpredictable.
When, in 1933, the National Government brought forward a Bill to
reform the Poor Law, these aspects of a court-centred system – defining
'needful sustentation' and the means test – finally entered into a public
review.

Rarely has any Scottish Bill undergone such a transformation and had
such a lengthy debate in its parliamentary progress. It made its first
appearance in November 1933, and required fifteen days work in Committee before it reached its final reading in July the following year. The
original Bill reflected the Department's desire for closer control over
local authority action and the need to 'recondition and discipline' certain
types of Poor Law claimant.[50] It not only gave the Department power to
regulate poorhouse management, the boarding-out of children and the
conduct of local government officers, but it also proposed draconian
powers of detention for the poorhouse 'in and out', the refractory inmate
and the 'physically incapacitated'. The law of settlement was also to be
abolished.

The Association of County Councils and the Convention of Royal
Burghs soon raised objections.[51] The counties were appalled at the
thought of the abolition of the law of settlement; they feared an influx
of city claimants. The burghs, for their part, disliked the increase in
Departmental 'rule and regulation'; their right to independent action

would be limited. Moreover both felt the proposal to have statutory 'disregards' for sickness benefit was a direct contravention of established Poor Law policy. The fact that this would have brought the Poor Law into line with the Government's own Transitional Payments for Unemployment Benefit was of little relevance to them. Noel Skelton, the Under-Secretary of State, after meeting the Association, agreed to withdraw the Bill and establish a Departmental Committee to review the law of settlement. Nevertheless in the Government's view the need for an interim measure remained. Both the proposed reform of the English Poor Law and of Unemployment Assistance would have meant the Poor Law in Scotland lagging behind in comparable provision. A new Bill was introduced without any reference to settlement.[52]

Unfortunately for Skelton, who introduced it into the Commons, the Bill had not taken into account either the change in public attitude towards poverty or acknowledged that the poor had well-established legal rights.[53] In less than an hour of Skelton sitting down, it was torn apart by an all-party alliance of backbenchers. A Labour MP, Neil Mac-Lean began the attack. The proposal to set the able-bodied to work was against the whole ethos of Scottish Poor Law practice. A National Liberal, J. MacPherson, then followed: detention powers implied 'poverty was a disgrace'. But it was left to a Conservative, C. Milne (West Fife), to effectively wreck the Bill's prospects. He told Skelton: 'we Scotsman are heirs of the Roman Law, and, accustomed as we are to the urbanity of a more civilised code, [than England's], those expressions [the Bill's clauses] are somewhat disconcerting'. Six other Government supporters also raised objections. So taken aback was the Lord Advocate, W. Normand, that he stated he would 'welcome any effective and more humane suggestions'.

Thus the debate between the Poor Law Commission's Reports had been brought to a head. Some method of weaving a path between overt Government control and discriminatory relief was necessary. In the backbenchers' opinion, increasing the powers of central Government would not have necessarily lead to a more humane and expansive system. The Left feared the perpetuation of a means-test system, while the Right feared the steady encroachment of Government on the transactions of everyday life. An independent judiciary and a continuance of local government autonomy were still regarded as a better guarantee of rights than civil servants answerable to no one but their section head.

The eventual Act balanced these perspectives. It greatly strengthened the legal rights of the poor by enabling them to appeal more effectively against the refusal and the inadequacy of relief.[54] Both the unemployed and the ordinary poor shared the same rights and the Department could, if a claimant appealed, order a higher allowance until the Court met. The more punitive clauses of the Bill were either abandoned or watered down. To complete the Act, those in receipt of sickness benefit as well as disability benefit could retain a part of it without deduction – virtually the same amount as Bonhill had argued for in 1923.

The Department was pleased with the result. It reported that the Act embodied a new philosophy: 'to secure that the interests of the poor receive paramount consideration and that the administration is carried out sympathetically'.[55] The philosophy was soon tested. Two court cases, one in 1934, as the Bill was being discussed, and the other in 1936, illustrated that even if the court was both progressive and humane, the other side of the equation – the attachment of many admininistrators to traditional philosophy – meant little prospect of a new consensus emerging.

The first case, Wilson v Mannarn, affected the right of claimants to pursue the political aim of improving their condition.[56] Walter Mannarn, an unemployed Lumphinans miner, decided to go on a hunger march to London. He told his wife where he was going, what route he was taking and then left her with all the money he had. As he was not available for work, the Labour Exchange cancelled his unemployment benefit. When he left, his wife applied for and was granted Poor Relief from Fife County Council. The local public assistance officer, a Mr Wilson, after hearing that benefit had been stopped, promptly issued a writ for Mannarn's failure to maintain his family. The council, by a narrow margin, approved his action. The local Sheriff, however, refused Fife's pleas: Mannarn was not guilty of neglect. The Court of Session also agreed. Lord Blackburn argued that the critical question was 'whether or not he was "able to do so" at a time when he failed to do so'. He considered that because Mannarn had little prospect of finding employment and was on public funds, he was not able to independently maintain his family. Lord Morison was of the same opinion. He concluded that there was no illegal conduct, because to go on a hunger march with the object of making representations to the Government 'was a lawful purpose'. The Poor Law could not be used politically to disenfranchise a claimant.

The second case, that of Duncan v Aberdeen County Council, was in fact a test case brought before the court because there had been so much confusion amongst local authorities on the question of deducting disability and other payments from Poor Relief.[57] Harry Duncan, an unemployed cabinet maker, who had lost his right leg and badly damaged an arm during the war, received a weekly £2 disability pension. On this he maintained a wife and five children. A few days after the 1934 Act came into operation, he applied for Poor Relief, believing that the maximum 'disregard' under the Act, £1, would entitle him to some assistance. Aberdeen County took a different view. It believed the Act was never meant to widen the scope of those legally considered poor. Any applicant would have to have an income below a local authority's needs level before they could be assisted. With an income of £2, one leg, one good arm, a wife and five children to support, Harry Duncan was over its scale of allowances.

The first judgment, the Sheriff's, went in favour of Mr Duncan, but the second, the Court of Session's, went in favour of Aberdeen. Lords Morison and Normand felt there was a distinction between deciding whether a person was poor and eligible for relief, and that of the 'quantum' of relief. Nothing in the Act entailed extending the class of 'pauperism', and an applicant's income from all sources would have to fall below the local authority's needs level before he could be assisted.

The judgment did not accord with the Department's (despite Lord Normand having drafted the Act) and a further appeal, backed by its Minute, was taken to the House of Lords. The five Law Lords rejected the the Court of Session's judgment and restored the Sheriff's decision. Lord Atkin made clear his view of the Act: 'They are obviously remedial provisions intended to make the position of the persons to whom they apply better than ordinary. . . [the pension] refers to income which the recipient has paid for by contributions or war service'. Lord Thankerton was even more forceful, expressing the view that 'public opinion had long been modifying the conception of a social stigma in the receipt of Poor Relief' and in his opinion the Act altered, 'not only the standard of adequacy of outdoor relief, but also the standard of poverty which is to give the legal right to that form of relief'.

'Needful sustentation' and the means test had taken on a new meaning. New needs, in this case the extra cost of being disabled, had been acknowledged as of legitimate concern for a means-tested service. However those needs could not be met by any discriminatory practice. They had to be seen in terms of broad categories of assistance, which detached the act of provision from the personal ideology of the administrator. Poverty was not a disgrace and rules and regulations ought to be devised and operated in a way that protected the poor from any shame and public humiliation. In that way the administrator's power would be reduced, and the claimant's increased.

Both cases illustrate that, despite departmental wishes, the old attitudes remained. Few could now maintain that a system of legal rights based on local administration could be instrumental in extending the Poor Law to encompass new needs. Adaptablity, broadening the categories of assistance and the quick implementation of new legislation were not its hallmarks. It had become a hindrance to, not a protector of, the poor. Indeed as the Mannarn case had shown, administrators were still prepared to use all the punitive powers within the Poor Law to implement a particular philosophy.

The Departmental Committee established to consider the question of settlement, although not recommending the abolition of the existing system, made it clear that further work was necessary to consider the Poor Law's future.[58] The Department in its review of the Committee's work was more forceful. There had been, it wrote, a qualitative alteration in public attitude towards poverty and the provision of benefits. The 'modern tendency' was to remove any hint of 'deterrence' and in discussing the prospect of future reform, it concluded by saying that 'experience has shown the risks run when Poor Law proposals are submitted if they do not promote the interests of the poor'.[59] In crude terms, the Department had recognised that the Poor Law's legitimacy as a welfare institution had evaporated; it was no longer seen as meeting need. The alternative, a system which hid poverty behind the rules and regulations of broad categories of assistance, and was administered by central Government, looked increasingly attractive. Two days after the war broke out all plans for the piecemeal reform of the Poor Law were shelved.

NOTES

1. Evidence of Murray, A., to *op. cit.* For illustration of a prosecution, see, Procurator Fiscal v Sinclair (3 and 4.5.93), in *Poor Law Magazine 1893*, pp.387-93. Barbara King, a noted 'in and outer', was found dead in an Orkney ditch. Sinclair, when contacted by the Police, refused to call the parish medical officer – King had previously declined Kirkwall Poorhouse. The original charge of culpable neglect of duty was reduced to one of technical neglect.
2. Berry, W. B. (Advocate), Comment on Glasgow Parish Council v Rutherglen Parish Council, in *Poor Law Magazine 1925*, p.2.
3. Evidence (13.1.08), to *op. cit.*
4. Evidence, to *ibid.*
5. Half-Yearly Report (1.7.95), in *Annual Report of the Local Government Board, 1894-5. C. 7786 (P.P. 1895 Vol. LII)* App.(A.) No.14, p.30.
6. MacPherson, *op. cit.*
7. The Inspector of Poor of Kilmartin v MacFarlane, 1885, *21 R. 713.*
8. Hoseason v Hoseason, 1870, *9 M. 37.*
9. Use of the Poorhouse as a Test (28.1.78), in *Annual Report of the Board of Supervision, 1877-8. C. 2166 (P.P. 1878 Vol. XXXVIII)* App.(A.) No.4, pp.18-9.
10. Forsyth v Nicholl, 1867, *5 M. 293.*
11. Hamilton v Hamilton, 1877, *4 R. 688.*
12. Maxwell v Lennox, in *Poor Law Magazine 1876*, pp.95-7; Inspector of Poor, Hawick v Inspector of Poor, Moncur, in *ibid. 1877*, pp.41-5; Campbell v Auld (3.5.83), in *ibid. 1883*, pp.387-8; Campbell v Campbell (8.2.87), in *ibid. 1887*, pp.274-7; Kilmaurs Parish Council v Maybole Parish Council (4.2.04), in *ibid. 1904*, pp.72-4.
13. For instance, Review of Applications, Bothwell Parish Council Minutes, 13.2.96, *SRA CO.1.23.6.*
14. *op. cit.*, p.11.
15. See, for instance, Half-Yearly Reports of Glasgow's Inspector of Poor (1905-09), Parish Council Miscellaneous Prints, *SRA*

T-PAR 1.4-12.

16. Evidence of Hawden, Miss E. (Edinburgh) (12.6.07), Martin, Mrs I. C. and Walker, Miss M. L. (both Dundee) (17.7.07), Aikman, Miss E. J. (Glasgow) (Appendix III) and Baird, W. (Glasgow) (Appendix IX), to *Poor Law Commission, op. cit.*
17. Abstracted from Leith Parish Council Minutes, 1900-10, *op. cit.*
18. Recommendation 35, in *op. cit.*
19. Glasgow Parish Council Minutes, 7.9.09, *op. cit.*
20. Relief of Widows with Children *op. cit.*
21. *Transactions of the Fourth International Home Relief Conference, 1904.* (Edinburgh, 1905); see also MacKay, G. A., A Scientific Basis for Parochial Relief, in *Poor Law Magazine 1904,* pp.73-7. MacKay was a Board clerk.
22. Evidence of Martin and Walker, to *op. cit.*
23. Evidence of Kerr, Mrs G. (14.6.07), to *op. cit.*
24. *op. cit.* pp.40-1.
25. Statistics and Aliments, Outdoor Relief, Memorandum II, suggestions by Mr. James Stewart, Glasgow Parish Council, 25.5.10, *op. cit.*
26. Memorandum IV, Inspectors General Observations, March 1910, *ibid.*
27. Memorandum by Inspector of Poor on Scale of Aliment, October 1910, Minutes, 11.11.10 and 5.12.10, *ibid.* The vote was seventeen to nine in favour; see Appendix 7 for scale. The means test calculations have been based on skilled workers' wages. Those on lower incomes would have contributed proportionately less.
28. Bothwell Parish Council Minutes, 28.3.19 and 29.3.20; also Govan Parish Council Minutes, 3.3.20, *SRA CO.1.23.18, D-HEW 5.1.*
29. Lindsay, D. E. *Report upon a Study of the Diet of the Labouring Classes in the City of Glasgow.* (Glasgow, 1913); Elderton, E. M. (1914) Height and Weight of School Children in Glasgow, *Biometrika 10,* pp.288-339; Ferguson, M. (1916-7) The Family Budgets and Dietaries of 40 Labouring Class Families in Glasgow, *Proceedings of the Royal Society of Edinburgh 37,* pp.117-32; (1917-8) A Further Study, *ibid. 38,* pp.40-51; Tulley, A. M. T. (1921) A Study of the Nutrition and Economic Conditions of Working Class Families in Glasgow in April 1921, *Lancet 1921(2),* pp.57-9; Paton, D. N. (1922) Rickets, the Part Played by Unhygenic Social Conditions, *Glasgow Medical Journal 97,* pp.129-44; Tulley, A. M. T. and Urie, E. M. (1922) A Study of the Diets and Economic Conditions of the Labouring Families in Glasgow in June 1922, *ibid. 98,* pp.353-68; Tulley, A. M. T. (1924) A Study of the Diets and Economic Conditions of Artisan Families in Glasgow in May 1923, *ibid. 101,* pp.1-13; Paton (et. al.) *op. cit.*
30. What is Adequate Relief?, in *Poor Law Magazine 1916,* pp.320-4 and The Causes of Pauperism, in *ibid. 1925,* pp.321-4.
31. Ballingry Parish Council Minutes, 10.3.20, *op. cit.* The Conference had taken place on 24.1.20.
32. Beath Parish Council Minutes, 27.4.20, *op. cit. 6.10.6.*
33. Board's letter of 2.7.20, Minutes, 9.7.20, *ibid.*
34. Letter of 4.12.20, Minutes, 14.12.20, *ibid.*
35. Letter of 13.5.21, Minutes 24.5.21, *ibid.*
36. Ballingry Parish Council Minutes, 6.9.21, *op. cit.*; Report (3.9.21),

in *Dunfermline Free Press,* p.2.

37. Memorandum by Inspector of Poor on Outdoor Relief Scale of Aliment, Glasgow Parish Council Minutes, 28.6.21 *op. cit.;* see also Appendix 8. Smith's needs level was now 36s., exclusive of clothing, soap, etc.. Glasgow's allowance was 39s. 6d.

38. Bothwell Parish Council Minutes, 1.11.21 and Old Kilpatrick Parish Council Minutes, 5.5.26 *SRA CO1.23.19, CO.4.20.34;* see also, *Annual Report of Board of Health, 1924, op. cit.,* pp.202-4. The Board, although it accepted scales as 'useful', remained adamant that they could only be a 'guide'. All circumstances had to be taken into account. The Department, after 1929, shared this view.

39. See, Cambuslang Parish Council Minutes, 12.5.27, Bothwell Parish Council Minutes, 2.9.29, Bonhill Parish Council Minutes, 22.2.29 and Govan Parish Council Minutes, 26.8.29 *SRA CO.1.25.23, CO.1.23.23, CO.4.12.4* and *op.cit.;* Scales of Relief and Deductions to the Ordinary Poor, Edinburgh Town Council Minutes, 26.2.31 *YJS 4245A2;* Evidence of Sir H. S. Keith for Convention of Royal Burghs (20.3.31), to *Royal Commission on Unemployment Insurance, 1933.* (1933, London).

40. Recommendations 1, 5, 38, 39, 40, 45, 53, 54 and 57.

41. Cuthill v Inverkeillor Parish Council (2.2.09 and 3.12.09), in *Poor Law Magazine 1909,* pp.177-85 and *ibid. 1910,* pp.6-13.

42. Paisley Parish Council v Greenock Parish Council (24.10.10), in *ibid.,* pp.102-4.

43. Glasgow Parish Council v Hamilton Parish Council (13.6.13), in *ibid. 1913,* pp.225-30.

44. Sorn Parish Council v Mauchline Parish Council (5.8.19), in *ibid. 1919,* pp.217-22.

45. Macpherson v Kilmore and Kilbride Parish Council (14.1.21), in *ibid. 1921,* pp.123-8. .

46. Melrose Parish Council v Gordon Parish Council (19.7.24), in *ibid. 1924,* pp.238-56. Alness was Robert Munro, the Coalition Liberal Scottish Secretary.

47. *Annual Report of the Department of Health, 1929. Cmd. 3529 (P.P. 1930 Vol. XIV)* p.176.

48. Stephens v Edinburgh Town Council and Caithness County Council (23.3.32), *1933, S.L.T. (P.L.) 9.*

49. Clark v the Public Assistance Officer of the District of Newbattle (8.3.33), *ibid. 14.*

50. *The Poor Law (Scotland) Bill, 1933;* Memorandum by the Secretary of State for Scotland on proposed Poor Law Legislation (27.4.33) and, Cabinet Meeting No. 62 (15.11.33), *PRO CAB 27.552, 23.77.*

51. Report of the Deputation appointed by the Association to meet N. Skelton (2.2.34); Letter of the Association to the Department of Health (23.2.34); Memorandum by the Convention of Royal Burghs on the Amending Bill, February 1934 *SRO CO.1 4.234;* Cabinet Meeting No. 4 (7.2.34), *PRO 23.78.*

52. *The Poor Law (Scotland) Bill, 1934.*

53. Second Reading (27.3.34), *Hansard 287 (Fifth Series),* pp.1829-1916.

54. Committee Stage and Third Reading (5.7.34), *ibid. 291,* pp.2087-2200; *Proceedings of the Standing Committee on Scottish Bills, 1933-4. (P.P. 1934 Vol. VIII);* Memorandum by Secretary of State for

198 THE COURTS, PARISHES AND THE MEANS TEST

Scotland on Treatment of Disablity Pensions (8.6.34), Cabinet Paper No. 155 and, Cabinet Meeting No. 24 (13.6.34), *PRO CAB 24.249, 23.79; The Poor Law (Scotland) Act, 1934. Ch. 52 (24 & 25 Geo. 5)*.

55. *Annual Report of the Department of Health, 1934. Cmd. 4837 (P.P. 1935 Vol. IX)* p.130.

56. Wilson v Mannarn (7.6.34), *1934, S.L.T. (P.L.)* 21; Fife County Council Minutes, 2.2.34, *op. cit.;* Fife Hunger March; Alleged Failure to Maintain (8.6.34), in *Glasgow Herald*, p.4.

57. Duncan v Aberdeen County Council (13.2.36 and 2.7.36), *S.L.T. (P.L.)* 4, 17; *The Annual Report of the Department of Health, 1935. Cmd. 5123 (P.P. 1935-6 Vol. XI)* p147; *ibid. 1936. Cmd. 5407 (P.P. 1936-7 Vol. XI)* p129; Soldier's Appeal (3.7.36), in *Scotsman*, p.7.

58. *Report of the Departmental Committee on the Poor Law (Scotland), 1937-8. Cmd. 5803 (P.P. 1937-8 Vol. XIV)*; Minutes of Meetings, Poor Law Enquiry, *SRO HH 61.105.*

59. Minute of 18.11.38, Office Committee to consider Report, *ibid. 61.101.*

9

CONCLUSIONS

By the beginning of the Second World War the philosophy and practice of Scottish welfare had seen a dramatic shift. Yet there remained many unresolved elements. National interests sat uneasily with local control; the administrative regulation of poverty was at odds with the spirit of legalism; and the development of a 'positive right' to welfare stood in contradiction to a popular understanding of the Poor Law's historical legacy. To understand the derivation of these tensions, and hence to appreciate the kinds of difficulties that war-time administrators faced in formulating policy, it is important to recognise two particular aspects of early 20th century Scotland. First, there was the existing philosophy of welfare with its heavy emphasis on minimal State interference in society's 'productive' forces. Thus although a legal right to welfare had been accepted as necessary to maintain order and secure working-class expectations, the middle classes developed an institutional framework strongly orientated towards voluntary care. Second, there was the way in which class and material interests had become articulated in an enfranchised society, one whose economy was undergoing a profound structural transformation. It was the fusion of these two elements, class interests and institutional framework, that led to the period before 1914 witnessing one of the most intense debates about welfare since the Old Poor Law in the 1840s.

Yet this debate had been sparked off, not by any working-class protest or agitation, but through a concern of Poor Law administrators that their strategy to reduce pauperism had failed. The fear that large sections of the working class had not been able to respond to the obvious advantages of a *laissez-faire* economy dominated their thoughts and actions. It was only later, with the deterioration of both the urban labour market and health standards, that other groups, most notably public health officers and independent working-class representatives, began to raise doubts concerning 'pauperism's' ability to sustain material well-being. In consequence, 'reformist' Poor Law administrators found that their rather individualistic interpretation of social ills and their policy of active but discriminatory relief was in conflict with the demands for a less stigmatising and a more humane form of welfare. Without such a change in policy, the more radical and Liberal administrator sensed that working-class support for a free, capitalist society would evaporate. If that occurred, they felt, there was a real prospect of a more serious breakdown in public order.

Thus the debate before 1914 essentially centred on not only how far the State should intervene to guarantee material well-being, but on what conditions – in what way it could determine the mode of conduct for those being assisted. Nevertheless for three reasons the period did not see any wholesale Poor Law reform. First, the existing form of welfare continued to retain considerable ideological support. With voluntary hospitals and other charities still capable of undertaking large-scale investment, property owners remained wary of a philosophy which stressed rate-supported welfare. Second, before 1906, the radical administrators and Labour representatives were not sufficiently powerful or numerous to carry through their policies. Only after that date, with Sinclair's appointment as Scottish Secretary and the election of greater numbers of Labour councillors, was the 'reformist' programme put to a more serious test. Thirdly, the intellectual elaboration of an alternative model, one that could remove the enfranchised worker from a position of 'moral' dependency had not been sufficiently developed. Despite war-time 'reconstruction', elements of middle-class 'reformism' still permeated the discussion. Traditional philosophy and practice had been severely weakened, but not extinguished.

It was therefore left to the inter-war period to resolve the issue and decide the future format of welfare. In this, three particular factors dominated the discussions. First, with the virtual collapse of the traditional industries of coal, steel and shipbuilding, Scotland's material progress, in comparison with England's, began to falter. As Walter Elliot noted, unemployment was higher, wages lower, housing poorer and deaths through childbirth far more prevalent.[1] By the mid-1930s it was estimated that Scotland had twice England's level of poverty.[2] This had important effects. On the one hand it meant there was a sharper and more acute sense of deprivation by those who were on the edge of poverty; the only future they had was a life on State benefits On the other, with the fluctuations in workers' subscriptions and the stagnation in middle-class contributions to voluntary hospitals, the marginal resources available to expand medical care declined. In a popular democracy, neither deepening poverty nor a deteriorating institutional framework was conducive to material well-being; it was the antithesis of 19th-century *laissez-faire* philosophy, economic progress matched by 'voluntaristic' social development.

Second, the 1920s witnessed the formal incorporation of the working classes into the structure of government. After the dramatic general and parish elections of 1922, the *Lennox Herald*, like other local newspapers, noted with some surprise that there had not just been a switch of party allegiances, but a revolution in attitude towards the prevailing system of industrial capitalism. All the 'old political landmarks' it said, 'have been swept away in a wave of popular disappointment'.[3] That meant Labour would have many more councillors, control larger numbers of parish authorities and possibly form a National Administration.

Third, with the successful overturning of the Poor Law's legitimacy came the emergence of a more assertive National Administration, one which believed the State had a duty to promote the material well-being of society. Indeed in 1919 this formed the cornerstone of the Board of Health's constitution. The methods it subsequently evolved, based on regulation rather than adjudication, and its perspective on 'positively' developing human capacities began to alter its position of supporting Capital over Labour. Thus by 1936, whatever the Government's financial orthodoxy, the Department felt that in regulating Scotland's 'social and economic affairs' its work was no more than a reflection of 'popular' demands for State intervention.[4]

These three factors – Scotland's relative material deprivation, the incorporation of working-class representatives into Government and the extension of National control – all stood uneasily with the continuance of 19th century practices. In particular, the failure of the voluntary movement to maintain a hospital service, the inability of local authorities to infuse their welfare services with a philosophy of non-discriminatory care and the expanding nature of material needs to be met, meant that there was bound to be considerable pressure on Government to take the initiative in formulating new welfare policy.

The first occasion when this was dramatically demonstrated was in 1921. Faced with mounting unemployment and prospect of widespread street disorder, the Government, once it had decided against shouldering the whole burden of relief, rapidly urged parish councils to break the law and assist the unemployed. As Churchill told his Cabinet colleagues, it was no longer 'possible for a civilised State. . . to leave a proportion of its citizens with neither work nor maintenance'.[5] A year later, after the 1922 elections, with the industrial situation showing little sign of improvement, the Government was forced to concede the intervention would not be a short-term affair. Acknowledging that 'workless men' would 'either receive assistance or starve', Lord Novar agreed that from then on, the Scottish Office's major function was the alleviation of unemployment.[6] Thus, although the Conservative administration professed a belief in a property-owning democracy (however small), the realities of securing working class support meant a much softer approach.[7]

The difficulties the Conservatives faced in maintaining both their ideology and electoral support was graphically illustrated by the events surrounding the 1926 miners' strike. Here they found the logic of promoting property ownership sharply at odds with the immediacies of preserving order. Whether or not there was collusion with the Court over delaying a decision is now a moot point, but there can be little doubt of the Opposition's amazement at the Government's willingness, despite the anger of many parish councils, to enforce its circular on relief. As Gilmour told the Commons, it had been the Government's 'undoubtable duty to give parish councils guidance'.[8]

The Conservatives' apparent willingness to promote new forms of welfare was underlined during the 1934 Poor Law Bill debates. At a time when Labour had only a handful of Scottish MPs, the Government found its proposals being destroyed by the troubled conscience of its own backbenchers. Worried about the continued deprivation of so many, they sought a policy which would emphasise a humane approach to the disbursement of relief. Again Labour were dumbfounded, Neil MacLean (Govan) actually thanking Skelton for the 'toleration' he had shown to Labour's successful amendments.

Just as dramatic was Collins's refusal to adopt a hard attitude towards Labour's policy of restoring the cuts. Although it is not known how he felt about the establishment of the Greenock Court of Enquiry (he did not think Glasgow's increases were 'extravagant'), there seems little doubt that he used Labour's attack on traditional principles both to substantiate his own claims for an improvement in benefit and to defeat a hardline 'property conscious' element within the Conservative establishment.[9] The Greenock Hospital affair only served to underline the shift in Conservative philosophy and the predicament they faced. In their view improved health care could only come through collectivised welfare, yet local ratepayers, their 'natural' supporters continued to remain attached to the utility of the old institutional framework.

Nevertheless it should not be assumed that there was a radical and consistent set of demands being presented by Labour. Whatever the action of the more militant councillors, and despite Maxton's notorious 1923 Commons speech, the Parliamentary Party emerged from the 1920s in a moderate, but somewhat confused state over the future direction of welfare.[10] For instance at the end of 1922, the Board was surprised to find Maxton, an ex-Glasgow Education Authority Councillor, declaring the restrictions on Scottish Educational welfare to be a 'purely local affair'.[11] Far from demanding a Commons debate on the matter, Maxton indicated he wished to proceed through Scottish administrative channels. A year later, when there was a potato famine in the Western Highlands, Labour MPs again demonstrated a willingness to follow the consensual line.[12] Adamson, when he entered office in January 1924, was quite content to use Lord Novar's plans to import foodstuffs as the basis of his own policy. Indeed the Board itself considered his and Stewart's activities during the first Labour Government were no more than a mixture of moderation and humanitarianism.[13] Although on the surface all these activities, together with Maxton's evidence to the 1926 Hospital Committee, reflected Labour's desire to capture the middle ground of Scottish politics, they did indicate a much deeper difficulty: an ambivalence over the future means of distributing welfare in a Socialist State. This was most forcefully illustrated during the 1929 Local Government Bill.

During the Second Reading, one of their MPs, W. M. Watson, described the proposed destruction of parish councils as 'undermining' the essential nature of Scottish democracy.[14] To Labour cheers, he added, the whole Bill 'was alien to the Scottish character'. Tom Johnston went further and suggested that the prospect of a greater local welfare bureaucracy would actually inhibit the meeting of real working-class needs. Yet in almost the same breath, he and other Labour MPs castigated the Government for not introducing clauses that would make rate-aided hospital development mandatory. At the end of the 1920s, Labour had singularly failed to resolve one of Socialism's basic dilemmas, the choice between preserving democratic accountablity and promoting a more efficient and centralised welfare programme. Indeed in the 1930s, when the Department attempted to introduce municipal hospitals, it remained an issue that Labour found difficult to resolve. Many Labour authorities, rather than accept the implications of nationally directed collectivism, preferred to promote the principles of local government autonomy, even if it did mean a loss of material well-being.

Both main parties had therefore encountered some difficulty in developing an electorally credible policy, the Conservatives unsure about incorporating working-class interests, and Labour ambivalent about the nature of central control. In consequence, defining one of the essential elements in the pre-1914 debates, the nature of the State's relationship to the recipient of welfare, could not be exhaustively undertaken. Yet in a popular democracy, which was demanding greater State intervention to guarantee material well-being, these were issues that could not be conveniently forgotten. Thus in late 1937 Elliot, alarmed at the prospect of the Conservatives losing their electoral majority, urged his Cabinet colleagues to develop new interventionist policies, to mitigate the worst effects of Scotland's bad housing and health.[15] For their part, Labour began to accept that the issue of meeting need was electorally far more vital than any socialist concern for accountablity and autonomy.[16]

This apparent convergence of perspectives was underlined by the conclusions of the 1938 Interdepartmental Committee on the Poor Law. Many public assistance committees, it argued, had experienced difficulty in incorporating new statutory duties within their existing administrative practice. Although the 1934 Act had obliged then to develop retraining programmes for the 'residuum' of unemployed, few had done so. The opportunity to reorganise and expand their Children's Department after the 1930 Adoption Act – which named the Inspector of Poor as the child's interim guardian, and the 1932 Children and Young Persons Act – which increased the age of child protection to nine – was

almost uniformly ignored. Added to this, an increasing number of sick
and disabled men were applying for relief, whether because sickness
benefit had run out or because it was inadequate for their family needs.
The same applied to widows and pensioners. It all seemed to much for
one local authority department.

By the beginning of the war, national administrators in particular
had come to accept that the lessons of the 1930s – the material deprivation
of so many, the failure to remove the 'taint of pauperism' and the lack
of local authority co-ordination – indicated that a radical shift in perspective was imperative. If working-class interests were to be guaranteed,
the economy regenerated, and public order maintained, meeting welfare
needs through the introduction of a more 'humanistic' ethic of care, a
redistribution of resources and direct central control had become a
necessity. Thus in 1941 the Determination of Needs Act, at the same
time as abolishing the family means test, transferred the majority of
widows and pensioners from the Poor Law to a nationally operated
Assistance Board. A year later, the Beveridge Report's recommendations
effectively removed the local authority from the sphere of providing
monetary assistance. The following spring, Johnston secured the
approval of his Secretary of State's Committee to ensure the continuance
of the State as a third party in hospital provision. But that still left local
authorities with the need to provide domiciliary and institutional support for a variety of other groups, including the elderly, children and
the disabled. Thus after a public scandal about the condition of children
under Poor Law care, the Government in 1945 established a Committee
on Homeless Children to provide a comprehensive review of existing
practice and suggest a framework for the continued involvement of local
authorities in the meeting of need.[17]

After hearing contradictory evidence from existing local authorities
and voluntary agencies on the benefits of the existing system, and from
the Department on the inadequacies of existing central control, the Committee began its own survey. Almost immediately Glasgow's policy of
fostering in the Highlands came under severe criticism. The Committee
member responsible for the investigation felt that the children were
often under the care of mothers who lacked even the most rudimentary
knowledge of hygiene and personal care.[18] An equally condemnatory
survey was reported of the Catholic Orphanage at Smyllum, Lanark.
There the member felt the untrained staff ran a very 'dismal' and 'spar-
tan' institution. In consequence there was little or no 'freedom' for the
child's character to develop.

These and other reports led to one conclusion: the existing form of
care under a single local authority department, staffed largely by
untrained workers, was incapable of generating a more expansive and
individually oriented form of welfare practice. Only a highly specialised
and integrated child service, which put care before the concept of

legalism, could further the promotion of need. In this way the dangers of discrimination and uninterest which had befallen many under the Poor Law's control would be averted. In any prospective legislation the complete removal of the 'parochial taint' was an immediate priority.

The direction of legislation and the type of practice within any new social service was quickly indicated by G.H. Henderson, the Department's Permanent Secretary. To a conference of local authorities in July 1946 he stated that, like the Department, they would have to develop a wider service than one of meeting purely material or 'disablement' need.[19] Moreover the conduct of officials would have to be on a different footing, one that did not imply disenfranchisement, moral stigma or punative treatment. Instead, officials would have to generate and sustain a client's belief that they were no more than a 'helping hand' in overcoming the difficulties of family life in a more complex and mature industrial society.

Some thirty years after the Poor Law Report, a formula for basing social welfare on the promotion of individual need without recourse to guilt or shame had been elaborated. The Government had struck a balance between promoting the 'rights' of individuals within a more advanced industrial society, guaranteeing working-class interests and ensuring the maintenance of order.

NOTES
1. The State of Scotland, SRO DD 10.292.
2. Department of Health, Report on Infant Mortality (Edinburgh, 1943).
3. Leader (18.11.22), in Lennox Herald, p.2.
4. Memorandum by the Permanent Under Secretary of State for Scotland, J. Jeffrey, (November 1936), Gilmour Committee on Scottish Administration, SRO HH 45.64.
5. Cabinet Paper No. 3345, The Unemployment Situation (28.9.21), PRO CAB 24.128.
6. Letter of Scottish Office to Board of Agriculture (10.1.23), SRO AF 43.203.
7. see Skelton, N., Constructive Conservatism (Edinburgh, 1924).
8. (17.6.26), Hansard 196 (Fifth Series), p.2546.
9. (5.7.34), ibid. 291 p.2186.
10. (27.6.23), ibid. 165 p.2382.
11. Minute of 22.11.22, SRO ED 7.7.7.
12. Distress in Western Isles, ibid. 7.7.6; AF 43.193-307, 62.1960-80, 67.378-388.
13. Activities of Scottish Departments since Advent of Labour Government, ibid. HH 45.54; AF 43.222.
14. (3.12.28), Hansard 223 (Fifth Series) pp.859-975.
15. SRO DD 10.292.
16. see for instance, Interim Report of the Labour Party Committee of Inquiry into Distressed Areas, Labour and Distressed Areas.

(London, 1937); Woodburn, A. (1940), Scotland – Plan or Perish, in *Plebs XXXII (1)*. pp.20-32; Johnston, T., *Memories*. (London, 1952).

17. *Report of the Committee on Homeless Children. Cmd. 6911 (P.P. 1946 Vol. XII).*

18. Report of Visits to Homes, *SRO ED 11.168*.

19. Meeting (29.7.46), Abolition of Poor Law, Glasgow Corporation Paper, *SRA D-TC 8.16B.32.1*; a later meeting (4.10.46) with the Secretary of State, J. Westwood, confirmed the Poor Law's abolition.

STATISTICAL APPENDICES

The Scottish Poor Law: Numbers asssisted and Annual Expenditure, 1859-1938.

1. Table showing Number of Ordinary Poor on Relief at 15 May each Year, and Annual Expenditure, 1859-1938.

	Males	Females	Total	Depts	Grand Total	Annual Expenditure	Per Cent of Population
1859	nk	nk	77,000	40,000	117,000	£546,000	3.9
1870	nk	nk	76,000	50,000	126,000	£684,000	3.8
1880	nk	nk	57,000	38,000	95,000	£645,000	2.6
1890	15,000	36,000	50,000	33,000	82,000	£605,000	2.1
1900	15,000	37,000	52,000	34,000	86,000	£731,000	1.9
1910	20,000	38,000	58,000	40,000	98,000	£1,139,000	2.1
1920	13,000	27,000	40,000	31,000	72,000	£2,500,000	1.5
1930	30,000	37,000	67,000	54,000	121,000	£2,900,000	2.5
1938	63,000	56,000	119,000	98,000	217,000	£5,175,000	4.3

Ordinary Poor were those both 'destitute and disabled' and included the sick, the infirm, the aged, widows, deserted wives, and orphan and deserted children. It excluded the insane.

2. Table showing Number of Able-Bodied Unemployed on Poor Relief at 15 May each Year, and Annual Expenditure, 1922-38.

	Males	Females	Total	Depts	Grand Total	Annual Expenditure	Per Cent of Population
1922	36,000	4,000	40,000	96,000	137,000	£1,190,000	2.8
1926	32,000	3,000	36,000	83,000	119,000	£1,350,000	2.4
1930	11,000	1,000	13,000	28,000	41,000	£340,000	0.8
1934	66,000	7,000	72,000	142,000	215,000	£2,420,000	4.4
1938	5,000	2,000	7,000	9,000	16,000	£350,000	0.3

3. Table showing Per Cent of Population on Ordinary Poor Relief, by Selected Counties, at 15 May each Year, 1869-1934.

	1869	1903	1934
Ross and Cromarty	4.9	3.7	3.7
Banffshire	5.0	2.0	1.7
Perthshire	3.7	1.4	1.1
Glasgow	3.3	2.3	6.6
Lanarkshire (excl. Glasgow)	2.9	1.9	5.2
West Lothian	3.5	1.9	4.5
Roxburghshire	3.0	1.5	1.0
Kirkcudbrightshire	5.0	2.3	1.2

Sources: *Annual Reports of the Board of Supervision, the Local Government Board, the Board of Health and the Department of Health.*

APPENDIX 2

Scottish Hospitals, 1840-1938

1. Scottish Hospitals; Number of Beds and Annual Expenditure, 1840-1938.

Date		Beds	Sector	Annual Expenditure
1840		2,000	Voluntary	£50,000
1890		6,000	Voluntary	£250,000
		4,500	Poor Law	£100,000
		1,500	Public Health	£50,000
	Total	12,000		£400,000
1914		10,500	Voluntary	£500,000
		6,900	Poor Law	£200,000
		7,900	Public Health	£400,000
	Total	25,300		£1,100,000
1938		14,100	Voluntary	£2,000,000
		5,600	Poor Law	£400,000
		15,400	Public Health	£1,600,000
	Total	35,100		£4,000,000

2. Scottish Hospital Admissions, 1870-1937; Numbers per Annum.

	Voluntary	Public Health	Poor Law
1870	24,000	nk	nk
1890	40,000	15,000	15,000
1913	79,000	50,000	33,000
1937	181,000	75,000	55,000

Beds, expenditure and admissions have been rounded as a number of Hospitals provided only estimates. Poor Law figures relate to officially classified sick beds.
Sources: *The Medical Directory for Scotland* 9 Vols. (London, 1852-60); Burdett, H. C., *Pay Hospitals and Paying Wards throughout the World* (London, 1880); *Hospitals and Asylums of the World* 4 Vols. (London, 1891-3); *Hospitals and Charities, Annual Reports* London, 1890-1930); *Hospital Yearbook, Annual Reports* (London, 1931-48); *Report on the Hospital and Nursing Services in Scotland Cmd.699 (P.P. 1920 Vol.XXII)*; The Department of Health *Report on the Hospital Survey of Scotland* (Edinburgh, 1946); *Annual Reports of the Board of Supervision, the Local Government Board, the Board of Health and the Department of Health.*

APPENDIX 3

Children under the Poor Law, Scotland, 1890-1945.

1. Number of Children under Poor Law Care at 15th May each Year.

	Orphan	Deserted	Separated from Parents	Total
1891	3165	1316	1190	5671
1900	2819	1175	2149	6143
1910	2802	1401	3730	7933
1914	2431	1503	4939	8873
1923	2446	1052	4338	7836
1933	1174	1227	6799	9200
1945	803	744	5700	7229

2. Number of Children Boarded Out at 15 May each Year.

	Boarded Out Separated	All Boarded Out
1891	700*	4883
1900	1821	5446
1910	3273	7106
1914	3967	7633
1923	3555	6841
1933	5863	8150
1945	4882	6343

* = estimate

Sources: *Annual Reports of the Board of Supervision, the Local Government Board, the Board of Health, and the Department of Health.*

APPENDIX 4

Work at Dundee Poorhouse; the Governor's Annual Report, 1905.

The work provided for the male inmates consists principally of wood-chopping and bunching, rope-teasing, yarn-winding, and field labour. A number of inmates are also employed at their respective trades, such as joinering, painting, shoe-making, tailoring, or plumber work, and smith work.

The most profitable works, financially, are firewood and rope-teasing, in which the ordinary inmates are chiefly engaged.

Table showing the numbe of Ordinary Inmates chargeable at 31st December 1905, and how those able for work were employed:-

Poorhouse and Hospital

	Males	Females	Children	Total
Working – Firewood and Bunching,	39			
Firelighters,	2			
Rope-teasing and yarn winding,	50	9		
Joiners,	2			
Plumbers,	1			
Painters,	3			
Shoemakers,	3			
Tailors, sewers, and knitters,	3	36		
Gate-keepers,	4			
In kitchen, sculleries, and stores,	5	16		
In straw shed,	3			
Scavengers,	3			
Coal carriers,	6			
Window Cleaners,	6			
Warders and cleaners,	36	55		
Laundry workers,	2	12		
Messengers,	9			
Field and garden workers,	2			
	189	128		317
Unable for Work –				
Hospital patients,	93	165	47	
Infirm inmates,	50	94		
In children's departments,	111			
	143	259	158	560
				877

Although rope-teasing is perhaps, not a very desirable occupation, when the constant demand for such is considered, and also the fact that, within the last

four years, the drawings from the sale of firewood alone have been more than doubled, I think the introduction of new work might be delayed in the meantime. I am, however, in favour of Mr Barclay's [the General Superintendent] suggestion, viz, the introduction of an automatic weaving machine, and may, perhaps, later on have an opportunity of requesting that his suggestion be adopted.
No structural alterations have been made during the year. The refitting of the Punsishment cell, and also the erection of the enclosure or shed in which the circular-saw has been fitted up have already been fully reported to the Parish Council. Before the circular saw was introduced some 24 men were constantly employed at cross-cutting wood by hand-saws. This work is now overtaken by 5 men. We are thus afforded a better opportunity of bringing the "test" into play by having those under "test" discipline isolated, and kept at stone-breaking or other work suitable for that class.

Admissions to the Poorhouse during the twelve months as under:

	Number	Total	
Entered for the	First time,	1382	1382
	Second time,	315	630
	Third time,	140	420
	Fourth time,	41	164
	Fifth time,	31	155
	Sixth time,	16	96
	Seventh time,	6	42
	Eighth time,	3	24
	Ninth time,	2	18
	Eleventh time,	1	11
	Thirteenth time,	1	13
	Fourteenth time,	1	14
	Total number of admissions,		2969

The following information (voluntarily given) was obtained:-

	Men	Women	Total
Drank heavily,	339	248	587
Drank moderately,	319	276	595
Total Abstainers,	94	258	352
			1534
Had been in Prison,	356	176	532
Never been in Prison,	396	606	1002

Left the Poorhouse rather than work,   41 men.

Source; Governer's Annual Report, 1905, in Dundee Parish Council Minutes, 12.2.06. *TRA TC.PCM.11.*

APPENDIX 5

Dietary Tables: Glasgow Poor Law Hospitals, 1904

Breakfast.
1. Ordinary.– Early Breakfast in bed, at 6.30 a.m., or thereby; Tea, ½ pint, with Bread and Butter.
   At 9 a.m.– Porridge, ½ pint; Tea, ½ pint; Milk, ½ pint; Bread Butter; or Coffee in place of Tea.
2. Special, or Low Diet.– Milk, 1½ pints; Bread, 6 oz.; Sugar, ½ oz., made into Sops when necessary.

Dinners.
1. Ordinary.– Lentil or Pea Soup, 1 pint; Rice Pudding, Bread.
   Broth, 1 pint; Meat, 6 oz.; Potatoes, 12 oz.; Bread.
   Stewed Meat, 6 oz.; Vegetables (mixed), 6 oz.; Potatoes, 12 oz.; Bread Pudding, Bread.
   Broth; Meat, 6 oz.; potatoes, 12 oz.; Bread.
   Rice soup, 1 pint; Meat 6 oz.; Potatoes, 12 oz.; Bread.
   Fish, 12 oz.; Potatoes, 12 oz.; Semolina Pudding, Bread.
   Potato Soup, 1 pint; Meat, 6 oz.; Potatoes, 12 oz.; Bread.
2. Special, or Low Diet.– Rice, Ground Rice, Sago, Semolina, Tapioca – one or other – 2 oz., dry, boiled in 1 pint sweet milk, with ¾oz. sugar, Milk, 1 pint; Bread, 2 oz.

Suppers.
1. Ordinary.– Tea, 1 pint; Bread and Butter, Cheese, 2 oz., or, tea, 1 pint, with Bread and Marmalade, or Jam.
2. Special or Low Diet.– Tea, 1 pint, with Bread and Marmalade, or Jam.
   (Quantities where not specified to be ad libitum)

Children's Dietary.
Children from 8 to 14, same as adults.
Children from 5 to 8 years, one-half thereof.
Children till 5 years of age, 1½ pints Sweet Milk, and 8 oz. Bread, to be increased according to age, and prepared as Medical officer may direct.

Instructions as to Preparation of Above Diets.
1. Tea, each pint to be made from ¼ oz. tea, 1 oz. sugar, and gill of milk.
2. Coffee, each pint to be made from oz. ground coffee, which may be 4 parts coffee to 1 part chicory, 3 oz. sugar, and gill milk.
3. Milk, in all cases, to be sweet, or entire milk.
4. Porridge, each pint to be made from 4 oz. of oatmeal.
5. Bread and butter, 1 oz. butter shall be spread on each 8 oz. bread; crust of bread to be cut off and ultimately used for bread puddings, and crumbs for other cooking purposes.

6. Marmalade or jam, 1 oz.

7. Lentil or Pea Soup of Sunday's dinner, each pint shall be made from 1 oz. marrow bone, or 1 oz. ox head, or oz. meat, and 2 oz. split peas or lentils, and 1 oz. fresh vegetables.

8. Broth, Rice Soup, and Potato Soup. These are to be prepared from the stock in which the meat of each day's dinner is boiled. If broth, each pint to contain 1½ oz. barely, ½ oz. peas, and 1½ oz. mixed vegetables; if rice soup, each pint to contain 1 oz. rice, and ¼ oz. onion; if potato soup, each pint to contain 4 oz. potatoes, ½ oz. onion, and 1½ oz. carrot and turnip.

9. Meat, to be either beef or mutton, and, except with Tuseday's dinner, to be boiled. The stated weight, 6 oz., refers to weight uncooked and without bone.

10. Stewed Meat, the meat, beef or mutton, to be stewed with the potatoes and mixed vegetables.

11. Fish, to be white fish or fresh herring, to be weighed uncooked, trimmed and cleaned; to be boiled or cooked in a steamer; to be served with a sauce, containing for each portion ½ oz. flour, and ½ oz. butter, and 3 oz. milk.

12. Puddings. Rice pudding to be made from 2 oz. whole or ground rice, and ¼ pint sweet milk, and 1 oz. butter; Semolina puddings as the foregoing, using semolina in place of rice; Bread pudding, to be made from 2 oz. bread, and ½ oz. currants, and ½ pint sweet milk, and 1 oz. sugar.

13. Potatoes to be weighed cleaned, and uncooked.

14. Stewed Fruits or Rubarb, or baked Apples, may, when in season, be served instead of puddings.

15. With all dishes, proper seasonings are to be served.

Source; Glasgow Parish Council Minutes, 15.2.04, in *GMLGR B514.701*.

APPENDIX 6

The Unemployed and Scales of Relief, Greenock, 1931.

Man	15s. 3d.
Wife	8s. 0d.
Child	2s. 0d.
Sons 16-17	5s. 6d.
Daughters 16-17	4s. 6d.
Sons 17-18	8s. 0d.
Daughters 17-18	7s. 0d.
Man 18-21 in lodgings	8s. 0d.
Woman 18-21 in lodgings	7s. 0d.
Man over 21 in model	10s. 0d. to 12s. 6d.
Woman over 21 in model	7s. 0d.
Man 18-21 with relatives	8s. 0d.
Woman 18-21 with relatives	7s. 0d.
Man over 21 with relatives	8s. 0d.
Woman over 21 with relatives	8s. 0d.
Maximum	37s. 6d.
Where two adults	23s. 6d.
Family earnings adult male; deduct all in excess of	12s. 6d.
Family earnings adult female; deduct all in excess of	10s. 0d
National Health Insurance; deduct all in excess of	7s. 6d.
Old Age, Widows and Orphans Pension; disregard	all
Blind Pensions; disregard	all
Lodgers and sub-letting; deduct all in excess of	5s. 0d.
or if idle	3s. 6d.
Savings, etc., disregard the first £100	
Casual Earnings, deduct one sixth of benefit.	
Disablement pensions, deduct	all

Instructions;
i – No relief, other than temporary relief, or relief in the poorhouse shall be granted by the sub-committee without the approval of the Public Assistance Committee, unless the applicant has resided within the Burgh for more than one year immediately prior to the date of application, and has been employed (otherwise than on relief work) for at least six months within that period.
ii – Outdoor relief shall not be granted to the following classes of Able-bodied Destitute Persons, namely – a) Residents in house over 16 years of age b) Single men in private lodgings c) Single women in private lodgings d) Men in models and farmed out houses, Unless the applicant proves to the satisfaction of the sub-committee – 1) that he has not been in receipt of relief for a longer period

than two years immediately prior to his application 2) that he has been employed, otherwise than on relief work, for at least six months in the last three years; and 3) that he has been genuinely seeking work, but has been unable to obtain employment.

III – Relief shall not be granted without the sanction of the Public Assistance Committee to any person 1) who has voluntarily left his or her employment, or has been dismissed for misconduct 2) who has been convicted of any offence or indictment, or has been convicted of any offence on a summary complaint on more than one occassion; or 3) who is shown to the the satisfaction of the sub-committee to have refused work.

IV – No person who enters into marriage while in receipt of relief or who applies for relief within six months of being married without having a reasonable period of employment immediately prior ro such marriage, shall be granted outdoor relief.

V – No outdoor relief shall be granted to a pregnant unmarried woman.

VI – No outdoor relief shall be paid to an unmarried man who admits that he is, or has been declared by the Court to be, the father of an illegitimate child.

VII – No unmarried person, whose parents are resident within the Burgh, shall recieve a larger sum of relief than he would have been entitled to had he been resident with his parents.

VIII – Relief payable to a person shall not be increased by reason of any of his children leaving the house, on obtaining employment and entering private lodgings within the Burgh.

IX – The Inspector in his sole discretion may relieve temporarily any recipient in kind, should he have any reason to believe that relief granted is being applied by the applicant otherwise than for the necessities of life.

X – No able-bodied inmate of the Poorhouse who is discharged therefrom, for misconduct or non-conformance to the rules of the Poorhouse while an inmate thereof, shall be granted any relief for a period of at least one month from the date of such discharge.

XI – Unless in exceptional circumstances no outdoor relief shall be granted to a married person living apart.

XII – No outdoor relief shall be granted to a married woman who has during chargeablity given birth to an illegitimate child, or to a married man who has admitted that he is, or been declared by Decree Court, to the the father of an illegitimate child.

XIII – In no case shall outdoor relief be graated without the sanction of the Public Assistance Committee, to any person a) who has been convicted of fraud upon the Parish Council, or b) who has wilfully withheld, or falsely represented, material facts in his applicatiuon, in order to obtain a larger grant of relief than he would otherwise have been entitled to.

XIV – No appeal by any applicant shall be comptetent unless the applicant can prove to the satisfaction of the Conveners of the Public Assistance Committee and the Sub-Committee, the Provost, and the Inspector, that the decision of the Sub-Committee is not in accordance with the foregoing instructions.

Source: Greenock Town Council Minutes, 1930-1, in *Greenock Public Library*; Evidence of Keith, Sir H. S. (20.3.31), to the Royal Commission on Unemployment Insurance, in *op. cit.*

APPENDIX 7

Glasgow Parish Council: Scale of Aliment, 1910.

I Persons with Dependants.
    a) 5s. per week for recipients, and in addition
       4s.6d per week for each son or daughter working
       4s.per week for one child under 14
       3s.6d per week for second child under 14
       3s.per week for third child under 14
       2s.per week for each additional child under 14
In addition, each child attending school to be given one suit or one dress, one pair of boots and stockings annually, with an outfit on obtaining work, if necessary.
    b) When recipient is the husband, his wife, if working, to be calculated as an adult worker, if not working as a dependant.
    c) A son or daughter able to work, but idle, no allowance to be made.
    d) When calculating earnings of recipient only ¾ (three-quarters) to be reckoned as income and deducted.
    e) Where recipient is in receipt of sick aliment from a Friendly Society 5s. per week to be deducted off same and remainder, if any, reckoned as income.
    f) Weekly earnings of sons and daughters of 4s.6d. and under to be reckoned as income
       5s. and 5s.6d. to be reckoned as income of 4s.6d.
       6s. and under 13s. to be reckoned as income of 1s. less
       13s. to be reckoned as income of 11s.6d.
       14s. to be reckoned as income of 12s.
       15s. to be reckoned as income of 13s. and deducted.
       16s. or 17s. to be reckoned as income of 13s.6d.
       18s. to 20s. to be reckoned as income of 15s.6d.
       21s. to 25s. to be reckoned as income of 16s.6d.
       26s. to 30s. to be reckoned as income of 17s.6d.
       Above 30s.to be reckoned as income of 18s.
       This will be the minimum that will be taken as income, and the employer's certificate to be the authority taken for wages earned.

II Destitute Old or Infirm Persons
    1) Living in their own houses, 5s. per week each; and all combined income above 2s.6d. per week to be deducted, but if recipeints' income is partly from Friendly Society, only that portion of income above 4s. to be deducted.
    2) In the case of a widow or widower with one of a family, and that member working, aliment to be granted as follows:-
If combined income is

5s. per week, allow aliment of 5s. per week
6s. per week, allow aliment of 4s.per week
7s. per week, allow aliment of 3s.6d. per week
8s. or 9s. per week, allow aliment of 3s.per week
10s. or 11s. per week, allow aliment of 2s.6d. per week
12s. per week, allow aliment of 2s. per week
13s. per week, allow aliment of 1s.6d. per week
14s. per week, allow aliment of 1s. per week
15s. or more, allow no aliment.

In no case must applicant's personal income including aliment, be more than 7s.6d. per week.

3) In the case of a married couple with one or two of a family the earnings of the family to be treated as in Section I.(f), and income going into house to be supplemented to 16s. for a household of three, and 20s. for a houshold of four.

4) Living with friends, 4s. per week each; all income of recipients to be deducted unless where the income is from a Friendly Society or Charitable Society, in which case allow 1s.6d. per week.

5) Living with son, daughter or grandchildren, maximum 4s. per week each; but less as household income warranted; all income of recipients to be deducted except allowance under clause 4.

6) Cases in Institutions, Homes, etc.; uniform rate of 3s. per week to be allowed.

III. Wives with Dependants, whose Husbands are in Asylum, Hospital, &c.
   To be treated as temporary cases and according to circumstances, but in no case must aliment be more than 15s. per week. If husband in Asylum for more than three months continuously wife and dependents to be treated as in Section I.

IV. Wives, with Dependants whose Husbands have Deserted them or are in Prison.
   To be offered indoor relief, but in very excpetional cases they would be treated as those under Section III.

Source: Glasgow Parish Council Minutes, 11.11.10, *op. cit.*.

APPENDIX 8

Glasgow Parish Council: Scale of Aliment, 1922.

Part I. Persons with Dependants.
a) 15s.6d. for recipient
8s. for wife if dependent and not working
6s. for first dependent child
5s. other dependent children.
2s. for pregnant mothers or children under two.
In addition, one suit, two pairs of boots and stockings, shirt and combinations
for boys at school; one dress, two pairs of boots and stockings, chemise,
petticoat and knickers for girls at school, also coat every two years to each.
b) Where wife and family in house and working, one third of all earnings to be
reckoned as income of recipient and aliment reduced accordingly, provided
not less than 18s. per week is left to the worker if earned. In the case of a wife
working, if earnings not equal to 8s., they will be supplemented by aliment
to that amount.
c) When calculating earnings of recipient, only two thirds to be reckoned as
income and deducted.
d) One half of all amounts received for board and lodgings to be treated as
income and deducted from aliment. One half for lodgers only.

Part II. Destitute Old and Infirm Poor.
a) Living alone in own house without family, 15s.6d.
A couple living alone in own house without family, 23s.6d.
If there is a family – Single Person. 12s.6d.
If there is a family – Couple. 20s.6d.
and all combined income above 3s. per week to be deducted.
b) Widow or widower with one of family working, and unmarried, 15s.6d., but
earnings deducted as on Part I (b).
c) Married couple with one or more of family working, relief to be given as in
Part I (a) and earnings Part I (b).
d) With friends 9s. each, but all income over 2s.6d. to be deducted.
e) With son or daughter or grandchildren, 9s. each; but less as household income
warrants. All income of recipients to be deducted.
f) Cases in Institutions, Homes etc., uniform rate 8s. per week each.
g) Where recipient is a compulsory insured person and in receipt of Benefit, as
ordained by Statute only amount over 7s.6d. of benefit to be deducted as
income. If a voluntary member of a Friendly Society, 10s. free of deduction,
but in all cases 10s. will be maximum amount to be reckoned. Where husband
or wife is maintained in a charitable or rate supported Institution, full Benefit
to be deducted.

Part III. Wife and Dependants and Husband in Hospital or other Institution.
To be treated according to circumstances, but not so liberally as in Part I, as they
are usually temporary cases. If however husband in for more than three months
then as Part I (a).

Part IV. Wife and Dependants and Husband Deserted or in Prison.
To be offered indoor relief, unless in very exceptional circumstances when treated
as in Part III.
Notes: the average cost of clothing (Part I) means an extra allowance of 2s. a
week to children who receive them. Adult poor – clothing only to be allowed to
aged and infirm without relatives, limited in value to £2 sterling per annum.

Source: Bonhill Parish Council Minutes, 1923, *op. cit.*

SOURCES AND SELECT BIBLIOGRAPHY

The Sources have been arranged as follows:
PART I   Manuscript Sources
A The Scottish Record Office
B The Public Record Office
C Local Archives and Libraries

PART II   Official Reports, Pamphlets and other Material
A Parliamentary Papers
B Non-Parliamentary Papers
C Acts of Parliament
D Bills presented before Parliament
E Hansard

PART III   Newspapers

PART IV   Contemporary Journals

PART V   Historical and other Scottish Works published before 1960

PART VI   Other Printed Works

PART I   Manuscript Sources
A SRO: Scottish Record Office (Edinburgh)
Lord Advocates' Department Papers (AD) 56.254, 276

Agriculture and Fisheries Department Papers (AF) 43.193-307, 62.1960-80,   388

County Council Papers (CO) 1.4; 2.97, 99

Development Department Papers (DD) 5.439, 693-721; 10.169, 182, 184, 192, 193, 237, 242, 243, 245, 246, 292, 363

Education Department Papers (ED) 7.1, 7; 11.155-276

General Papers (GD) 40.16

Home and Health Department Papers (HH) 1.471, 486, 496-507, 915; 2.15, 16; 9.3, 5, 24, 25, 35, 54; 23.1-23; 26.1; 28.2; 31.36; 40.1-242; 45.54, 62, 64, 65; 50.166; 56.15, 19; 60.65; 61.101, 105; 64.51, 151, 161; 65.49-53, 62-7, 70-2, 93, 94;

Sheriff Court Papers (SC) 36.7

B PRO: Public Record Office (London)
Cabinet Minutes 1921-36 (CAB 23)
Cabinet Papers on Unemployment and the Scottish Poor Law, 1921-36 SCAB 24T
Cabinet Papers of the Committee on the Regulations of the Unemployment

c Local Archives and Libraries
ADA: Ayrshire District Archives (Ayr)
Ardrossan Parish Council Minutes CO.3.21
Auchinleck Parish Council Minutes CO.3.22
Galston Parish Council Minutes CO.3.38
Irvine Parish Council Miniutes CO.3.40
Old Cumnock Parish Council Minutes CO.3.52
Stevenston Parish Council Minutes CO.3.59
Kyle Combination Poorhouse Minutes CO.3.65

Central Regional Archives (Stirling)
Falkirk Parish Council Minutes FA.1.8
Logie Parish Council Minutes XA.2.2
St. Ninians Parish Council Minutes XA.2.1

Edinburgh District Archives
Edinburgh City Parochial Board Minutes
Edinburgh Parish Council Minutes
Edinburgh City Corporation Minutes
Kirkliston Parish Council Minutes

EPLER: Edinburgh Public Library (Edinburgh Room)
Edinburgh Parish Council Minutes qYHV 251
Edinburgh City Corporation Minutes YJS 4245A2
Leith Parish Council Minutes qYHV 243L

FRCR: Fife Regional Council Records (Glenrothes)
Ballingry Parish Council Minutes 6.8
Beath Parish Council Minutes 6.10
Culross Parish Council Minutes 6.19
Fife County Council Minutes 3.11
Wemyss Parish Council Minutes 6.56

GMLGR: Glasgow Mitchell Library (Glasgow Room)
Glasgow Parish Council Minutes B514.79
Glasgow City Corporation Minutes
Govan Parish Council Minutes G352.04143
Lamond, R. P., Memorandum on the Children and Education Acts, 1908 G362.7
Memorandum Regarding Procedures adopted by the Parish Council of Glasgow
    and its Inspector of Poor of the Children's Act, 1908. (1911) G362.7
    Supplementary Memorandum by Inspector of Poor on the Children's Act,
    1908, June 1910 G362.7

Inverclyde District Library (Greenock)
Greenock Town Council Minutes
Midlothian District Council Records (Edinburgh)
Cranston Parish Council Minutes
Newbattle Parish Council Minutes
Renfrew District Library (Paisley)
Paisley Parochial Board Minutes 57.7

SRA: Strathclyde Regional Archives (Glasgow)
Avondale Parish Council Minutes CO.1.20
Cadder Parish Council Minutes CO.1.24
Barony Parish Council Minutes D-HEW 2.2
Barony Parochial Board Minutes D-HEW 2.2
Blantyre Parish Council Minutes and Inspector's Letter Book CO.1.22

Bonhill Parish Council Minutes and Inspector's Letter Book CO.4.12
Bothwell Parish Council Minutes Council CO.1.23
Cambuslang Parish Council Minutes CO.1.25
Dalziel Parish Council Minutes CO 1.37
Douglas Parish Council Minutes CO.1.39
Dunbartonshire County Council Minutes CO.4.4
Glasgow Parish Council Minutes D-HEW 1.2
Glasgow Parochial Board Minutes D-HEW 1.2
Glasgow Parish Council Miscellaneous Prints T-PAR
Glasgow City Corporation Minutes C.1.3
Glasgow City Corporation Miscellaneous Health Department Papers D-HE 1.1
Glasgow City Corporation Town Clerk's Papers D-TC 8
Govan Parish Council Minutes D-HEW 5.1
Old Kilpatrick Parish Council Minutes CO.4.20
Omoa Combination Parish Council Minutes CO.1.23
Renfrewshire County Council Minutes CO.2.3
Rutherglen Parish Council Minutes CO.1.53

TRA: Tayside Regional Council Archives (Dundee)
Dundee Parish Council Minutes TC.PCM

West Lothian Public Library (Bathgate)
West Calder Parish Council Minutes 2.1
Uphall Parish Council Minutes 1.1

PART II. Official Reports, Pamphlets and other Material
A Parliamentary Papers
Annual Reports of the Board of Supervision (1846-94)
Annual Reports of the Local Government Board for Scotland (1894-1919)
Annual Reports of the Scottish Board of Health (1919-1928)
Annual Reports of the Department of Health for Scotland (1929-48)
Annual Reports of the Board of Commissioners in Lunacy (1858-1914)
Annual Reports of the Board of Control (1915-38)
    Report of the Royal Commission on the Poor Law (Scotland). (P.P. 1844 Vols.
    XX-XXV)
Select Committee of the House of Lords on the Laws relating to Parochial
    Assessments, 1850. (P.P. 1850 Vol. XVI)
Royal Commission on Lunacy (Scotland). (P.P. 1857 Vol. V)
Return of Able-Bodied Poor. . . Occasional Relief. (P.P. 1865 Vol. XLVIII)
Select Committee on the Poor Law (Scotland), 1869. (P.P. 1868-9 Vol. IX)
Report of the Select Committee on the Poor Law (Scotland). (P.P. 1870 Vol. XI)
Henley, J. J., Report on the Boarding-Out of Pauper Children in Scotland. (P.P.
    1870 Vol. LVIII)
Report of the Civil Departments (Scotland) Committee. C. 64 (P.P. 1870 Vol. XVIII)
Report of the Royal Commission on the Sanitary Laws. C. 281 (P.P. 1871 Vol.
    XXXV)
Skelton, J., Report as to the Boarded-Out Pauper Children in Scotland. C. 1382
    (P.P. 1875 Vol. XXXII) (in the Board of Supervision's Annual Report, 1874-5)
Peterkin, W. A., Report to the Board of Supervision on the System of Boarding
    Pauper Children in Private Dwellings. C. 7140 (P.P. 1893-4 Vol. XLIV)
Report by the Board of Supervision on the Measures taken by Local Authorities
    for the Relief of Able-Bodied Unemployment. C. 7410 (P.P. 1894 Vol. LXX)
Report on Local Taxation in Scotland. C. 7575 (P.P. 1894 Vol. LXXIV)
The Third Report from the Select Committee on Distress from Want of
    Employment. (P.P. 1895 Vol. IX)

Royal Commission on the Aged Poor, Evidence. C. 7684-II (P.P. 1895 Vol. XIV)

Report of the Departmental Committee on Habitual Offenders, Vagrants, Beggars, Inebriates and Juvenile Delinquents. C. 7753 (P.P. 1895 Vol. XXXVII)

Report of the Departmental Committee on Poor Law Schools, Evidence. C. 8027-1 (P.P. 1896 Vol. XXXVII)

Report of the Departmental Committee on Reformatory and Industrial Schools, Evidence. C. 8290 (P.P. 1897 Vol. XLII)

Dunlop, J. C., Report on Prison Dietaries. C. 9514 (P.P. 1899 Vol. XLII)

Report of the Departmental Committee on Prisons (Scotland), Evidence. Cd. 219 (P.P. 1900 Vol. XLII)

Dunlop, J. C., Report on the Dietary of Pauper Lunatics. Cd. 955 (P.P. 1902 Vol. XLI)

Report of the Departmental Committee on the Nursing of the Sick Poor, Evidence. Cd. 1366 (P.P. 1902 Vol. XXXIX)

Report on the Physical Examination of 600 Edinburgh Schoolchildren, in The Royal Commission on Physical Training (Scotland). Cd. 1507 (P.P. 1903 Vol. XXX)

Royal Commission on Physical Training (Scotland), Evidence. Cd. 1508 (P.P. 1903 Vol. XXX)

Report of the Departmental Committee on Poor Law Medical Relief (Scotland). Cd. 2008 (P.P. 1904 Vol. XXXIII)

Report of the Departmental Committee on Poor Law Medical Relief (Scotland), Evidence. Cd. 2022 (P.P. 1904 Vol. XXXIII)

Parish Trusts (Scotland) (No.1), Parish Trusts (Scotland) (No.2) and Burgh Trusts (Scotland). (P.P. 1905 Vol. LXVIII)

Return of Parish Medical Officers (Scotland). (P.P. 1905 Vol. LXVIII)

Report on the Methods of Administering Poor Relief in Certain Large Town Parishes of Scotland. Cd. 2524 (P.P. 1905 Vol. LXVII)

Report of the Select Committee on the Education (Provision of Meals) (Scotland) Bill. (P.P. 1906 Vol. VIII)

Report of the Departmental Committee on Vagrancy, Evidence. Cd. 2891 (P.P. 1906 Vol. CIII)

MacKenzie, W. L. and Foster, A., The Physical Condition of Children Attending the Public School of the School Board of Glasgow. Cd. 3637 (P.P. 1907 Vol. LXV)

Royal Commission on the Care and Control of the Feeble-Minded (Scottish Report). Cd. 4202 (P.P. 1908 Vol. XXXIV)

Royal Commission on the Care and Control of the Feeble-Minded, Scottish Evidence. Cd. 4217 (P.P. 1908 Vol. XXXIV)

Kay, A. C. and Tonybee, H. V., Report on Endowed Voluntary Charities in Certain Places, and the Administrative Relations of Charity and the Poor Law (for the Poor Law Commission). Cd. 4593 (P.P. 1909 Vol. XV)

Report of the Inspector for Scotland under the Inebriates Acts, 1908. Cd. 4682 (P.P. 1909 Vol. XXIV)

Report of the Departmental Committee on the Law Relating to Inebriates and their Detention. . . Cd. 4766 (P.P. 1909 Vol XXVI)

Report of the Royal Commission on the Poor Law. . . for Scotland. Cd. 4922 (P.P. 1909 Vol. XXXVIII)

Royal Commission on the Poor Laws, Scottish Evidence. Cd. 4978 (P.P. 1910 Vol. XLVI)

Royal Commission on the Poor Laws (Unemployment Evidence). Cd. 5068 (P.P. 1910 Vol. XLIX)

Pringle, J. C., On the effects of Employment or Assistance given to the Unemployed since 1886. . . (for the Poor Law Commission). Cd. 5073 (P.P. 1910 Vol. LII)

Parsons, T. C., The Condition of Children who are in Receipt of the Various

Forms of Poor Relief in Certain Parishes in Scotland (for the bPoor Law Commission). Cd. 5075 (P.P. 1910 Vol. LII).

Parsons, C. T., Report on the Physical Condition of Able-Bodied Male Inmates of Certain Scottish Poorhouses, and English Workhouses and Labour Yards (for the Poor Law Commission). Cd. 5076 (P.P. 1910 Vol. LII)

Statistical and Other Documents (Scotland) (for the Poor Law Commission). Cd. 5440 (P.P. 1910 Vol LIV)

Return of Civil Service Appointments. (P.P. 1912-3 Vol. LVI)

Royal Commisison on the Civil Service, Third Report, Evidence. Cd. 6740 (P.P. 1913 Vol. XVIII)

Report on the Hospital and Nursing Services in Scotland. Cmd. 699 (PP 1920 Vol. XXII)

The Interim Report of the Scottish Consultative Council on Medical and Allied Services, in A Scheme of Medical Service for Scotland. Cmd. 1039 (P.P. 1921 Vol. XXX)

Report of the Departmental Committee on Local Taxation in Scotland. Cmd. 1674 (P.P. 1922 Vol. VIII)

Proposals for Reform in Local Government in Scotland. Cmd. 3135 (P.P. 1928 Vol. XIX)

Report of the Committee on Local Expenditure (Scotland). Cmd. 4201 (P.P. 1932-3 Vol. XIV)

Proceedings of the standing Committee on Scottish Bills, 1933-34. (P.P. 1934 Vol. VIII)

Report of the Committee on the Scottish Health Services. Cmd. 5204 (P.P. 1935-6 Vol. XI)

Report of the Departmental Committee on Scottish Administration. Cmd. 5563 (P.P. 1937 Vol. XV)

Report of the Departmental Committee on the Consolidation of the Poor Law (Scotland). Cmd. 5803 (P.P. 1937-8 Vol. XIV)

Report of the Committee on Post-war Hospital Problems in Scotland. Cmd. 6472 (P.P. 1942-3 Vol. IV)

Report of the Committee on Homeless Children. Cmd. 6911 (P.P. 1946 Vol. XII)

B Non-Parliamentary Papers

Royal Commission on Housing in Scotland (Evidence). (London, 1920)

Report of the Scottish Consultative Councils, A Reformed Local Authority for Health and Public Administration. (Edinburgh, 1923)

Royal Commission on National Health Insurance, Evidence, 1925. (London, 1925)

Report on the Hospital Services of Scotland, 1926. (Edinburgh, 1926)

Royal Commission on Local Government, Evidence, 1928. (London, 1928)

Board of Trade, An Industrial Survey of Scotland. (London, 1932)

Department of Health, Consultative Council on Medical and Allied Services Report on Hospital Services. (Edinburgh, 1933)

Royal Commission on Unemployment Insurance, Evidence, 1933. (London, 1933)

The Department of Health, Report on Infant Mortality in Scotland. (Edinburgh, 1943)

The Department of Health, The Scottish Hospital Survey. (Edinburgh, 1946)

C Acts of Parliament

Poor Law (Scotland) Amendement Act. Ch. 83. (8 & 9 Vict. 1845)

Lunacy (Scotland) Act. Ch. 71. (20 & 21st. Vict. 1857)

Public Health (Scotland) Act. Ch. 101. (30 & 31 Vict. 1867)

Secretary for Scotland Act. Ch. 61. (48 & 49 Vict 1885)

Prevention of Cruelty to, and Protection of, Children Act. Ch. 44. (52 & 53 Vict. 1889)

Local Government (Scotland) Act. Ch. 50. (52 & 53 Vict. 1889)
Custody of Children Act. Ch. 3. (54 & 55 Vict. 1891)
Prevention of Cruelty to Children (Amendment) Act. Ch. 27. (57 & 58 Vict. 1894)
Local Government (Scotland) Act. Ch. 37. (57 & 58 Vict. 1894)
Public Health (Scotland) Act. Ch. 38. (60 & 61 Vict. 1897)
Infant Life Protection Act. Ch. 57. (60 & 61 Vict. 1897)
Poor Law (Scotland) Act. Ch. 21. (61 & 62 Vict. 1898)
Inebriates Act. Ch. 60. (61 & 62 Vict. 1898)
Prevention of Cruelty to Children Act. Ch. 15. (4 Edw. 7. 1904)
Education of Defective Children (Scotland) Act. Ch. 10. (6 Ewd. 7. 1906)
Children Act. Ch. 12. (8 Ewd. 7. 1908)
Education (Scotland) Act. Ch. 63. (8 Edw. 7. 1908)
Mental Deficiency and Lunacy (Scotland) Act. Ch. 38. (3 & 4 Geo. V. 1913T
Scottish Board of Health Act, 1919. Ch. 20. (9 & 10 Geo. V. 1919)
Poor Law Emergency Provisions (Scotland) Act. Ch. 64. (11 & 12 Geo. V. 1921)
Local Authority (Emergency Provisions) Act. Ch. 6. (13 & 14 Geo. V. 1923)
Poor Law Emergency Provisions Continuance (Scotland) Act. Ch. 9. (14 & 15
    Geo. V. 1924)
Poor Law Emergency Provisions Continuance (Scotland) Act. Ch. 35. (15 & 16
    Geo. V. 1925)
Poor Law Emergency Provisions (Scotland) Act. Ch. 3. (16 & 17 Geo. V. 1927)
Re-organisation of Offices (Scotland) Act. Ch. 34. (18 & 19 Geo. V. 1928)
Local Government (Scotland) Act. Ch. 25. (19 & 20 Geo. V. 1929)
The Adoption of Children (Scotland) Act. Ch. 37. (20 & 21 Geo. V. 1930)
The Children and Young Persons (Scotland) Act. Ch. 47. (22 & 23 Geo. V. 1932)
Poor Law (Scotland) Act, 1934. Ch. 52. (24 & 25 Geo. V. 1934)

D Bills Presented to the House of Commons
The Local Government (Scotland) Amendment Bill. No. 80, 1902
The Local Government (Scotland) Amendment (No. 2) Bill. No. 102, 1902
The Detention of Poor Persons (Scotland) Bill. No. 286, 1902
The Detention of Poor Persons (Scotland) Bill. No. 19, 1903
Poor Law (Scotland) Bill. No. 244, 1905
Education (Provision of Meals) Scotland Bill. No. 92, 1906
Education (Provision of Meals) Scotland Bill. No. 14, 1907
The Poor Law (Scotland) Bill. No 175, 1933
The Poor Law (Scotland) Bill. No. 52, 1934

E Hansard

PART III Newspapers
Clydebank Press
Dundee Advertiser
Dunfermline Free Press
Edinburgh Evening News
Falkirk Herald
Falkirk Mail
Forward
Glasgow Herald
Govan Press
Greenock Telegraph
Hamilton Advertiser
Lennox Herald
Scotsman
Stirling Journal

PART IV Contemporary Journals
Biometrika
British Medical Journal
Edinburgh Medical Journal
Glasgow Medical Journal
Journal of the Royal Sanitary Institute
Lancet
Poor Law Magazine
Plebs
Proceedings of the Royal Philosophical Society of Glasgow
Proceedings of the Royal Society of Edinburgh
Public Health
Scots Law Times
The County and Municipal Record
The Sanitary Journal of Scotland
The Scottish Medical and Surgical Journal
Transactions of the Obstetrical and Medico-Churigical Society of Edinburgh

PART V Historical and other Scottish Works Published before 1960.
Aitchison, R. S., Effects of Diets upon Kidneys. (Edinburgh, 1896)
Alison, A., The Principles of Population and their Connection to Human
    Happiness. (Edinburgh, 1840)
Alison A., Autobiography of Sir A. Alison. (Edinburgh, 1883)
Alison, S. S., Report on the Sanitary Condition and General Economy of the
    Town of Tranent. (N.P., after 1840)
Alison, W. A., Observations on the Management of the Poor in Scotland.
    (Edinburgh, 1840)
Arnot, R. Page, The History of the Scottish Miners. (London, 1955)
Association for Improving the Condition of the Poor (Glasgow), Report on
    Labour Colonies. (Glasgow, 1892)
Black, W. G., A Handbook of Scottish Parochial Law. (Edinburgh, 1893)
Bowie, J. A., The Future of Scotland. (Glasgow, 1939)
Bridie, J., One Way of Living. (London, 1939)
Browne, W. A. F., What Asylums were, are, and ought to be. (Edinburgh, 1837)
Bunglass, D. G., The Classification of Poorhouse Inmates. (Edinburgh, 1875)
Burdett, H. C., Hospitals and Charities, Annual Reports. (London, 1890-1930)
Burdett, H. C., Pay Hospitals, and Paying wards throughout the World. (London,
    1880)
Carnegie Trust (United Kingdom), Family Diet and Health in Pre-war Britain.
    (Dunfermline, 1955)
Chalmers, A. K., The Health of Glasgow, 1818-1930. (Glasgow, 1930)
Chalmers Association for Diffusing Information on Important Social Questions,
    Pauperism and the Poor Law. (ed. T. Ivory) (Edinburgh. 1870)
Chalmers, T., On the Sufficiency of the Parochial System, without a Poor Rate,
    for the Right Management of the Poor. (Glasgow, 1841)
Comrie, J. D., The History of Scottish Medicine. 2 Vols. (London, 1927-32)
Cormack, A. A., Poor Relief in Scotland. (Aberdeen, 1923)
Day, J. P., Public Administration in the Highlands and Islands of Scotland.
    (London, 1918)
Dundee Social Union, Report on Housing and Industrial Conditions and Medical
    Inspection of Schoolchildren. (Dundee, 1905)
Dunn, C. L., The Emergency Medical Services. (London, 1952)
Easterbrook, C. C., The Chronicle of the Crichton Royal. (Dumfries, 1940)
Edinburgh Charity Organisation Society, Report on the Physical Condition of
    1400 Schoolchildren. . . Edinburgh. (London, 1906)

Ferguson, T., The Dawn of Scottish Social Welfare. (Edinburgh, 1944)
Ferguson, T., Scottish Social Welfare, 1864-1914. (Edinburgh, 1958)
Gibson, H. J. C., The Dundee Royal Infirmary, 1798-1948. (Dundee, 1948)
Glasgow City Parish, Parochial Law. (Glasgow, 1885)
Glasgow City Parochial Board, Report on the Boarding-Out of Orphan and
    Deserted Children and Insane. (Glasgow, 1872)
Graham, J. E., The History of the Poor Law of Scotland. (Edinburgh, 1921)
Haddow, W. M., My Seventy Years. (Glasgow, 1943)
Haddow, W. M., The Labour Party in Scotland. (Glasgow, 1920)
Halliday, A., A Letter to Lord Binning. (Edinburgh, 1818)
Halliday, A. A., A General View of the Present State of Lunatics. (London, 1828)
Hamilton. T., Poor Relief in South Ayrshire. (Edinburgh, 1942)
Hatch, Life Story of William Quarrier. (Glasgow, 1900)
Hospital Yearbook, Annual Reports, 1931-48. (London, 1931-48)
Interim Report of the Labour Party Committee of Inquiry into Distressed Areas,
    Labour and Distressed Areas. (London, 1937)
Johnston, T., The History of the Working Classes in Scotland. (Glasgow, 1929)
Johnston, T., Memories. (London, 1952)
Kelynack, T. N., Defective Children. (London, 1915)
Kerr, H. L., The Path of Social Progress. (Edinburgh, 1912)
Lady Balfour, Lord Balfour of Burleigh. (London, 1924)
Lady Pentland, Memoir of Lord Pentland. (London, 1928)
Lamond, R. P., The Scottish Poor Laws. (Glasgow, 1893)
Lindsay, D. E. Report upon a Study of the Diet of the Labouring Classes in the
    City of Glasgow. (Glasgow, 1913)
Lindsay, W. L., A General History of the Murray Royal Institution, Perth. (Perth,
    1878)
MacArthur, W., F., A History of Port Glasgow. (Glasgow, 1932)
MacDougall, J. P. and Dodds, J. M., A Parish Council Guide for Scotland.
    (Edinburgh, 1894)
MacGregor, A. S. M., Public Health in Glasgow, 1905-46. (Edinburgh, 1966)
MacKay, G. A., The Practice of the Scottish Poor Law. (Edinburgh, 1907)
MacKay, G. A., The Management and Construction of Poorhouses. (Edinburgh,
    1908)
MacKenzie, T. C., The Story of a Scottish Voluntary Hospital. (Inverness, 1946)
MacKenzie, W. L., The Medical Inspection of Schoolchildren. (Edinburgh, 1904)
MacKenzie, W. L., The Health of the Schoolchild. (London, 1906)
MacKenzie, W. L., Health and Disease. (London, 1911)
MacKenzie, W. L., Mothers and Children: The Carnegie Trust Report on Physical
    Welfare (Scotland). (Dunfermline, 1917)
Mackintosh, D. J., The Construction, Equipment and Management of a General
    Hospital. (Edinburgh, 1909)
MacPherson, J. M., The Kirk's Care of the Poor. (Aberdeen, 1941)
Marwick, W. H,. Economic Development in Victorian Scotland. (London, 1936)
Mechie, S., The Church in Scottish Social Development. (London, 1960)
Medical Directory of Scotland. 9 Vols. (London, 1852-60)
Milne, D., The Scottish Office. (London, 1957)
Milne, D. M., Scotch Poorhouses and English Workhouses. (Edinburgh, 1873)
Monnypenny, D., Remarks on the Poor Laws in Scotland. (Edinburgh, 1834)
Ness, R. B., The Western Infirmary of Glasgow. (Glasgow, 1940)
No Author, Origin and Development of the Victoria Infirmary of Glasgow.
    (Glasgow, 1938)   .
Paton, D. N. (et al), A Study of the Diet of Labouring Classes in Edinburgh.
    (Edinburgh, c.1901)
Paton, D. N., Poverty, Nutrition and Growth. (Medical Research Council Special

Series) (London, 1926)

Patrick, J., A Short History of Glasgow Royal Infirmary. (Glasgow, 1940)

Pearson, D. A. (ed.) Conference on Charity and the Poor Law. (Glasgow, 1885)

Presbytery of Glasgow, Report of the Commission on the Housing of the Poor. (Glasgow, 1891

Scott, W. R. and Cunnison, J., Industries of the Clyde Valley During the War. (Oxford, 1924)

Sellar, G., Forms for Sherrifs and Sherrif-Clerks. (Glasgow, 1880)

Skelton, J., The Handbook of Public Health. (Edinburgh, 1892)

Skelton, N., Constructive Conservatism. (Edinburgh, 1924)

Smith, J. G., A Digest of the Laws of Scotland relating to the Poor, the Public Health and other Matters managed by Parochial Boards. (Edinburgh, 1878)

Stark, W., Considerations of the Affairs of the Poor. (Edinburgh, 1824)

Transactions of the Fourth International Home Relief Conference, 1904. (Edinburgh, 1905)

Tuke. D. H., Chapters in the History of the Insane... (London, 1882)

Turner, A. L., The Royal Infirmary of Edinburgh, 1798-1929. (Edinburgh, 1929)

Watson, D. C., Food and Feeding in Health and Disease. (Edinburgh, 1910)

Webb, B., Our Partnership. (London, 1948)

Webb, S. and B., History of English Local Government. (London, 1929)

Webb, S. and B., English Poor Law Policy. (London, 1929)

PART VI Other Printed Works

Abel-Smith, B., The Hospitals, 1800-1948. (Harvard, 1964)

Adler, M. and Asquith, S., Discretion and Welfare. (London, 1981)

Ayers, G. M., England's First State Hospitals, 1867-1930. (London, 1967)

Behlmer, G. K., Child Abuse and Moral Reform in England, 1870-1908. (Stanford, 1982)

Brand, J. L., Doctors and the State, (Baltimore, 1965)

Briggs, A and Saville, J. (eds.), Essays in Labour History, 1918-1939. (London, 1977)

Brown, K. D., Labour and Unemployment. (Newton Abbot, 1971)

Brown, E. H. Phelps and Browne, M., A Century of Pay. (London, 1968T

Brown, G., Maxton. (Edinburgh, 1986)

Bruce, M. (ed.), The Rise of the Welfare State. (London, 1968)

Cage, R. A., The Scottish Poor Law, 1745-1845. (Edinburgh, 1981)

Campbell, A. B., The Lanarkshire Miners. (Edinburgh, 1979)

Campbell, R. H., The Rise and Fall of the Scottish Economy. (Edinburgh, 1981)

Checkland, E. O., Philanthropy in Victorian Scotland. (Edinburgh, 1980)

Checkland, E. O. and Lamb, M. (eds.), Health Care as Social History. (Aberdeen, 1982)

Checkland, S. G. and O., Industry and Ethos. (London, 1984)

Coates, A. W. (ed.), The Scottish Poor Law, 1815-1870. (Farnborough, 1973)

Crowther, A., The Workhouse System, 1834-1929. (London, 1981)

Deacon, A., In Search of the Scrounger. (London, 1976)

Deacon, A. and Bradshaw, J., Reserved for the Poor. (Oxford, 1983)

Dickson, A. (ed.), Capital and Class in Scotland. (Edinburgh, 1982)

Dickson, A. (ed.), Scottish Capitalism. (London, 1980)

Digby, A., Pauper Palaces. (London, 1978)

Donajgrodski, A. P. (ed.), Social Control in the 19th Century Britain. (London, 1977)

Emvy, H. V., Liberals, Radicals and Social Politics. (Oxford, 1973)

Ferrier, A., The Greenock Infirmary, 1906-1968. (Glasgow, 1968)

Fraser, D., The Evolution of the British Welfare State. (London, 1973)

Fraser, D. (ed.), The New Poor Law in the Nineteenth Century. (London, 1976)

Freeden, M., The New Liberalism: An Ideology of Social Reform. (London, 1978)
Gauldie, E., Cruel Habitations. (London, 1974)
George, V. and Wilding, P., Ideology and Social Welfare. (London, 1985)
Gilbert, B. B., British Social Policy, 1914-1939. (London, 1970)
Ginsberg, N., Class, Capital and Social Policy. (London, 1979T
Gordon, G. (ed.), Perspectives of the Scottish City. (Aberdeen, 1985)
Harris, J., Unemployment and Politics. (London, 1972)
Harvie, C., No Gods and Precious Few Heroes. (London, 1981)
Hay, J. R., The Development of the British Welfare State. (London, 1978)
Hill, M., Understanding Social Policy. (London, 1980)
        History of the Aberdeen Association of Social Services. (Aberdeen, 1971)
Hutchinson, I. G. C., A Political History of Scotland, 1832-1924. (Edinburgh, 1986)
Irving, G., The Dumfries and Galloway Royal Infirmary, 1776-1975. (Dumfries, 1975)
Knox, W., Scottish Labour Leaders. (Edinburgh, 1984)
Kerr, C. (et. al.), Industrialism and Industrial Man. (London, 1966)
Langton, J. and Morris, R. J., Atlas of Industrialising Britain, 1780-1914. (London, 1986)
Levitt, I., Scottish Government and Social Conditions, 1845-1919. (in press)
Levitt, Ian and Christopher Smout, The State of the Scottish Working Class in 1843. (Edinburgh, 1979)
Lindsay, J., The Scottish Poor Law; its Operation in the North-East from 1745-1845. (Ilfracombe, 1975)
McLean, I., The Legend of Red Clydeside. (Edinburgh, 1983)
MacDonald, M., The Glasgow Royal Informary. (Glasgow, 1971)
MacDougall, I., Militant Miners. (Edinburgh, 1981)
MacGregor, A., Public Health in Glasgow, 1905-46. (Edinburgh, 1966)
MacIntyre, S., Little Moscows; Communism and Working Class Militancy in Inter-War Britain. (Cambridge, 1980)
MacKenzie, N., Letters of S. and B. Webb, Vol II. (Cambridge, 1978)
MacKenzie, N. and J., The First Fabians. (London, 1977)
MacQueen, L. and Kerr, A. B., The Western Infirmary of Glasgow, 1874-1974. (Glasgow, 1974)
MacShane, H. and Smith, J., Harry MacShane; No Mean Fighter. (London, 1978)
Middlemas, K., The Clydesiders. (Glasgow, 1965)
Mishra, R., Society and Social Policy. (London, 1981)
Morris, M. (ed.), The General Strike. (Penguin, 1976)
Pinker, R., English Hospital Statistics, 1861-1938. (London, 1966)
Pinker, R., The Idea of Welfare. (London, 1979)
Room, G., The Sociology of Welfare. (Oxford, 1979)
Rose, M. E., The Relief of Poverty, 1834-1914. (London, 1974)
Rose, M. E., The Poor and the City: The English Poor Law in its Urban Context, 1834-1914. (Leicester, 1985)
Searle, G. S., The Quest for National Efficiency. (Oxford, 1971)
Skelley, J. (ed.), The General Strike. (London, 1976)
Slaven, A., The Development of the West of Scotland Economy. (London, 1973)
Smout, T. C. (ed.), The Search for Wealth and Stability. (London, 1979)
Smout, T. C., A Century of the Scottish People, 1830-1950. (London, 1986)
Stevenson, J., Social Conditions in Britain between the Wars. (Penquin, 1977)
Sullivan, M., Sociology and Social Welfare. (London, 1987)
Taylor-Gooby, P. and Dale, J., Social Theory and Social Policy. (London, 1981)
Thane, P., The Foundations of the Welfare State. (London, 1982)
Thane, P., The Origins of British Social Policy. (London, 1978)
Thompson, A. W. M., The Glasgow Eye Infirmary, 1824-1962. (Glasgow, 1963)
Transactions of the 5th World Congress of Sociology. (London, 1964)

Treble, J. H., Urban Poverty in Britain, 1830-1914. (London, 1979)
Urwin, D. W., Politics and the Development of the Unionist Party in Scotland.
    (Manchester, 1963)
Walker, W. H., Juteopolis: Dundee and its Textile Workers, 1885-1923.
    (Edinburgh, 1979)
Watt. O. M., Stobhill Hospital. (Glasgow, 1972)
Young, J. D., The Rousing of the Scottish Working Class. (London, 1975)

INDEX